Rabbi
SCHNEUR ZALMAN
Of Liadi

A BIOGRAPHY

by
NISSAN MINDEL

CHABAD RESEARCH CENTER
KEHOT PUBLICATION SOCIETY
770 Eastern Parkway / Brooklyn, NY 11213

RABBI SCHNEUR ZALMAN OF LIADI

A BIOGRAPHY

Published and Copyright © 1969

Fifth Printing 2002
By

KEHOT PUBLICATION SOCIETY
770 Eastern Parkway • Brooklyn, New York 11213
(718) 774-4000 • FAX (718) 774-2718

Order Department:
291 Kingston Avenue • Brooklyn, New York 11213
(718) 778-0226 • FAX (718) 778-4148
www.kehotonline.com

ISBN 0-8266-0416-1

CONTENTS

NOTES

PREFATORY NOTE

The present volume is the first of two volumes which deal with the life and thought, respectively, of Rabbi Schneur Zalman, known among Chasidim as the "Alter Rebbe" ("Old Rabbi") and to others as the *Rav* of Liadi, author of the *(Rav's) Shulchan Aruch* and the *Tanya*, and founder of the *Chabad* philosophical system and way of life.

Rabbi Schneur Zalman's contribution to Jewish thought will be dealt with more fully in the forthcoming volume.

The present volume is concerned with the story of Rabbi Schneur Zalman's life and the dual historical role which he played: Leader of Russian Jewry in the second half of the 18th century and for more than a decade of the 19th century, while at the same time being the founder and head of the Chabad-Chasidic school during the formative years of the Chasidic movement in general; both roles harmoniously and inseparably merging into one.

This biography should be of interest not only to the student of Jewish history, but also to the contemporary lay reader who has often asked: What is it that moves and motivates the Chabadniks, more popularly known as Lubavitchers, in their dynamic activity to revitalize Jewish life in all parts of the world, often at great personal sacrifice, and—in countries behind the Iron Curtain—with complete disregard to adverse circumstances?

A clue to this phenomenon will be found in this biography, bearing in mind that Rabbi Schneur Zalman was the progenitor of the Chabad-Lubavitch dynasty of Jewish leaders, setting the pattern, by example and precept, for both the leaders and followers of the Chabad school of thought and way of life.

In presenting this biography, the author has endeavored to avoid embellishment, and to use a minimum of personal commentary, letting the events speak for themselves.

The author wishes to acknowledge his indebtedness to the Chabad Research Center for making available to him manuscripts and material from the archives of the Lubavitcher Rebbe's library. Grateful acknowledgment is extended also to his associates, whose helpful cooperation has made his task much easier.

NISSAN MINDEL

24th of *Tevet*, 5729

FOREWORD

by
Rabbi Menachem M. Schneerson
זצוקללה"ה נבג"מ זי"ע
the Lubavitcher Rebbe

(to first edition)

The moral person must strive to bring his personal life and daily conduct in full harmony with his convictions; to live up to the standards of morality and ethics which he would like others also to adhere to. This is particularly true of the Jewish religious person, since the Jewish religion is a way of everyday life, and considers the *deed*—the actual conduct in the daily life—as the essential thing and the ultimate purpose of knowledge. The Chasidic philosophy goes a step further. While considering the deed essential, it demands that the deed be permeated with vitality and inwardness. Insisting that there can be no substitute for the actual fulfillment of duty, Chasidus insists at the same time that such action be animated; that the act have a "soul." It is only on this level that a person can achieve true harmony in every aspect of his daily life, physical, emotional and intellectual; harmony of all his "components"—his Divine soul, animal soul and physical body, as well as harmony with the world in which he lives.

As one studies the biography of the Alter Rebbe, the exponent of the Chasidic teachings of the Baal Shem Tov and the founder of the Chabad school of Chasidus, one cannot but marvel at the complete accord between his personal life and his philosophy and teachings. Indeed, he was the living embodiment of all that he taught, and more. It is for this reason also that we find him to be a person of many accomplishments, down to small detail. He strove to develop himself in every way. From his very early youth he was known to recite his daily prayers with the *kavanot* of the saintly *SheLoH* (Rabbi Isaiah Hurwitz), based on the Kabbala of the *Ari HaKadosh* (Rabbi Yitzchok Luria), and all his daily activities were deeply probed and carefully measured.

IX

Making *Ahavat Yisrael*—in its *immediate application in actual practice*—a cornerstone of his ethical system, he misses no opportunity of applying it in his own life. Thus, no sooner does he come in possession of a sum of money (quite substantial in those days), than he dedicates *all* of it, in accordance with a prior stipulation, as a fund for constructive economic help to needy families. He was the *Baal Kore'*, reading the Torah in his congregation, with particular attention to pronunciation and grammatical rules; he was also the *Baal Toke'a*, sounding the *shofar* on Rosh Hashanah. In composing his *Shulchan Aruch*, he personally checked and counterchecked weights and measures defined by Jewish Law. He studied algebra, geometry and astronomy in order not to have to rely on others in making calculations essential to the study of the Talmud and the making of legal decisions. Knowing the value of *neginah* in the attainment of *devekut*, he himself composed *nigunim* and sang them with soulful ecstasy. Meticulous in all his ways, he sifted scores of prayer books (according to one tradition—no less than sixty different versions) to produce a prayer book punctilious in version and grammar.

The English reader is now fortunate in having been given access to both the philosophy and biography of the Alter Rebbe, in whom, as already mentioned, the former is fully reflected in the latter, for his life was a living example of what he taught; and both complemented each other. In regard to the philosophy, the student of Chabad is no longer dependent upon secondary sources (which are in any case very scarce). He can study the basic work of Chabad, the *Likutei Amarim (Tanya)* in English translation. As for the life-story of the author, the present volume fills a longfelt need, for it is the first comprehensive biography of the Alter Rebbe in the English language.

Dr. Nissan Mindel, who has the distinction and the *zechut* of being the first to introduce the classic of Chabad philosophy, the *Likutei Amarim (Tanya)* of the Alter Rebbe, to the serious minded student who finds its easier to study it in English than in the Hebrew original, has now followed it up with another "first," the present biographical volume. For this noteworthy contribution the author and the Chabad Research Center are to be highly commended.

MENACHEM SCHNEERSON

Yud-Tet Kislev, 5729

INTRODUCTION

(HISTORICAL BACKGROUND)

General *Chasidut,*[1] as we will call the parent movement in distinction from *Chabad*[2] *Chasidut,* its offshoot, arose in the second quarter of the 18th century,[3] and became one of the outstanding developments in the history of Jewish religious thought in modern times. It was founded by Rabbi Israel Baal Shem Tov (1698-1760), a native of Podolia, at present a part of the Ukraine, but at that time belonging to Poland. From Podolia, where the Baal Shem Tov (popularly known by the abbreviation BeShT, or Besht) first began to preach his doctrine, the movement rapidly spread to the neighboring provinces of Wolhynia, the Ukraine, Galicia, and other parts of Poland. Thence it branched out to White Russia, Lithuania, Rumania and Hungary. In due course, through the mass emigration of Eastern European Jews to the West during the period of 1881-1914, the Chasidic movement established itself in virtually all parts of the world. Today, two hundred years after the death of its founder, it continues to constitute a vigorous religious and social force in Jewish life.

The phenomenal growth of the Chasidic movement, which within a century from its inception embraced half of the Jewish population of Eastern Europe,[4] was induced by various factors, which had their roots in the social, cultural and economic conditions of Eastern European Jewry in the period under discussion. These will be briefly reviewed in due course. At the same time some of the basic doctrines of the Baal Shem Tov, with their intrinsic appeal to the masses, contributed in no small measure to their widespread popularity. Yet some of the factors which contributed towards the rapid expansion of the Chasidic movement were also partly responsible for the early opposition to the movement. A detailed analysis of the relative role which each of the pertinent factors played in the early history of Chasidut would take us beyond our task. But whatever weight one may be inclined to attach to any particular factor, it is as a religious philosophical movement that Chasidut must be viewed above all else. Needless to say, the early history of the movement could not be understood without reference to the position of Eastern European Jewry in the period under review, and this must now be briefly outlined.

The calamitous year of 1648 may well serve as a starting point. In that year, exactly half a century before the birth of the Baal Shem Tov, the Cossack insurrection under Hetman Bogdan Chmielnicki broke out in all its savagery against the Poles and the Jews. From the Ukraine the Cossack and Tatar hordes swept through Poland, leaving a horrible train of death and desolation behind them. For several years these massacres and atrocities went almost unchecked, before the hordes were finally turned back to the steppes whence they came. Yet the surviving Jews were given no respite. They were soon overwhelmed by the ravages of war in the wake of the Russian and Swedish invasions into Poland. Many areas which had escaped the Chmielnicki holocaust found themselves in the path of invading armies. As if the cup of woe for the Jews of Poland had not been filled to overflowing, there ensued a period of the so-called "tumults" and outbreaks against the Jews of Poland, fanned by religious intolerance, which lasted to the end of the seventeenth century.

These tragic upheavals throughout the second half of the seventeenth century left the Jewish population of Poland fearfully decimated, economically ruined, and spiritually quite dazed.

Nor was Poland the only place where Jews had suffered. The Thirty Years War (1618-48) had devastated many a prosperous community in Central Europe; religious persecution was rampant in Austria, and the position of Jews in other countries was extremely precarious.

Under these circumstances, it is small wonder that the self-styled Messiah, Shabbatai Tzvi (1626-1676), found the time opportune for his pseudo-Messianic movement. He declared the Chmielnicki massacres as the "birth-pangs of the Messiah," and himself as the Messiah. He gained many adherents, and excitement ran high among Jews in various parts of the world. In the beginning of his career, even some prominent rabbis were impressed with Shabbatai Tzvi. However, before long the rabbis realized that Shabbatai Tzvi and his movement constituted a grave danger to the Jewish people, and they began to oppose him. But numerous Jews were prepared to follow him blindly. The Messianic expectations had taken such firm hold on the imagination of many Jews that not even the downfall of Shabbatai Tzvi and his conversion to Islam could eradicate them. Despite an all-out effort on the part of leading rabbis to suppress the movement, it continued to hold sway over many Shabbatian followers, especially in Poland, where it erupted again, half a century later, in the form of the notorious Frankist sect. Its leader, Jacob Frank, was a contemporary of the Besht and also a native of Podolia. Eventually, he and most of his sect converted to Christianity.

Although these abortive pseudo-Messianic movements died a natural, if not very peaceful, death, their after-effects lingered on in the suspicion and mistrust which they had aroused within the ranks of the Rabbinate. The tragic experience of Rabbi Moses Chaim Luzzato (1707-1746) accused of pseudo-Messianic doctrines, the controversy around Rabbi Jonathan Eybeschutz (1690-1764) accused of Shabbatian leanings, and other major and minor controversies among the leading rabbis of the period, are all symptomatic of the Shabbatian aftermath. In all these cases, the delving into the mysticism of the Kabbala was blamed for the trouble.

As was to be expected, Kabbala fell into disrepute as a result of the above-mentioned events, and its study, which had previously been quite popular among many rabbis and in leading Talmudic academies in Poland and elsewhere,[5] became well nigh proscribed.[6]

A direct result of the material impoverishment of the Jewish communities of Poland was, of course, the general deterioration of the cultural level of the masses, which accentuated a social problem of long standing. This was an important factor in the early history of the Chasidic movement, a point that must be further elaborated.

Traditionally, the pursuit of knowledge was placed above that of material riches in Jewish life. Poverty did not constitute as serious a social stigma as ignorance. As far back as Talmudic times there was a marked social distinction between the *chaver* or *talmid-chacham* (scholar) and the *am ha'aretz* (ignoramus).[7] The contempt of the former for the latter became a calculated attitude after the destruction of the Second Temple, when the study of the Torah and religious observances assumed additional importance as the main factors of national unity and survival.[8] Realizing that the Jewish people, deprived as it was of its soil and political independence, could not survive among the nations of the world except through the preservation of its cultural heritage, the rabbis sought all means of disseminating the study of the Torah and of discouraging ignorance through contempt and shunning of the ignorant. This attitude naturally evoked a reciprocal feeling of hostility on the part of the *am ha'aretz* towards the scholar.[9] However, with the passing of the centuries, as the general standards of Jewish education attained relatively high proportions, this mutual antagonism tended to fade. While poverty was always rampant, poverty did not necessarily mean ignorance when Jewish communal life was well organized, since some provision was usually made for the support of the poor student. Moreover, the common practice by families of moderate means to take learned sons-in-law and to support the young couple for a number of years after marriage, in order to enable the student to devote his time exclusively to his studies, further tended to ameliorate the mutual attitude between the learned and the unlearned.[10]

However, things changed radically during the period under discussion. The communities (*kahals*) were too impoverished to provide free education for the masses. Only in the larger communities were there *yeshivot* (Talmudic academies), but attendance was necessarily limited. The vast majority of Jewish children and youth remained uneducated, and the gulf between the unlearned masses and the learned minority widened considerably. This cleavage extended to every facet of the social and religious life, which greatly added to the miseries of the masses. Thus from every point of view, economic, cultural and social, Jewish life in the Polish provinces had reached a very low ebb in the aftermath of the tragic second half of the seventeenth century. A pall of gloom had descended upon the Jewish population, and the people yearned for spiritual guidance and uplifting.

Such was the general setting when Rabbi Israel Baal Shem Tov appeared on the scene.

Being acutely conscious of the educational problem of the young and of the widespread spiritual depression among the adults, the Besht set out to help his co-religionists through a two pronged campaign, directed at both the young and the old. However, mindful of the prevailing climate, he did not begin his work openly. Himself a follower of another "Baal Shem," namely, Rabbi Adam Baal Shem of Ropshitz,[11] a disciple of Rabbi Joel Baal Shem of Zamosc (Zamoshtz),[12] the Besht first began his activities underground. As a young man of eighteen, while he was a member of a group of "secret servicemen," itinerant mystics (nistarim), followers of Rabbi Adam Baal Shem, whose mission was to wander through the towns and villages to bring cheer to the Jewish people and help uplift their religious and moral standards, the Besht became closely acquainted with conditions of Jewish life and with the need for more widespread education of the young. He himself became an assistant teacher for a period of time, dedicating himself to the education of the very young children.[13] After the death of Rabbi Adam Baal Shem, the Besht became the leader of the nistarim, who spread his doctrines among the masses. When, at the age of thirty-six, the Besht revealed himself as the leader of the new Chasidic movement, he already had a number of nuclei of followers in various communities in Poland, who had prepared the ground for the movement to a considerable extent. These included a number of outstanding scholars, but the Besht remained a popular teacher, never losing contact with the masses. For this reason he made ample use of parables, metaphors and aphorisms, whereby he was able to convey many a profound doctrine in simple terms.

We must now review some of the Beshtian doctrines which, as we mentioned earlier, were in themselves a potent factor in the popularity of the movement.

The Besht taught that it was everyone's duty to serve the Creator, and that this duty embraced every aspect of the daily life and was not confined to the study of the Talmud exclusively. He emphasized the importance of prayer and obedience to the Law, above the study of the Law, where such study tended to degenerate into nothing more than intellectual exercise.

Contrary to some of the classical Jewish philosophers who made Divine Providence commensurate with the knowledge of G-d, the Besht insisted that Divine Providence extends not only to every individual, but to every particular, even in the inanimate world. "A leaf torn from a tree and swept by the wind from place to place reflects the Divine Will and Providence."[14] This is a corollary of his doctrine of Continuous Creation, which he explains by the principle that "G-d is All and all is G-d,"[15] there being no other Reality but G-d. The true reality of all things is the "word" of G-d which brought all things into being, and which continually keeps them in existence. Without this creative and active principle which is the "soul" of every particle of matter, all things would revert to their previous state of nonexistence.[16]

In the tradition of the Kabbala, the Besht taught that the goal of Divine worship is attachment to G-d (devekut), which is essentially a service of the heart rather than the mind. For, ultimately, G-d cannot be apprehended rationally, and it is by means of emotional commitment and obedience to the Divine will, rather than by intellectual speculation, that the human being can come closest to his Creator. Hence his emphasis on the maxim, "G-d desires the heart," i.e., the intention of the heart (kavanah) in the performance of the Divine precepts. Here the Besht took the notion of kavanah out of its mystical context and placed it in the simple frame of devoutness and self-surrender to G-d. To attain devekut, the Besht preached, it is not necessary to dwell on the meaning of the prayers and psalms, or the significance of the religious precepts; the sincere recitation of the holy words and the simple performance of the precepts are in themselves sufficient to establish contact with G-d, provided this desire for communion was the object of the worship. This was a concession to the most illiterate, the *am ha'aretz*, as the Besht taught that none is excluded from Divine service.

But the Besht went even further than that, teaching that in some respects the simple, unlearned worshipper, unaware of the esoteric or even elementary functions of the precepts, has a two-fold advantage over the scholar. In the first place, the unlearned Jew possesses a greater measure of natural humility and, in the second place, it is possible for him to attain the very heights of passionate worship, often beyond the reach of the cool, intellectual, and sophisticated scholar. For, whereas the scholar finds an outlet for his religious feelings through his prayers and the study of the Torah which he is able to understand, the non-scholar continues to be consumed by the fire of his passionate yearning to cleave to G-d, like a "burning bush which is not consumed."[17] It is out of this humble bush that G-d first spoke to Moses, indicating—so the Besht taught—that it is among the humble but sincere folk that the presence of G-d is most evident.[18]

Let no one feel slighted, the Besht pointed out, at being called *am ha'aretz* (lit. "people of the land"). This epithet which had become so derogatory in reference to the common people was not originally intended to be used in that sense. On the contrary, in the Holy Scriptures we find nothing derogatory about it, and the whole Jewish people were referred to affectionately in similar terms, viz., "For you shall be a land of delight."[19] The Besht went on to explain the metaphor: The earth is trodden upon, yet it contains the greatest treasures; so does every Jew, even the humblest of the humble, contain great spiritual treasures, which only have to be brought to the surface.[20] Foremost among these spiritual treasures the Besht placed the simple virtues which he found inherent in the common people: faith, sincerity, humility, love and benevolence. He urged the cultivation and exercise of these traits, by word and deed. A whole life's mission may depend on a single good act. "A soul may descend from its heavenly abode to live in this material world for seventy/eighty years,[21] for the sole purpose of doing a good turn to a fellow-Jew, materially or spiritually," was one of his characteristic maxims.[22]

Above all, the Besht endeavored to instill the quality of joy in Divine service. To "serve G-d with joy"[23] is a biblical precept which the Besht made a cornerstone of his popular religious philosophy. Indeed, being conscious of the proximity of the Creator everywhere and at all times, being aware that G-d is the essence of goodness, whose benevolent Providence extends to every individual and every particular, and having the opportunity to serve the Creator in so many ways in everyday life, the Besht could not see how any Jew sharing these feelings could experience anything but a perpetually happy frame of mind.

Finally, a word about his Messianic concept. The Baal Shem Tov had no personal Messianic aspirations,"[24] nor did he lay claim to having discovered a shortcut to the advent of the Messiah. One might venture to suggest that he consciously relegated the Messianic idea to the background, mindful of the perversion of this ideal by Shabbatai Tzvi and Frank. The Besht did not believe that the advent of the Messiah should be hastened by any artificial (i.e., kabbalistic) means. Rather did he postulate a gradual process of personal redemption as the sine qua non of the Messianic Redemption, except that he understood "personal redemption" in terms of his own teachings. A Chasidic tradition has it that the Messianic Era will be ushered in "when the fountains of the Baal Shem Tov will have been diffused abroad,"[25] that is, when his teachings will be accepted and put into practice by the Jewish people throughout the Diaspora.

So much for the Baal Shem Tov's basic doctrines, which are scattered in various books of his disciples, as he himself did not leave any written works.[26] We shall have occasion to see how some of the Beshtian doctrines received a systematic and homogenous, though sometimes modified, exposition in the system of Chabad.

At any rate, from all that has been said about the Baal Shem Tov's teachings it is clear that they did not contain any heterodox doctrines to which objection might be raised from the point of view of Jewish Law. Indeed, with the exception of his doctrine of Continuous Creation and the related concepts of Divine

Immanence and Providence, in which the Besht steers a new course in Jewish philosophy, there are virtually no basic doctrinal innovations in the Besht's system. His philosophy rests otherwise on a shift of emphases, primarily intended to raise the moral and ethical standards of the illiterate Jew and to enrich his daily religious experience. His doctrinal innovations, too, far from shaking the foundations of the orthodox beliefs, could only have the effect of deepening and strengthening the old faith.

Nor did the Besht conceive of his movement in terms of a "sect" in the strict sense of the term. On the contrary, from its very inception it was envisaged by him as a mass movement which, necessarily starting with individuals and groups, hopefully intended to include all classes of the Jewish people.

Nevertheless, it was inevitable that the Chasidic movement should assume certain sectarian characteristics, partly because of some tenets germane to it, and largely because of the intolerance of the opposition.

As already mentioned, the climate which had been induced by Shabbatai Tzvi and Frank was saturated with suspicion and fear of any new movement that was even remotely connected with the Kabbala, or smacked of sectarianism. Besides, some of the Besht's doctrines, such as tended to erase the distinction between scholar and layman, or the emphasis on the emotional rather than the intellectual, were considered quite radical notions. Such doctrines, the opposition claimed, could constitute a threat to the established communal order and indirectly, even to the authority of the Rabbinate itself. Finally, some Beshtian doctrines appeared grossly pantheistic to the uninitiated, and provided additional grounds for objection to the movement as a whole.

The fight against the Baal Shem Tov and his movement broke out while the Baal Shem Tov was still alive. The first assault on the new "sect" (kat)—the epithet itself imputing to it Shabbatian leanings—was made in 1755,[27] and two years later a ban (cherem) was pronounced against it in Vilna in conjunction with representatives of the Rabbinates of Slutzk and Shklov.[28] However, the opposition gained momentum only after the death of the Baal Shem Tov (1760), when his scholarly disciples, par-

ticularly his successor, Rabbi Dov Ber of Mezritch, began to disseminate Chasidism on a wider scale, eventually also by means of
the printed word. In 1772, coincidental with the death of Rabbi
Dov Ber, the ban against the Chasidim was reiterated in Vilna.
Still stricter was the ban pronounced against the Chasidim at a
rabbinic convocation in Zelva, in 1781. The opponents (mitnagdim) were particularly incensed by the Chasidic book, Toldot
Ya'acov Yosef, by Rabbi Jacob Joseph HaKohen of Polonnoye, a
disciple of the Besht, which had appeared in that year. The book
was highly polemical, contrasting the barrenness of contemporary non-Chasidic life with the quickening vitality of the
Chasidic doctrine. It fanned the flame of opposition, which now
resorted to more radical sanctions against the "sect." The
Chasidim were branded as heretics; their meat and wine were
outlawed; intermarriage with them was prohibited. These stringent measures were not effective, however, to suppress the movement or stem its tide. The Rabbinates found it necessary to reaf-
firm their stringent opposition to the movement in 1784, in
Mohilev, and in 1796, in Vilna. In the meantime, Rabbi Schneur
Zalman had, reluctantly at first but later boldly, assumed the
leadership of the Chasidic movement, while at the head of the
opposition stood the celebrated Gaon of Vilna, Rabbi Elijah
(1720-1797). Concurrently, the center of the struggle had shift-
ed to Czarist Russia, since the former Polish territories of
Lithuania and White Russia had been ceded to Russia after the
partitions of Poland in 1772, 1793 and 1795. The real crisis for
the Chasidic movement came when Rabbi Schneur Zalman was
denounced to the Czar as a dangerous rebel in 1798 (after the
appearance of the Tanya) and again in 1800. We will have more
to say about these events later. However, with the exoneration of
the Chasidic leader and his movement by the Russian government, the opposition gave up all further concerted efforts against
the Chasidic movement. As the mitnagdim began to realize that
their suspicion of the new movement was unfounded, and their
hostility to it unjustified, opposition soon gave way to a mutual
rapprochement. Already about the year 1808, we find leaders of
both sides as joint signatories on a haskamah (approbation) on
the printing of the Talmud in Kopust, something which would

have been unthinkable a decade earlier. The breach was healed at last. The Chasidim were accepted as full-fledged co-religionists, and the movement was likewise accepted as an integral part of traditional Judaism. Moreover, the Chasidim came to be regarded as representatives of the ultra-orthodox position in Jewry. As such, they became the object of a renewed frontal attack, this time from the direction of the Haskalah movement. But this development largely lies beyond the limits of our historical review.[29]

Thus, the history of the Chasidic movement, in the course of only several generations, evolved from suspected heterodoxy to co-existent orthodoxy to accepted ultra-orthodoxy—a unique phenomenon in Jewish history.

What has been said of the Chasidic movement as a whole is equally true of the history of the Chabad movement in particular. Its founder, Rabbi Schneur Zalman, did not consider his system as a branch of Chasidut, or a version of it. To him it was Chasidut par excellence, just as Chasidut itself was to the Besht Judaism par excellence. This is not surprising in view of the fact that Rabbi Schneur Zalman regarded himself as the spiritual legatee of the Baal Shem Tov.[30] Indeed, for a time at least, Rabbi Schneur Zalman was regarded by both the Chasidim and their opponents as the leader and spokesman for the Chasidic movement as a whole, before the latter fragmented into a number of dynastic groups, each headed by a direct descendant of the Baal Shem Tov, or of one of his disciples. Owing to this position, Rabbi Schneur Zalman bore the brunt of the attack against Chasidut in its most violent outbreaks, and, as already noted, his victory over the opposition was not only a triumph for Chabad, but for Chasidut in general.

CHAPTER I

RABBI SCHNEUR ZALMAN'S BIRTH AND CHILDHOOD

Schneur Zalman (Boruchovitch)[1] was born on the 18th day of *Elul*,[2] in the year 5505, corresponding to September, 1745.[3] He was born in Liozna, a small Polish town in the province of Mohilev, lying some 50 miles from the county town of Orsha, on the highway from Smolensk to Vitebsk. His parents, Baruch and Rivkah,[4] had three other sons, all of whom became outstanding Talmudic scholars and held rabbinic posts.[5] Schneur Zalman spent his earliest childhood in the lap of nature, on a fair-sized estate in the vicinity of Liozna, operated by his father.

Schneur Zalman's father was apparently a man of some means. He was a member of, and contributor to, the *Chevrah Kadisha* (Burial Association)[6] of Liozna. Moreover, he was an imaginative philanthropist, helping a number of Jewish refugee families from Bohemia to settle on the land in the vicinity of Liozna. Baruch himself was born in a family that had originally lived in Bohemia, tracing its ancestry to the famous rabbi and kabbalist, Yehuda Lowe of Prague (1512-1609).[7]

As in the case of many other great personages in Jewish history, the birth of Schneur Zalman is surrounded with an aura of auspicious omens, reaching into the realm of the mystical and supernatural.

Chasidic tradition and family records have the following to say about Schneur Zalman's parents and the circumstances surrounding the birth of the founder of Chabad.

1

Baruch was a member of the society of the followers of the Baal Shem Tov, who, at that time, carried on their "missionary" activities among their fellow-Jews in secret, as already referred to earlier.[8] So secretive was the work of these *nistarim* in the early period of the Besht's leadership, that their identity was concealed even from each other. Only the Besht and, later, Baruch's wife Rivkah, knew of Baruch's membership in the *Nistarim* society.[9]

Baruch's wife Rivkah was a learned woman, who had daily study-periods, which was quite unusual for women of those days. She was the daughter of Abraham, a learned and pious Jew of Liozna, who had declined the career of a rabbi in order to earn his livelihood by the "toil of his hands," as a gardener. At one time Baruch was employed by Abraham as a watchman. The earnest and quiet youth had made an impression on his employer, and, at the latter's suggestion, Baruch accepted the proposal that he marry his daughter.[10]

Baruch and Rivkah were married on a Friday, the 17th of *Elul*, 5503 (1743). When a year had passed by and the young couple were not blessed with a child, Baruch and his wife went to see the Baal Shem Tov, to ask him for his blessing.

It was the Besht's custom to celebrate his birthday every year (on the 18th of *Elul*). At the repast on that auspicious day, the Besht blessed them and promised them that, exactly a year later, they would become the parents of a boy. Not even the Besht knew at that time that the soul which was destined to descend into Baruch's son was a *new* and unblemished soul which had never yet been on earth. Such souls are rare, since most souls descending to earth are reincarnations, sent down to make amends for wrongs or omissions in a life which had once, or even more than once, been spent on earth.

The Besht, for whom the celestial halls (*hechalot*) were open, had known for some time that a new soul was to descend to earth, since such a soul undergoes a three-year period of preparation prior to its descent (while all other souls require only one year's preparation). However, the identity of that soul had not been revealed to him, and he did not know that it was to be Baruch's son.

On Rosh Hashanah of that year (5505/1745) the Besht's disciples noticed a radical change in the manner of their master. Usually, the "Period of Awe" began with the Besht from the first day of *Elul*, and lasted through Yom Kippur (Day of Atonement, 10th of *Tishrei*). This period corresponds to the third period of forty days which Moses spent on Mount Sinai, when he evoked the "Thirteen Attributes of Mercy," and attained Divine forgiveness for the Israelites for the sin of the Golden Calf. It was on the 10th of *Tishrei* that Moses came down from Sinai, carrying the second Tablets with the Decalogue.

These were solemn days for the Besht, when his Divine service was solemn and awe-inspiring. However, from the termination of the Day of Atonement until after Simchat Torah (the Day of Rejoicing with the Torah), it was the "Season of Rejoicing"—a period of sublime joy, when his Divine service was manifestly joyous. It was therefore most unusual to see the master in a state of obvious rejoicing during that particular Rosh Hashanah. This was evident when he wished everyone the traditional blessing of *Shanah Tovah*—"to be inscribed unto a good year," and during his Torah discourse at the repast, as also during the *Tekiot* and *Mussaf*. His joy grew in intensity from the termination of Yom Kippur through Succot (Feast of Tabernacles). The Besht's disciples wondered what the cause of that extraordinary joy was, but could find no explanation.

Baruch and Rivkah spent the entire period of Holy Days in Miedzibosz. Before departing for home they saw the Besht again. Their faces were beaming with joy, and when the Besht repeated his blessing, Rivkah fervently promised that she would consecrate her son to the dissemination of Torah and the Chasidic doctrine and way of life as taught by the Besht.

Rivkah, as has been mentioned previously, was well versed in Jewish learning and devoted some time every day to the study of Torah. She kept this, however, from her husband's knowledge. Now she decided to intensify her sacred studies, and she visited her sister-in-law, her husband's sister, who was married to the rabbi of Vitebsk, to ask her for guidance as to prayer and study during her anticipated pregnancy.

In due course Rivkah was able to tell her husband that she had conceived. Though they were certain that the Besht knew that his blessing was beginning to be fulfilled, they decided to let the Besht know about it.

At the beginning of the month of *Adar-Sheni*, Baruch went to Miedzibosz again, to inform the Besht that his wife was pregnant. The Besht wished him *Mazal-Tov* and gave him certain instructions to convey to his wife. Baruch left for home in a blissful frame of mind.

On the fourth day of the third week of *Elul*, on the 18th day of the month, which was his birthday, the Besht displayed an extraordinary elation. He personally led the prayers, which he chanted in joyous melodies. It was clear that the Besht was observing that day as a festive day. During the repast which followed the prayers, the Besht told his disciples:

On the fourth day of Creation the luminaries were set in the sky. Today, the fourth day of the week, a week related to the *haftorah*, "Arise, shine forth" (Isa. 60), a new soul descended on earth, a soul which will illuminate the world with the revealed and esoteric teachings of the Torah, and will successfully disseminate the Chasidic way with selfless dedication, preparing the way for the arrival of the Messiah.

The Besht proceeded to give a discourse on the verse "This one will console us" (Gen. 5:29), taking his text from *Midrash Tanhuma*.

The following Shabbat, on which the Torah reading was the *Sidrah Tavo* (Deut. Chaps. 26-29:8), the Besht again gave a discourse during the repast, the theme being the reading from the Prophets, dwelling on the verse, "Arise, shine forth, for your light has arrived, and G-d's glory shines upon you" (Isa. 60:1).

On the 25th day of *Elul* (when the circumcision of Schneur Zalman took place in Liozna), the Besht arranged a feast and held a discourse on the verse "On the eighth day his uncircumcised flesh shall be circumcised" (Lev. 12:3), and three days later, on the Shabbat, when the *Sidrah Nitzavim* (Deut. Chap. 29:9-31) was read, he again gave a discourse on the verse "I shall surely rejoice in G-d" (Isaiah 61:10—the *Haftorah* of the week), and he was in a manifestly elated frame of mind. All of which presented a mystery to his disciples and followers.

4

Many years later, when Schneur Zalman, as a young man, came to Rabbi Dov Ber, the *Maggid* of Miezricz, the disciple and successor of the Besht, the Maggid related to his son Rabbi Abraham, the "Angel,"[11] the reasons for the extraordinary conduct of the Besht on those occasions, as was revealed to him by the Besht himself.

What the Besht's disciples witnessed in those days was nothing else but their master celebrating the birth of Schneur Zalman, his entrance into the "Covenant of Abraham," and the critical third day of circumcision. Moreover, the various discourses which the Besht delivered on those occasions were connected with the newborn's destiny.

"'The reason I am telling you all this,' my master, the Besht, told me, 'is that he—Schneur Zalman—belongs to you'"; the Maggid concluded his story to his son, the "Angel."

For the Day of Atonement, 5506, Baruch came to Miedzibosz to be with his master. He had been forewarned not to tell anybody about the birth of his son, nor the name which had been given to him. Again, before leaving for home, he received from the Besht a set of instructions as to the discipline which was to surround the child, and the careful watch which was to be kept over him at all times, keeping him away particularly from the eyes and ears of idle gossipers.

The following year Baruch came, as usual, to the Besht for the Solemn Days. The Besht inquired about the little boy in great detail, and repeated his admonition about taking special care of child.

After Succot, when Baruch was ready to leave for home, the Besht again cautioned him to shelter the boy, and not to repeat any of his clever acts or sayings, as some parents are fond of boasting about their children.

Another year passed by. Once again Baruch made his annual pilgrimage to Miedzibosz. Baruch reported to the Besht that, upon returning home from Miedzibosz after Succot, his wife told him that there was a noticeable change in the boy on his second birthday. His speech and vocabulary had considerably improved.

During the year, the parents discovered that the boy had an extraordinary memory, and whatever he heard once, he never forgot. The Besht gave Baruch further instructions concerning the boy. Upon Baruch's request for permission to bring the boy to the Besht on his third birthday for the traditional "haircutting" ceremony,[12] the Besht told him that the boy should be accompanied by his mother, and his aunt Dvorah Leah, and they should come to him on the 18th of *Elul*, after the Morning Prayers.

Arriving home, Baruch found that the boy had made further strides in the two months of his absence from home. Little Schneur Zalman could now recite many psalms by heart, and his memory and mental grasp were astonishing.

According to plan, Rivkah and her sister-in-law, Dvorah Leah, brought the boy on his third birthday to the Besht. The Besht cut off a few locks of hair, leaving *peyot* (side locks) according to custom, and he blessed the boy with the three-fold Priestly Blessing (Num. 6:24-26). He then sent the visitors home, with his blessings for a safe journey and for the new year.

All the way home, little Schneur Zalman kept on asking his mother who the old Jew was who had cut his hair. "That was *Zaida* ('grandfather')," was her reply. Little did he then know that some day he would come to regard the Besht as his "grandfather" in a very real sense, namely, as the master of his master, the Maggid of Miezricz, to whom he owed his spiritual fulfillment.[13]

In his fifth year, Schneur Zalman was enrolled as a junior member in the Burial Association (*Chevrah Kadisha*). This honor entailed an annual contribution of a certain quantity of wood and money to the local synagogue for a period of eight years, until the boy reached the age of Bar Mitzvah, when he would become a full-fledged member. This was duly recorded in the *Pinkas* (Register) of the Chevrah Kadisha of Liozna on the 15th day of *Kislev*, 5510.[14]

From his fifth birthday, Schneur Zalman began to display a phenomenal mental grasp in his advanced Torah studies. Together with his insatiable thirst for knowledge, he experienced a great love for people. He revered Torah scholars for their scholarship, and he respected and loved ordinary folk for their simple faith and piety.

Many years later, he once told his grandson Rabbi Menachem

Mendel (subsequently the famed author of the Responsa *Tzemach Tzedek* and successor to the throne of Chabad): "All through my youth I found my Torah studies very easy, without my having to make any real effort. This was disconcerting to me, for the *mitzvah* of 'toiling in the Torah' eluded me. It was only when I reached the age of fifteen that I learned who I was and what the purpose of my soul's descent to earth was."[15]

At first, little Schneur Zalman was tutored by local *melamdim* (teachers). After several years, his father decided to send him to study in nearby Lubavitch,[16] under the tutelage of Rabbi Yissachar Dov,[17] also known as Yissachar Dov Kobilniker, a Torah scholar of note. Schneur Zalman studied under his guidance until he reached the age of eleven years. Then his teacher brought him back home, informing the boy's father that the boy could continue studying on his own. Rabbi Yissachar Dov prepared a program of studies in Talmud and Kabbala for the boy, and also a discipline of daily conduct.

Back home, in the country atmosphere of his father's estate, Schneur Zalman continued his studies. His father, and also his grandfather, both of whom were profound Talmudic scholars, took time out for Talmudic and Halachic sessions with young Schneur Zalman. During the long summer days the young scholar spent most of his time studying under the shade of the fruit trees in his father's orchard. His grandfather asked him once what he liked best in the orchard. "The pure, unpolluted air," was his reply.[18]

His love for the fields and meadows expressed itself in a practical way, in his efforts to encourage his brethren to engage in agricultural pursuits. According to a chronicle by Rabbi Schneur Zalman's son Moshe—who cites as his source an eye-witness account of an aged Chasid, Shlomo Ivansker—Schneur Zalman once stationed himself on a wagon and addressed a crowd of Jews who had come to the fair at Liozna. The young "Liozna Prodigy," as Schneur Zalman was known, urged his brethren to abandon their peddling and trading, and engage in farming and manual occupations. Schneur Zalman was then eleven years old. The impassioned plea of the young scholar had its effect. A number of Jewish families, refugees from Prague and Posen, did in fact settle on the estate of Schneur Zalman's father Baruch, with the latter's help. Other Jewish refugees from Bohemia formed an agricultural settlement in the vicinity of Byeli Rutchei ("White Spring"), adjoining Baruch's estate.[19]

Incidentally, the discovery of the "White Spring" was credited to Schneur Zalman. According to a legend current in the vicinity, the origin of the spring was as follows:

The well on the outskirts of Liozna, which had provided water for man and beast, had suddenly become polluted and unwholesome. A sorcerer named Akim was blamed for it, for it was believed that he had cursed the water of that well. One day Schneur Zalman was sitting in the orchard when his younger brother, Yehuda Leib, came running up to ask him what blessing of grace to recite after eating an apple. It was a new orchard, in its fourth year, when the fruits are forbidden (Lev. 19:23-24). Schneur Zalman told his younger brother never again to eat or drink anything before making sure it was permitted. Then he said to him that it would be well for him to cleanse himself with pure spring water. Schneur Zalman explained to his brother the importance of ritual immersion, which serves as an act of purification from spiritual contamination, and also as a symbolic transition to a higher degree of holiness, as the case may be. Schneur Zalman said he, too, would immerse himself in the water. He then led him to the foot of a nearby hill near a quarry of white limestone. The two boys began to dig. Soon, they uncovered a spring of fresh water. The quarry was filled with the water of the spring, and the two boys bathed in it. Eventually the spring became known as the "White Spring," and it was said to have healing powers, having cured both humans and beasts affected by the accursed well.[20]

During these early years, Schneur Zalman was introduced also to mathematics, geometry, astronomy, and philosophy, by two learned brothers, refugees from Bohemia, who had settled in the vicinity of Liozna.[21] One of the two brothers was a Kabbalist, who was said to be in possession of manuscripts by Rabbi Yitzchok Luria.[22]

When Schneur Zalman attained his Bar Mitzvah (the age of thirteen) and, in accordance with custom, delivered his first public discourse, he was acclaimed as an outstanding Talmudic scholar. He was thereupon elected as an honorary member of the local Chevrah Kadisha and entered in the *pinkas* of the community with titles and honors accorded only to ordained scholars of exceptional merit.[23]

Shortly after his Bar Mitzvah, Schneur Zalman went to Vitebsk, to spend a few months with his uncle Rabbi Yosef Yitzchak. Schneur Zalman, as he later related, was greatly impressed and influenced by the extraordinary Talmudic knowledge and brilliant mental grasp of his uncle. Under his lucid tutelage Schneur Zalman deepened his knowledge and enhanced his methods of study. Rabbi Yosef Yitzchak opened new horizons for the young Schneur Zalman in the interpretation of the text of the Bible, and of the sayings of the Sages in the *Aggadah* and *Midrash*. It was only later that Schneur Zalman discovered that much of the brilliant interpretations and revelations which he had heard from his uncle was actually derived from the teachings of the Baal Shem Tov, who was, as yet, unknown to Schneur Zalman.

The Besht, for reasons best known to himself, and much to his regret, kept himself out of direct contact with Schneur Zalman. He did not permit Baruch to take his son with him on his visits to Miedzibosz, and he enjoined Rabbi Yosef Yitzchak from telling his nephew anything about him, the Besht.

"Schneur Zalman is not destined to be my disciple," the Besht said. "He belongs to my successor."

Rabbi Yosef Yitzchak used to visit the Besht once a year or once in two years, on the occasion of the Festival of Shavuot. Each time, the Besht inquired about Schneur Zalman, and reiterated his admonition to keep Schneur Zalman in ignorance of the Chasidic way and of its leader. For the last time, Rabbi Yosef Yitzchak visited the Besht in the year 5520 (1760), the year of the Besht's demise. On the Shabbat before Shavuot the Besht said to the Maggid of Miezricz in the presence of Rabbi Yosef Yitzchak:

> From the day that the new soul was to descend from its abode in the realm of *Chochmah d'Atzilut* (the highest supernal sphere) to be clothed in a body on this earth, in

9

the person of the son of my saintly disciple Baruch and his wife Rivkah, I staked my life for him. He is yours, but he must come to you of his own volition, without external influence. Eventually he will come to you, and you should then realize what a "receptacle" he is. Be careful in guiding him, in order that he should successfully accomplish his destiny.[24]

That year (5520) Schneur Zalman was as yet unaware of the Besht. It was only in the month of *Elul* of that year (after the demise of the Besht) that Rabbi Yosef Yitzchak told Schneur Zalman of the Besht, and conveyed to him some of the teachings of Chasidut and the Chasidic way.

The fame of the young '*iluy*' (prodigy) reached Vitebsk, where one of its most prominent Jews, Yehuda Leib Segal, a man of considerable wealth and scholarship, wished to have him as his son-in-law. He approached Schneur Zalman's father and the match was duly arranged.

S chneur Zalman was fifteen years old when he married Sterna. She turned out to be a worthy mate, who stood by him throughout a lifetime of many tribulations.

The marriage was solemnized on Friday, the eve of *Shabbat Nachamu*, 5520. Schneur Zalman had made it a condition of his consent to the marriage, that the amount of 5,000 gold coins, which the father of the bride had promised by way of dowry, should be placed entirely at his, Schneur Zalman's, disposal, to do with as he saw fit.

Within the first year of their marriage, Schneur Zalman, with his wife's consent, placed the entire amount in a fund to help Jewish families settle on land and engage in agricultural pursuits. They were aided in the acquisition of farmland and farming implements, in flour milling, spinning and weaving wool and linen, and in similar pursuits of a livelihood. Thanks to this help many Jewish settlements sprang up in the vicinity of Vitebsk, along the banks of the River Dvina. Schneur Zalman continued to preach publicly, from time to time, to encourage Jews to give up peddling and take up, instead, some agricultural pursuit. He also visited the Jewish settlements and urged the

Jewish farmers to arrange periodic study groups for the adults for the study of *Chumash*, *Midrash* and *Aggadah* on their own level.[25]

Schneur Zalman's endeavors to encourage Jews to settle on land were in line with the general policy of the government in Poland and Lithuania. Facing the growing hostility of the urban classes towards the Jews, whose competition in trade and commerce they feared, the government offered various incentives to induce more and more Jews to settle in the country and villages.[26]

As a result, many Jews with no definite trade turned to mixed farming and agriculture for their livelihood.

In Vitebsk, Schneur Zalman was in proximity to his distinguished uncle Rabbi Yosef Yitzchak, and the latter introduced him to the teachings of Chasidut and the Chasidic way of Divine service, as taught by the founder of Chasidut, the Besht, and continued by his disciple and successor, the Maggid of Miezricz. Their sessions lasted over a period of two years.

Rabbi Schneur Zalman's prominent father-in-law, who had dealings with members of the landed nobility, introduced his brilliant son-in-law to members of the nobility and high officialdom. Two episodes are related of Rabbi Schneur Zalman at that time, which greatly enhanced his reputation as a scientist among the local nobility. One was the occasion when Rabbi Schneur Zalman solved the problem of a truant sundial which adorned the garden of the governor of Vitebsk. The sundial, which had been working perfectly, suddenly ceased to function during part of the afternoon in cloudless skies. The governor, so it is related, called in several scientists, but they failed to solve the mystery. The young Rabbi Schneur Zalman was then called in and he succeeded in placing the cause of the malfunction in an obstruction created by trees that had grown tall on a hill at a certain distance away. The other episode concerned a mathematical problem which the head of the local higher academy, a certain Prof. Marcel, had been struggling with for a long time, and Rabbi Schneur Zalman solved it for him.[27] Rabbi Schneur Zalman's reputation and acquaintance with the local nobility stood him in good stead in his work in behalf of his brethren, and in the crucial periods of his career.

By the time Schneur Zalman was eighteen years old, thanks

to his extraordinary assiduity and brilliance of mind, he had become "proficient in the entire Talmudic literature, with all its commentaries and early and late codifiers."[28] At the same time he studied the classics of Jewish philosophy and Kabbala literature, especially the *Zohar* and the *Shenei Luchot HaBerit* (ShaLoH) of Rabbi Isaiah Hurwitz.

Rabbi Schneur Zalman gathered around him a group of young men of excellent scholarship, and led them in the study of the Talmud as well as in the discipline of the Kabbala. They organized a *minyan* (small congregation) and worshipped in the manner of the saintly ShaLoH. For three years he led this group, and Schneur Zalman's reputation as a brilliant scholar and teacher was further enhanced.

Schneur Zalman had already conceived a new system of Divine service, based on the central principle that love of G-d and fear of G-d must derive from an intellectual approach, with a profound comprehension of the greatness of G-d. He also elaborated the methods of attaining this end by the application of the principle "from my flesh I see G-d" (Job 19:26), an inductive method leading from the microcosm to the macrocosm, and from the analogy of the soul powers in man to the Divine categories of the *En Sof*, using the attributes of the human soul as counterparts of the Divine categories. This system was eventually perfected in his *Likutei Amarim* (*Tanya*).

CHAPTER II

RABBI SCHNEUR ZALMAN'S "CONVERSION" TO CHASIDUT

The vast knowledge which Schneur Zalman had acquired gratified him intellectually, but his sensitive soul still yearned for fulfillment. He had yet to find a way to establish an equilibrium between the rational and emotional sides of his nature. It was then, at the age of about twenty years, that Rabbi Schneur Zalman decided to leave home for a period of time in search of a teacher and guide. Two centers of learning beckoned his attention. One was Vilna, the Lithuanian capital, the center of Talmudic scholarship, with the famed Vilna Gaon[1] at its head. The other was Miezricz, the seat of Rabbi Dov Ber, the "Maggid of Miezricz,"[2] heir to Rabbi Israel Baal Shem Tov, the leader of the still young Chasidic movement. For Rabbi Schneur Zalman, Miezricz was both geographically and intellectually the more distant place, but he had heard about the great scholarship of Rabbi Dov Ber, and the new way of Divine service which he was teaching. Rabbi Schneur Zalman had to make a momentous choice. It is recorded that Rabbi Schneur Zalman said, "I have already been exposed to Talmudic discipline; I have yet to learn the discipline of prayer,"[3] and he decided in favor of Miezricz. The decision was, of course, the turning point of his life.

Rabbi Schneur Zalman's decision to go to Miezricz aroused his father-in-law's vehement opposition, to the extent of depriving his daughter and son-in-law of any further financial support. But Rabbi Schneur Zalman's wife stood by him, and agreed to his

13

going there, on condition that if he decided to stay, he would not extend his stay beyond eighteen months. She raised a little sum of money with which to buy a horse and cart. Soon after Pesach (5525), Rabbi Schneur Zalman left for Miezricz, accompanied by his brother Rabbi Yehuda Leib. Having made their way to Orsha, a distance of some fifty miles, the horse collapsed. On learning from his brother that the latter had left home without his wife's consent, Rabbi Schneur Zalman urged him to return, while he himself continued his journey to Miezricz on foot.[4]

His first impressions were not encouraging. Schneur Zalman closely observed the Maggid of Miezricz and his senior disciples. He discovered that they devoted considerable time to the daily prayers and in preparation before the prayers, inevitably reducing the time left for Torah study. To the intellectual that he was, this emphasis on prayer seemed extravagant. He decided that Miezricz was not for him. Rabbi Dov Ber made no attempt to detain him.

As Schneur Zalman left Miezricz, he remembered that he had forgotten one of his belongings in the *Beit Medrash* of the Maggid. Returning there, he found the Maggid engaged in the examination of a Halachic question. The brilliant analysis by the Maggid of all aspects of the question, which displayed his extraordinary erudition in the realm of Halachah, made a profound impression on Schneur Zalman, and he decided to stay a while longer in Miezricz. Thereupon, the Maggid told Schneur Zalman that his saintly master, the Baal Shem Tov, had revealed to him that one day the son of Rabbi Baruch would come to him (the Maggid), would leave him, and then return again. Then he (the Maggid) was to tell him about the great destiny that was linked to Schneur Zalman's soul. The Besht further predicted that Schneur Zalman's path in life would be hazardous, but that he, the Besht, would intercede in his behalf, and in behalf of his followers, so that "his end would be exceedingly great" (Job 8:7).

Schneur Zalman was deeply moved by what he heard, and he decided to cast in his lot with the new Chasidic movement.[5]

Soon, new horizons began to unfold before him.

One particular episode, involving a brief discourse by Rabbi Dov Ber, "converted" him. The episode is of sufficient importance to merit recounting here, in approximately the same terms as the episode was described by Rabbi Schneur Zalman to his brother Rabbi Yehuda Leib.

Rabbi Schneur Zalman once happened to witness an intimate discussion by the "Holy Society," that is, the group of senior disciples of Rabbi Dov Ber. The subject matter of the discussion was in the realm of the Kabbala. They spoke of the various categories of the supreme angels, of the Divine Chariot, and of the array of the hierarchy of Divine Emanation. The main topic of the conversation centered on the perpetual state of love and fear (awe), of advance and retreat, which those heavenly creatures experience in the presence of the Divine Majesty. As the discussion progressed, it so fired the vivid imagination of the participants that they seemed to be carried away to those very sublime spheres which they were depicting, where but a thin veil separates the pure spirits from the Infinite Light. They worked themselves up into a state of rapturous ecstasy, where the desire for the mystical union with the Infinite (*En Sof*) becomes so overpowering as to bring one to the verge of soulful consummation (*Kelot Hanefesh*). Rabbi Schneur Zalman himself was deeply touched and, as he related, for the first time felt the consuming passion of this mystical experience. At that very moment the sound of the master's footsteps brought them back to earth. They came out of their reverie and rose to their feet in anticipation of their master's appearance. Presently Rabbi Dov Ber entered the room, took his accustomed place at the head of the table and began:[6]

[It is written] "I made the earth and man thereon created" (Isa. 45:12). *Anochi* ("I"), He Who is the true "I," unknown and concealed even from the highest emanations, clothed His Blessed Essence through numerous contractions (*tzimtzumim*) in order to give rise to emanations and creatures, the various categories of angels, and worlds without number. Through countless condensations "I made this physical world, and man thereon created." Man is the ultimate purpose of creation. *Barati* ("I have created") is the numerical equivalent of 613 [the number of biblical commandments], the end-purpose of man. As the [book of]

Pardes (Portal 22, ch.4) quotes from the book of *Bahir*, "Said the attribute of *Chesed* (Kindness) before the Holy One, 'Master of the Universe, since the days of Abram on earth I have had no work to do, because Abram is serving in my place.'" Thus Abraham, a soul clothed in a body, occupying himself with hospitality to wayfarers as a means of disseminating the idea of G-d on earth, is higher in quality and rank than the attribute of Kindness itself in its most supernal state. The "complaint" of Kindness was the expression of that attribute's "envy" of our Patriarch Abraham.

Concluding his words, Rabbi Dov Ber retired to his quarters. His brief discourse had a calming effect on his disciples, and gave them food for thought. It contained the doctrines which form the underlying basis of the theology and ethics of Chasidut, which Rabbi Schneur Zalman was surely not slow in grasping, namely: (1) The Divine "I" is unknowable even to the highest supernal creatures. (2) The pure spirits and intellects, namely, the supernal spheres and emanations, are not the end of Creation, but a means to it. (3) The purpose of Creation is man, a soul in a body, on this physical earth. (4) The purpose of man is obedience to the Divine Law. (5) Man is superior to angels. These doctrines eventually found an elaborate and systematic exposition in the *Tanya*. But what mostly impressed Rabbi Schneur Zalman on that occasion was Rabbi Dov Ber's demonstration of that perfect equilibrium and harmonious synthesis of the mystic and rationalist which was the object of Rabbi Schneur Zalman's quest. To quote Rabbi Schneur Zalman: "Two things I saw then: The sublime ecstasy of the Holy Society on the one hand, and the remarkable composure of our master Rabbi Dov Ber on the other, which enthralled me completely. That is when I became a Chasid."[7]

Once the young *"Litvak"* (native of Lithuania) became attached to Rabbi Dov Ber, the latter began to give him special attention, though he was the youngest and newest of the disciples. Rabbi Dov Ber arranged that his son, Abraham,[8] (who because of the saintliness of his character had earned the appellation *Malach* ["Angel"]), initiate the new disciple into the eso-

teric doctrines of the Kabbala and Chasidut, as had been taught
by the Besht and himself, in return for instruction in Talmudic
study. Rabbi Schneur Zalman's time was now equally divided
between the study of the Talmud and Chasidut, which he studied with his customary diligence. He also closely observed the
master, Rabbi Dov Ber, and his distinguished disciples, in an
effort to emulate their day-to-day behavior and refinement of
character. Here was a group of scholarly mystics who exemplified
Chasidut at its best. This is what Rabbi Schneur Zalman had
been looking for.

Schneur Zalman found among the disciples of the Maggid
some two score elders who had been the Baal Shem Tov's close
followers. Some of them knew the Besht even before he revealed
himself, and knew also his father, Rabbi Eliezer. These sages
related to Schneur Zalman many episodes and events about the
Besht, to which they had been witness.

Schneur Zalman found the nights too short to record all that
he heard during the day. His notes grew into many volumes of
manuscripts. Unfortunately, most of his manuscripts, including
those he had acquired while in Miezricz from members of the
Maggid's "Holy Society"—altogether twenty-four bound volumes and numerous bundles of loose folios—were destroyed in
the fire which broke out in Liadi in 5570 (1810), when Rabbi
Schneur Zalman happened to be in Berditchev. In that fire the
major part of his *Shulchan Aruch* was also destroyed.[9]

Schneur Zalman considered himself very privileged when he
was included in the list of the senior disciples of the Maggid who
attended on their master. The Maggid, in turn, showed him
affectionate consideration. Occasionally, the Maggid consulted
his youngest disciple as to the level of scholarship on which to
preach to the followers who came to listen to him, and reviewed
with Schneur Zalman the intended lecture. On several occasions, as Schneur Zalman related to his grandson the Tzemach
Tzedek, the Maggid reduced the level of his lecture no less than
four times, when Schneur Zalman found it still too high for the
visitors, and only the fifth version of it received Schneur
Zalman's approval.[10]

Being the youngest of the Maggid's disciples, and imbued

with a goodly measure of humility, Schneur Zalman attended also on his senior colleagues, observing their conduct and emulating their ways. Soon, they realized that the new disciple excelled them in scholarship and in the breadth of his grasp of their master's teachings. They called him, affectionately, the "Young Sage."[11]

When Rabbi Schneur Zalman returned home, after the eighteen months had elapsed, he was asked by his erstwhile colleagues in Vitebsk whether he had found it worthwhile to go so far away while Vilna was so much nearer. Rabbi Schneur Zalman answered: "In Vilna you are taught how to master the Torah; in Miezricz you are taught how to let the Torah master *you!*"[12]

Upon his return to Vitebsk, Schneur Zalman immediately set out to disseminate the teachings of the Baal Shem Tov and of the Maggid of Miezricz, with particular emphasis on prayer. He also began to concern himself with the ordinary Jewish folk and *amei-ha'aretz* in accordance with the Chasidic doctrine.

The "conversion" of the "Liozna *Iluy*" to Chasidut created a stir in the Jewish community of Vitebsk. Complaints were lodged against him before the *Beit Din*. On his part, Schneur Zalman informed the *Beit Din* that he was prepared to debate the issue and defend the way of the Baal Shem Tov and of the Maggid of Miezricz. Moreover, he challenged the validity of the bans and excommunications against the Besht which had been made public in the year 5517 (1757).

The *Beit Din*, in conjunction with the leading scholars of Vitebsk, decided to accept the challenge of Reb Yehuda Leib Segal's son-in-law, whose attitude they regarded as overbearing and presumptuous.

The public debate lasted for about a week. It gave Schneur Zalman an opportunity to expound the basic teachings of the Baal Shem Tov and of his successor the Maggid, which resulted in the winning over a number of young men of the scholarly set to his side. On the other hand, many expressed open hostility to the new Chasidim, and the community found itself divided.

Schneur Zalman's "conversion" to Chasidut, his complete preoccupation with intellectual problems, his extraordinary assiduity, his devoutness in prayer and eccentric ways, aroused his father-in-law's disappointment. The latter began to have serious misgivings as to the mental soundness of his son-in-law. Both father and mother pressed their daughter Sterna to divorce her husband, on the ground of the latter's "unbalanced mind." The young wife, however, remained loyal to her husband. Life became difficult for the young couple in the home of her parents. The latter often denied their son-in-law candles, so he would not be able to study through the night, but Schneur Zalman continued his studies by moonlight. In the long, wintry nights the young couple suffered cold and privations, but the pressures applied by his parents-in-law did not dampen Schneur Zalman's spirits, nor cause him to change his ways.

Rabbi Schneur Zalman did not remain in Vitebsk very long. The atmosphere was charged with open hostility on the part of his in-laws and other members of the community, though Rabbi Schneur Zalman made a number of converts among the younger scholars of his age. These, in turn, suffered the same treatment, unless they succeeded in concealing their adherence to the Chasidic way. Rabbi Schneur Zalman returned to Miezricz, and he continued to visit his master from time to time, following him also to Rovno and Anipoli, where Rabbi Dov Ber moved towards the end of his life.

The years of privation and abuse for Rabbi Schneur Zalman ended when in 1767 he was summoned to become *Maggid*[13] in his home town Liozna. Rabbi Schneur Zalman accepted the post, which he held for the next thirty years, until he moved to Liadi (in 1801), following his second arrest and exoneration, as will be recounted later.

In 1770, when Rabbi Schneur Zalman was barely twenty-five years old, Rabbi Dov Ber assigned to him the task of re-editing the code of Jewish Law, the *Shulchan Aruch*. It was almost exactly two hundred years since Rabbi Yosef Caro had written his famous masterpiece. During this time much halachic material had been added in rabbinic literature, often giving rise to divergent opinions as to the practical application of the Jewish Law in given circumstances. It was Rabbi Schneur Zalman's task to examine and sift all the new material, make decisions where necessary in the light of the earlier codifiers and Talmudic literature, and finally embody the results into his new edition of the *Shulchan Aruch*, thus bringing it up to-date. Needless to say, it was an enormous and responsible task, requiring extraordinary erudition and mastery of the entire Talmudic and Halachic literature as well as a boldness to arbitrate and make decisions in disputed cases involving the opinions of the greatest masters of Jewish Law up to his time. Rabbi Schneur Zalman superbly acquitted himself of this task, which at once immensely enhanced his reputation in the rabbinic world, and gave him an honored place among the great codifiers of Jewish Law. The work became known as the *"Rav's" Shulchan Aruch*, in distinction from its forerunner.[14]

Two years after he began his work on the *Shulchan Aruch*, Rabbi Schneur Zalman began to work on his system of Chabad philosophy, which was eventually embodied in his *Likutei Amarim* or *Tanya*. He worked on it intermittently for twenty years.[15]

Chapter III

The First Crisis

The Chasidic movement, under the leadership of the Maggid of Miezricz, was generally not given to excesses. The synthetic blend of the inner rational and emotional forces, as exemplified in the leader, kept the mystical susceptibilities of his followers more or less in check. There was one exception, however, among the disciples of the Maggid of Miezricz. He was Rabbi Abraham of Kalisk.[1] By nature a highly temperamental individual, he was carried away by some of the teachings of the Maggid. Rabbi Abraham Kalisker gathered around him a group of brilliant young men, whom he inspired to ecstatic states of Divine worship, which, as he taught, was attainable only under extreme self-effacement. For about two years he taught this group a rigorous discipline of austerity, selfmortification and saintliness. Their mode of prayer was ecstatic and rapturous, often giving way to frenzy. During prayer they were prone to paroxysms of dancing, gesticulation and boisterousness. They were impatient of the opponents of Chasidut, particularly the type of dispassionate Talmudists, who carried about them an air of staidness and gravity, which, to these passionate mystics, betrayed insensibility and arrogance. They took upon themselves the task of exposing them to ridicule, in order to rouse them out of their complacency, as they thought.

In the year 5530 (1770) the activity of this group reached its height, when a young man, a member of the group, came to Shklov and requested permission from the local rabbi to preach in the synagogue. The rabbi engaged the stranger in a Talmudic

21

discussion and was satisfied with the visitor's erudition and piety. So, permission was granted.

The lecture was attended by the rabbi and lay leaders, as well as a large gathering of the local community. The preacher held the audience spellbound throughout his lecture. His scholarship and eloquence were impressive indeed. However, towards the end of his lecture, the preacher switched his theme in a subtle manner and began to heap abuse upon certain rabbis and Talmudists whose opposition to Chasidut in the name of piety was, in his words, nothing but a cloak covering their arrogance and self-interest. His accusations were so thinly veiled as to leave no doubt in the minds of his audience that he was attacking some of the most prominent spiritual leaders who were in the forefront of the assault upon the Chasidic movement. The young preacher's concluding remarks left the audience shocked and dumbfounded. In the ensuing commotion the young man disappeared, leaving the town agog.

The admiration of the audience for the eloquence and brilliance of exposition of the unknown preacher gave way to indignation at his audacity and brashness. A committee was at once formed in Shklov to actively combat the spread of the Chasidic movement, and delegates were dispatched to other centers such as Minsk and Vilna to coordinate the combat forces against the followers of the Besht and his successor, the Maggid of Miezricz.

A report of the episode, and the consequent intensification of the opposition, reached the Maggid. He summoned all his disciples, including Abraham of Kalisk, to a special conference. The latter was severely rebuked, and a decision was adopted to put an end to any extravagant mode of religious conduct such as had been conceived by Rabbi Abraham Kalisker.[2]

In order to evaluate the rise of the opposing forces, and to counteract them in some measure, the Maggid of Miezricz sent Rabbi Schneur Zalman on a secret mission to the centers of the opposition. In the late autumn of 5531 (1771), we find Rabbi Schneur Zalman in Shklov, appearing there as an itinerant young scholar. Arriving in one of the local synagogues, weary and cold from the journey, the stranger settled down near the oven to warm up and rest. As in most other Lithuanian towns and townlets—and Shklov was one of Lithuania's most out-standing Torah centers—a daily Talmud class was in session. It was led by the *gaon* Rabbi Yosef Kolbo, whose fame extended far and wide.

When the class was over, attention centered on the wayfar-er. A lively Talmudic discussion ensued, in which the stranger's erudition in the vast Talmudic literature amazed the *gaon* and the other scholars. Rabbi Schneur Zalman was persuaded to extend his visit for several days, and he was invited by the *Rosh-Av-Beit-Din* of Shklov, Rabbi Henoch Schick, to give a lecture in Talmud. Rabbi Schneur Zalman's logical exposition and method of study made a profound impression upon all present. When asked who he was, and what was his name, Rabbi Schneur Zalman evaded direct answers and did not reveal his identity.

The mystery surrounding this visitor, his obvious scholar-ship, piety and humility, were the talk of the day for the people of Shklov. It was only some days after Rabbi Schneur Zalman's departure from Shklov that the community learned that he was the Maggid of Liozna, and one of the youngest disciples of the Maggid of Miezricz.[3]

Rabbi Schneur Zalman visited many other Jewish communi-ties, in some of them concealing his identity, in others openly professing to be a disciple of the Maggid of Miezricz. Everywhere he won personal admirers and, what was more important to him, admirers for the Baal Shem Tov and the Chasidic movement which he represented.

Upon completing his mission, Rabbi Schneur Zalman reported to the Maggid and his Saintly Society on the high stan-dard of learning and piety in all the communities of Lithuania he had visited. He further declared that wherever there was opposi-tion, it was primarily due to misunderstanding or sheer ignorance of the Chasidic way. He advocated a policy of restraint and for-bearance towards the opposition, suggesting, also, that the way to win over the opposition would be to match their level of Talmudic learning.[4]

In the meantime, the wave of opposition grew unabated. In 5532 (1772) a public debate on Chasidut was arranged in Shklov. Rabbi Schneur Zalman and Rabbi Abraham of Kalisk were designated by the Maggid of Miezricz to defend the Chasidic movement at this public debate. The two Chasidic emissaries successfully warded off all attacks against the new movement. However, they had no defense against the complaint centered on the Chasidic group of Kalisk, namely their frenzied ways, including somersaulting in public, their brazen attitude towards Torah scholars who did not join the ranks of the Chasidim, and the scandalous conduct of one of them in the town of Shklov two years previously, which had not been forgotten, nor forgiven.

Far from winning over the rabbinic authorities of Shklov, or at least softening their opposition, the debate ended in their downright condemnation of the Chasidic movement as a menace to the established order and norms of Orthodox Judaism. A report to that effect was dispatched by the Beit-Din of Shklov to the Gaon of Vilna. The Chasidim were described in most reprobate terms, as rebels and heretics with pagan tendencies. The fact that the condemnation was really leveled against a small group of Chasidim who were the exception rather than the rule, was ignored. The Gaon of Vilna adjudged the whole Chasidic movement as heretical, and therefore subject to proscription. Accordingly, a ban against the Chasidim was published on the 8th day of *Nissan* of that year, 5532 (1772), over the signatures of the Gaon of Vilna and the entire *Beit-Din* of Vilna.[5]

About the same time, a virulent anti-Chasidic pamphlet entitled *Zemir Aritzim*[6] appeared, containing various manifestos and bans against the Chasidim.

This was a very critical period for the fledgling Chasidic movement, which was faced with a frontal assault, both from the side of Orthodoxy as well as that of the Haskalah movement. The latter already had begun to make serious inroads into the larger Jewish communities.

One of the early casualties of the Mitnagdic attacks was the saintly Rabbi Levi Yitzchak of Berditchev, who, at that time, was the Rabbi and *Av-Beit-Din* of Pinsk. A strong opposition to him developed in his community for his attachment to the Maggid of Miezricz. His community was split, and embroiled in a heated controversy. While he was visiting the Maggid, the opposition got the upper hand. In his absence, he was ousted from his post, and another rabbi—Avigdor[7]—was appointed in his place. The new rabbi, as it turned out later, was an ambitious individual, and not altogether scrupulous. In order to entrench himself firmly in the community, and to preclude the former spiritual leader from claiming his post, he applied all sorts of pressures against the wife and children of Rabbi Levi Yitzchak to induce them to leave town. The distressed family appealed to Rabbi Levi Yitzchak by letter after letter to get them out of their predicament.

All these circumstances presented a very serious challenge to the Maggid of Miezricz and his disciples. The leading disciples gathered together to weigh the situation, in order to decide upon ways and means of counteraction. They decided to counter the ban against them by pronouncing a ban against those who issued the ban against them, especially against the new rabbi of Pinsk who had usurped the position, contrary to the *din* (Jewish Law).

Chasidic tradition has it that the Maggid of Miezricz, on learning of the action taken by his disciples, said that it had shortened his life. Nevertheless, he predicted that the cause of Chasidut would triumph.[8]

The Maggid of Miezricz felt that the time of his returning his soul to heaven was drawing near. On his last Shabbat on earth, the Shabbat of the weekly *Sidrah* of *Vayyishlach* in the year 5533 (1772), he delivered a Chasidic discourse to his disciples while he was confined to his bed. On the following day (the 17th of *Kislev*) he told Rabbi Schneur Zalman that during the last three days before the soul's returning to heaven, it was possible to perceive the creative word of G-d in every physical thing, which is its true essence and reality. That night he further told Rabbi Schneur Zalman that he would be blessed with a son, his first-born, whom he should name Dov Ber, after him, and he gave him special instructions as to the manner in which he should take care of his newborn son from the day of his birth until after the *Brit* (circumcision).[9]

On the third day of the week, the 19th of *Kislev*, 5533 (1772), Rabbi Dov Ber, the Maggid of Miezricz, disciple and successor of the Baal Shem Tov, returned his soul to its Maker. He passed away in the town of Anipoli, where he was laid to rest. A year later, on the 9th of *Kislev*, 5534 (1773), Rabbi Schneur Zalman's wife gave birth to a son, who was named Dov Ber, after the Maggid of Miezricz.

Upon the Maggid's demise, the disciples cast lots as to how to divide among them the *taharah* (purification of the body) of their saintly master. The *taharah* of the head fell to the lot of Rabbi Schneur Zalman. To the rest of the disciples this served as an obvious omen, not only of Rabbi Schneur Zalman's special merits, but also as a harbinger of his succession to the leadership.[10]

N ow that the leader was gone, the Chasidic movement faced its greatest crisis. The smoldering opposition which had erupted violently shortly before the death of the Maggid of Miezricz, could be expected to continue in full force. On the other hand, the question of succession to the Maggid reached an impasse. The Maggid's son, Rabbi Abraham, refused to accept the leadership. Besides, his aloofness from the world hardly made him a fitting leader at this critical time. In order of seniority, the vacant chair of leadership should have been given to Rabbi Menachem Mendel Horodoker,[11] senior disciple of the Maggid. But, out of deference to the Maggid's saintly son, he refused to accept the succession. Under the circumstances, the disciples decided to form an administrative committee, under the chairmanship of Rabbi Schneur Zalman. It was empowered to work out a program for the future of the movement. The plan was to include a geographical distribution of the Chasidic forces, with various centers from which the Maggid's disciples would carry on their work, each one in his own territory. To Rabbi Schneur Zalman was assigned the task of visiting these local Chasidic centers from time to time, as well as other towns and communities, with a view to strengthening and expanding the movement's influence. Thereupon the disciples parted, each one having been assigned a certain territory in which to spread the teachings of Chasidut.

Rabbi Schneur Zalman's task was the most difficult one, for he was to capture the stronghold of the opposition, the province of Lithuania, with Vilna, the seat of Rabbi Elijah himself. This he was expected to accomplish in cooperation with Rabbi Menachem Mendel Horodoker.

Rabbi Schneur Zalman set out to acquaint himself more closely with the prevailing conditions in the very strongholds of the opposition. During the years 1772-75 he revisited such centers as Shklov, Minsk, Vilna, at times and in some places concealing his identity. Wherever possible he sowed the seeds of Chasidut, organized new Chasidic nuclei, and strengthened the movement in various communities.

Seeing that the opposition threatened to turn the conflict into an irreparable schism, Rabbi Schneur Zalman and his colleagues decided to do their best to avert it. In 1775, Rabbi Schneur Zalman accompanied his senior colleague Rabbi Menachem Mendel to Vilna in the hope of convincing Rabbi Elijah that his opposition to Chasidut was based on a misconception. Twice they unsuccessfully sought an audience with the Gaon, and when some influential community leaders persisted in their appeal to Rabbi Elijah to meet with the two leaders of the Chasidim, Rabbi Elijah left town and stayed away until the two emissaries had departed.

Dismayed but not discouraged, the two emissaries went to Shklov, in the hope of once again engaging the leaders of the opposition there in a public debate, but their efforts proved fruitless there also.

Recounting these efforts in a letter to his followers in Vilna in the year 1797,[12] nearly a quarter of a century later, Rabbi Schneur Zalman describes in detail the circumstances of this fruitless attempt and refers also to the ideological differences between him and Rabbi Elijah in regard to certain Kabbalistic doctrines. It is noteworthy that although Rabbi Schneur Zalman was deeply disappointed by Rabbi Elijah's refusal to see him and his colleague, he defends the attitude of the "saintly scholar" on the ground that the latter had been misled by distorted testimony which he had unsuspectingly accepted as trustworthy. Characteristically, Rabbi Schneur Zalman's references to Rabbi Elijah were always highly respectful, referring to him as *HaGaon HaChasid* (the "saintly *Gaon*"). The text of the letter (with abbreviations) follows:

. . . May my opening words fall upon attentive ears to hear truthful words of genuine truth in regard to the dispute with our opponents.

If it had been possible for me to bring the matter to a proper conclusion with them—surely there is no greater *mitzvah* than establishing peace among Jews. But what was there for us to do that we did not do? We have tried very hard in this matter, but we did not succeed. We are innocent before G-d and Israel.

With prior notice we went to the house of *HaGaon HaChasid*, long may he live, to debate with him and to remove his censures from us. I was there together with the *Rav* and Chasid Rabbi Mendel Horodoker of saintly memory, but he [the Gaon of Vilna] shut the door to us twice. When the notables of the community spoke to him, "Master, behold, their famous *Rav* came to debate with your Torah Eminence; and should he be defeated it will certainly bring peace upon Israel," he staved them off by various pretexts. But when they began to implore him persistently, he disappeared, leaving the city and staying away until the day we left the city, as the elders of your city know.

Subsequently, in our province, we went to the community of Shklov, again to seek a debate, and we did not succeed. They did unto us things that should not be done, reneging upon the promise they had promised us not to mistreat us. But seeing that they had nothing with which to refute us, they resorted to violence, purporting to rely on the authority of *HaGaon HaChasid*, long may he prosper.

In truth, we judged him in the scale of merit, inasmuch as the matter had been completely resolved in his mind, without a doubt or any shadow of a doubt, and he had arrived at a verdict on the testimony of many trustworthy witnesses insofar as a man can see superficially. Accordingly, when he heard a word of Torah quoted to him by the notorious provocateur[13] who interpreted it, he did not look upon it favorably or try to justify it, perchance the agent had slightly misquoted it. For, as is well known, a minor change in language may alter the matter from one extreme to the very other. It certainly could not have occurred to him that they [the Chasidic leaders] might be in possession of the word of G-d received from Elijah [the Prophet] of saintly memory, to interpret and sublimate the material [language] of the holy *Zohar* in a mystical manner that had eluded him, since it can be transmitted only directly from mouth to mouth, and not through the said agent. But because the attainment of such a high level [to merit the revelation of Elijah] required a very great and profound sanctity, diametrically opposed to that [level] which had been confirmed to him by witnesses whom his Eminence considered trustworthy—and usually people do not err to such an extent, from one extreme to another—he refused to accept from us any argument, answer or defense whatsoever, or any explanation of the word of Torah which he had heard [in our name], nor anything else whatever.

And why should this day be different? For even now nothing has been heard from him in the way of a retreat and regret from [his position in] bygone days, to indicate that any doubt has now arisen [in his mind] perchance they [the opponents] had been wrong. On the contrary, the money is the proof, namely, the fact that he demanded two thousand *adumim* for *tzedakah* or other worthy cause. This was because he did not wish to waste his time. For, as you know, I have answers to all the questions, which are well-known in our provinces; but they did not accept the answers, as we have personally witnessed in the community of Shklov. Now, therefore, why should I toil in vain? For the dictum of our Sages of blessed memory is well known: "Just as it is a *mitzvah* to say a thing that will be heeded, so it is a *mitzvah* not to say a thing that will not be heeded."[14] . . . Especially after the many evil deeds which have been perpetrated against our Chasidic fellowship in the province of Lithuania and Little Russia on the basis of the expressed opinion of *HaGaon HaChasid*, particularly to his disciples; and a friend has a friend. I have seen with my own eyes a letter written by one of his disciples in Vilna in the name of his teacher [containing] things which I do not wish to put in writing out of respect for the Torah.

Now, from the content of your esteemed letter it is evident and clear to me that all the above has not escaped your esteemed selves, and you were fully aware of it. Nevertheless, you relied primarily on the possibility of there being two esteemed men who could adjudicate [the dispute] and decide who is right, etc. But there is no wisdom in this suggestion. For their esteem would certainly carry no weight whatever were they to adjudicate against the opinion of *HaGaon HaChasid* which he placed in the mouth of his emissary R' Saadiah,[15] who always speaks in the name of his master, and certainly not in his own name; particularly in regard to the interpretation of the book of *Likutei Amarim* and its like, which are based on the lofty sacred teachings of the *Ari* of blessed memory. Insofar as is known, there is not one person in the province of Lithuania who would dare to maintain an opinion contrary to that of *HaGaon HaChasid*, and declare openly that he erred, G-d forbid, except in the distant countries such as Turkey, Italy, most of Germany, Greater Poland and Minor Poland (Galicia). This I would welcome indeed, especially in matters of faith; for according to the rumor in our provinces [stemming] from his disciples, it is precisely in this area that *HaGaon HaChasid* found objection to the book of *Likutei Amarim* and its like, where the concept of G-d's "Presence in all the world" and "no place is devoid of Him" is interpreted in a very *real* sense, whereas in his esteemed opinion it is absolute heresy to say that G-d, blessed be He, is to be actually found in very lowly things, for which reason, according to your esteemed letter, the well-known book was burnt,[16] whereas they have their own mysterious and unique interpretation of the said dicta, namely, "the whole earth is full of His glory" refers to [G-d's] watchfulness, etc. Would that I could know him and guide him, and present to him our case, to remove from ourselves all his philosophical censures and objections in the footsteps of which he has followed, according to his said disciples. If, however, he would find it hard to retract from the path to which he has been accustomed since his youth, and my words will not be accepted by him, then his greatness should be matched by his modesty, to explain fully all his objections to us in regard to this tenet, spelled out clearly in writing by one of those who are close to him, and signed by himself personally; and I will follow it up and answer all his objections, also over the signature and seal of my own hand. Both letters would then be copied and sent to all the wise men of Israel, both near and far, to express their opinion thereon. For Israel has not been forsaken by G-d, and there will be found many with perfect knowledge of the Torah and with a mind inclined to adjudicate, without partiality to either side. Then the majority will rule, and peace in Israel will be established thereby.

As for the book *Likutei Amarim* and its like, in the matter of the "elevation of the sparks" from the *kelipot,* etc.,[17] the essential concept of this sublimation and the elevation of the sparks has been mentioned for the first time only in the Lurianic Kabbala, but not by previous Kabbalists, nor [is it found] explicitly in the holy *Zohar.* We know with absolute certainty that *HaGaon HaChasid,* long may he live, does not accept the tradition of the *Ari* of blessed memory in its entirety, that it has all been revealed by Elijah, of blessed memory, but only a small portion of it; While the rest is of his [the *Ari*'s] own great wisdom; consequently, there is no imperative to accept it, etc; moreover, the writings [of the *Ari*] came down in a most defective form, etc.[18] A person who holds this view is entitled to make his own choice to choose that which to him is good and fitting, out of all the sacred writings of the *Ari,* of blessed memory, saying, "This tradition is nice, and stems from the mouth of Elijah, and this one is not from the mouth of Elijah, of blessed memory." What can we say, and what can we speak, and how can we justify ourselves in his presence? Even if he interprets something in the writings of the *Ari,* of blessed memory, at variance with our interpretation, anyone with brains in his skull can understand that one who does not believe in a certain thing is no authority to judge and rule on that matter. But the adjudicators should be "the great" in Israel who are noted for their acceptance of the tradition of the *Ari*, of blessed memory, in its entirety, that it is all from the mouth of Elijah, of blessed memory, such as the Sephardic *Chachamim* and their like. And this, too, would be of no avail, unless the claimants and contestants against us also accept the tradition of the *Ari*, of blessed memory, in its entirety, like ourselves, and were leading scholars of Israel in *Nigleh* ("revealed," i.e. Talmud, etc.) and *Nistar* ("esoteric," i.e. *Kabbala*), and adjudication be required between them and the leaders of Israel among our Chasidim who are renowned in Poland and Germany.[19] But so far we have heard nothing of this.

As for the burning of the well-known book,[20] it is not for you to fight for the cause of the Baal Shem Tov of saintly memory and to provoke strife, G-d forbid. This is neither the city nor the road in which G-d delights. If in your eyes it is something new, it has already happened before. Remember the days of old. For who was greater to us than Moshe in his generation, namely, the Rambam, of blessed memory, who in his country, Spain, rose in high repute, growing ever greater, so that while he was yet alive they used to include in the text of the *Kaddish* "in your life, and your days . . . and *in the life of our master Moshe*, and in the life of all the house of Israel," etc., for they saw his esteem and his holiness and piety; yet in distant lands, where they had not heard nor seen his esteem, he was considered a heretic and denier of our holy Torah, and his books were publicly burnt, viz. the first book of his Code, by order of men wise in their eyes, who objected to what he had written in the Laws of *Teshuvah*, and it did not occur to them to ascribe it to the deficiency of their knowledge and understanding of his sacred words, as subsequently clarified by the Ramban (Nachmanides) and RaDaK (Rabbi David Kimchi) of blessed memory. However, with the passing of time their hatred also disappeared, and the truth appeared on the surface and all Israel knew that Moshe was true and his teaching was true. So will it be with us, speedily in our time. Amen.[21]

It is clear from the above letter that the weight of the opposition to the Chasidic movement, insofar as the Gaon of Vilna was concerned, rested on formal testimony presented to the Gaon by persons whom the Gaon had no reason to suspect of deliberate distortion. Such testimony undoubtedly included the excesses of the Kalisk group, which could have been sufficient to arouse the ire of the Sage of Vilna. However, unless this testimony was presented to him as representative of the *whole* Chasidic "sect" rather than as an *exception*, the Gaon of Vilna would not have consented to a general ban against the Chasidic movement as a whole. There must also have been other deliberate misrepresentations which the Gaon in his saintly innocence could not conceive as half-truths. Thus, Chasidic lore relates the following episode which may serve as an illustration of the kind of "testimony" presented to the Gaon: Two Jews, whose reliability as witnesses could not be doubted, testified on oath that they had seen the leader of the Chasidim sitting at a joyful repast on *Tisha b'Av* (the Fast of the 9th day of *Av*) with a female on his lap! The testimony was true insofar as it went, except for two things: It happened to be on Shabbat, when the Fast is postponed for the following day, and the "female" happened to be a baby grandchild. It cannot be ascertained whether the said episode actually took place, or is no more than a legend. But it is nevertheless characteristic of the manner in which "testimony" could have been presented to the Gaon to obtain his condemnation of the sect. It need not surprise us that the Gaon should have accepted such testimony in good faith, for the Shabbatians and their heirs, the Frankists, were known to indulge in all sorts of immorality and misconduct, and the Chasidim were sometimes branded as secret followers of those notorious though defunct sects.

In addition to whatever testimony may have been presented to the Gaon about the conduct, or misconduct, of the Chasidim, it is clear from the above document that there were also certain deep-rooted philosophical and doctrinal differences which sepa-

rated the Gaon of Vilna from the teachings of the Baal Shem
Tov, particularly those expounded in the *Likutei Amarim*
(*Tanya*). These differences could have been resolved through a
direct confrontation between the Gaon of Vilna and Rabbi
Schneur Zalman, but the Gaon persistently refused to meet with
his younger defendant, as we have seen. Moreover, by reason of
the immense stature of the Gaon of Vilna, both as a Talmudist
and as a Kabbalist, there could not be found a person commanding similar authority within reasonable precincts, who could act
as an arbiter in the dispute. Under the circumstances there
appeared little likelihood for the rift to be healed during the lifetime of the Gaon of Vilna, unless he reversed himself, which did
not seem to be within the realm of probability.

The following year (1776), the leading disciples of the late
Rabbi Dov Ber of Miezricz conferred on the situation. It was
decided that Rabbi Menachem Mendel's wish to emigrate to
Palestine be granted, and that Rabbi Schneur Zalman was to
become the leader of the Chasidim in White Russia and
Lithuania. However, Rabbi Schneur Zalman refused to accept
the leadership in an official capacity as long as his senior colleague lived, despite the latter's repeated appeals.[22] Only after
Rabbi Menachem Mendel died in 1788 did he accept the leadership officially. In the meantime, Rabbi Schneur Zalman was
actively engaged in preaching and disseminating the Chasidic
doctrines according to his own interpretation. During his extensive travels many followers were attracted to him, not only from
the masses but from the ranks of scholars as well. He established
a school of selected disciples in his own town. The students were
divided into three groups (*Chadarim*) and many of them became
distinguished scholars and Rabbis. The *Chadarim*, established by
Rabbi Schneur Zalman in Liozna during the years 1773-1778,
admitted only selected students of high scholastic ability for
intensive studies of both Talmud and Chasidut. The faculty
included, in addition to Rabbi Schneur Zalman himself, his
three learned brothers, Rabbi Yehuda Leib, Rabbi Mordechai,
and Rabbi Moshe. This academy of higher learning existed for
twenty years, and produced Chasidic rabbis of outstanding cal-
iber, who widely disseminated the Chabad doctrine.[23]

In the year 5537 (1777) Rabbi Schneur Zalman experienced a traumatic personal crisis. It was towards the end of that year that Rabbi Menachem Mendel of Vitebsk, with two of his colleagues, Rabbi Abraham of Kalisk and Rabbi Israel of Polotzk,[24] together with a group of their followers, were due to leave for the Holy Land. Rabbi Schneur Zalman felt a great urge to join them and likewise emigrate to Palestine. By nature a peace-loving man, Rabbi Schneur Zalman did not cherish the battle which awaited him, and which he would have to wage single-handedly after his colleagues were gone. Moreover, he was imbued with a profound love for his fellow-Jews in general, and with deep respect and affection for Torah scholars in particular. The strife between the Mitnagdim and Chasidim was very painful to him, and seeing no prospects of immediate reconciliation and peace, he was sorely tempted to escape from it all.

For three months he wrestled with the agonizing problem as to whether or not to join his colleagues and emigrate to the Holy Land. Finally, during *Chol-HaMoed* Pesach he reached a decision. He informed his family and immediate circle of followers and disciples that he would be leaving for the Holy Land right after Pesach.

The Jewish community of Liozna consisted of ordinary, simple, pious Jews. They revered the great Chasidic leader, and his learned brothers, who graced their humble community with their presence. Now, the community was deeply grieved to learn of the impending departure of all its glory. Hastily, the seven elders of the Community Council convened to deliberate on what to do to preserve, at any rate, the institutions of learning which Rabbi Schneur Zalman had set up. The following resolutions were adopted:

(a) The houses occupied by Rabbi Schneur Zalman and his brothers and their families would be kept in good repair and readiness for their original occupants, should they decide to return.

(b) The Council pledged to maintain and support all the married scholars and younger students of the *Chadarim* of Rabbi Schneur Zalman, who would choose to remain in Liozna for at least one year.

(c) The community at large would further provide maintenance for an additional fifty new students, if the seminarians
would agree to provide instruction and guidance for them.

Rabbi Schneur Zalman was gratified to see the sincere concern of the community to maintain his seminaries. He urged his
disciples to remain in Liozna and avail themselves of the community's generous hospitality. He arranged for them a curriculum
of studies to be followed in his absence.

The whole town turned out to bid farewell to Rabbi Schneur
Zalman and his brothers. In the courtyard of the main *Beit
Hamidrash*, a platform was set up, from which Rabbi Schneur
Zalman addressed his farewell message to the community,
exhorting them to support the Talmudic students with esteem
and affection. He blessed them to have sons and sons-in-law who
would be "learners" and scholars of the Torah.

In the beginning of the month of *Iyar*, Rabbi Schneur
Zalman, with his family and his brothers, Rabbis Yehuda Leib,
Mordechai and Moshe, with their families, as well as some of the
disciples of the upper two *Chadarim*, left Liozna. They made their
way to Mohilev, on the Dniester River.

On the way, Rabbi Schneur Zalman tarried in various towns
where he gave public discourses in Talmud, and homiletic lectures in *Mussar*, inspiring the large audiences who flocked to listen to him with love and awe for G-d and closer adherence to
the Torah and Mitzvot.

To all pleadings that he not forsake his flock, and remain to
guide their lives and destinies, Rabbi Schneur Zalman replied:
"Our Sages have ruled, 'Your own life has priority.'"[25]

Some of his leading disciples, however, remained to settle
down in various towns on the way.

Throughout the whole summer of that year 5537 (1777),
Rabbi Schneur Zalman tarried in the districts of Podolia and
Wolhynia, taking leave of many followers with parting lectures
and sermons.

Arriving, finally, in Mohilev, his senior colleagues Rabbi
Menachem Mendel of Horodok and Rabbi Abraham of Kalisk
did not disguise their displeasure at their colleague's intention of
abandoning his post. They urged him to reconsider his decision,

asserting that he had no right to leave the land, and thus deprive the Chasidim of his leadership at such a critical time. They also reminded him of the destiny which the Maggid of Miezricz had foreseen for him, with the assurance of the eventual success of his life's mission.

Rabbi Schneur Zalman spent three weeks in Mohilev in the company of his senior colleagues. During the last week of their sojourn together Rabbi Schneur Zalman spent long hours each day in private discussions with Rabbi Menachem Mendel. They finally left without him, and he remained in Mohilev for two more weeks which he spent in seclusion. Then he let it be known that he would return to Lithuania. Upon hearing of this momentous decision, his brothers hastily returned to Liozna with their families, although it was not known yet with certainty whether Rabbi Schneur Zalman would also return to Liozna, or take up residence in some other town. There was some speculation that he might settle in Horodok at the behest of Rabbi Menachem Mendel, or in Kalisk, at the behest of Rabbi Abraham, or perhaps in a larger Jewish community, such as Minsk or Shklov.

Arriving in Liozna, Rabbi Schneur Zalman's brothers were pleased to find the scholars and students engaged in diligent study, according to the prescribed curriculum of Rabbi Schneur Zalman. Moreover, there were a number of new young faces, mostly from the vicinity of Liozna, who had taken advantage of the community's offer to maintain fifty additional students.

The return of Rabbi Schneur Zalman's brothers to Liozna revived the fervent hope of the community that Rabbi Schneur Zalman, too, would return and settle in their midst. However, in view of the conflicting rumors as to Rabbi Schneur Zalman's ultimate choice of residence, the Liozna Community Council called a general meeting in the main *Beit Hamidrash*. Before the appointed time, the *Beit Hamidrash* was filled to overflowing, and the women's gallery, too, had a capacity attendance.

Rabbi Schneur Zalman's brothers also attended the meeting. They informed the community that their illustrious brother had, indeed, decided to return to Lithuania, but had not decided, as yet, where to make his residence. However, pending final arrangements, he intended to come first to Liozna, where his house was so thoughtfully kept in readiness for him and his family.

The announcement brought cheers from all present. Several resolutions were immediately adopted:

(a) To send a delegation to greet Rabbi Schneur Zalman and extend to him an urgent invitation to make Liozna his residence again.

(b) To provide lodgings and board for up to one hundred seminarians on a year-round basis.

(c) To provide free board and lodgings for thirty visitors each week-end for three days, that is, for the Shabbat and the day before and after. On *Shabbat-Mevorchim* (when *Rosh Chodesh* is blessed) this hospitality would be extended to fifty visitors, as also during the festival seasons. Finally, during the month of *Tishrei*, when a large influx of Chasidim could be expected for the Solemn Days and Succot, the community pledged to provide free board and lodgings for up to five hundred visitors.

The members of the Community Council thereupon appealed to Rabbi Schneur Zalman's brothers to join the delegation that was to be sent to greet their illustrious brother, and to convey to him the community's pledges. To this they agreed, choosing Rabbi Yehuda Leib to go with the delegation.

In due course the delegation returned with the happy tidings that Rabbi Schneur Zalman had favorably accepted the community's proposals, and consented to take up his residence again in Liozna.

About the time that the first Chasidic émigrés arrived in the Holy Land (5th of *Elul*, 5537/1777), Rabbi Schneur Zalman and his entourage left Mohilev and began the long wagon-trail bound for Liozna. Rabbi Schneur Zalman's caravan, including scores of coaches and wagons, augmented by new disciples and followers, moved at a leisurely pace from town to town, stopping to rest for a day or two in each town. They celebrated Rosh Hashanah and the whole festival-season in the midst of this journey, and it was not until the middle of *Shevat* (5538/1778) that Rabbi Schneur Zalman finally reached Liozna.[26]

By this time, the turbulence of anti-Chasidic agitation had

abated considerably. The lull lasted for about three years. During this time Rabbi Schneur Zalman was able to concentrate his attention on his seminaries and on the dissemination of the teachings of Chasidut.

CHAPTER IV

THE CHASM WIDENS

T he period of the years 1781-1788 saw Rabbi Schneur Zalman again engaged in defending the position of the Chasidim and the Chasidic doctrine against attack. As has already been mentioned,[1] the battle against the Chasidim was renewed with much vigor in 1781, following the publication of the book *Toldot Yaakov Yosef* by Rabbi Joseph HaKohen of Polonnoye. This book is believed to be the first published Chasidic work by a disciple of the Baal Shem Tov which was openly critical of certain aspects of the Rabbinate. It raised a storm of protest among the Mitnagdic extremists, who caused the book to be burnt publicly in Vilna, Brody, and elsewhere. Chasidic books were also burnt in some Jewish communities in Bohemia, where the well-known Rabbi Ezekiel Landau, Chief Rabbi of Prague, was the formidable antagonist of the Chasidic movement.[2] However, the central figure of the opposition was Rabbi Elijah of Vilna, the greatest Talmudic authority of the period. In the late summer of 1781 Rabbi Elijah was co-signatory with Rabbi Shmuel, head of the Ecclesiastical Court of Vilna, on a manifesto calling for the most stringent measures against the Chasidic "sectarians." This appeal sparked the strict ban against the Chasidim which was pronounced, with all the paraphernalia of the dreaded *cherem*, at the rabbinic convocation in Zelva, and by the Rabbinates of Brisk, Slutzk, Shklov and other Mitnagdic strongholds.

These attacks were more effective in causing the Chasidim to close their ranks than in curbing their movement. The

40

Chasidim were forced into greater separation. If, in the past, the Chasidim tended to hold their own congregational services by reason of their adoption of the Lurianic rite in prayer (the so-called *Nusach Ari*), they were nevertheless often permitted to share the same houses of prayer.[3] The wave of intolerance, however, forced the Chasidim to establish separate synagogues, which began to spring up in growing numbers.[4] Then there was the question of the ritual slaughter of animals (*shechitah*). Rabbi Schneur Zalman insisted on the use of a specially honed slaughterer's knife for this purpose.[5] The Chasidim, therefore, would either have their own trained and qualified slaughterer, or they would rather do without meat. In view of the fact that the meat-tax was an important source of revenue for the *kahal*, the problem of the Chasidic meat-boycott was sometimes solved by permitting the installation of a Chasidic slaughterer in the communal slaughter-house.[6] But with the rise of antagonism against the Chasidim, such cooperation was well-nigh impossible, and the schism tended to become more intensified.

The issue of the *shochet's* (slaughterer's) knife played an important role in the controversy between the Chasidim and Mitnagdim, and calls for some clarification.

Jewish law requires that the knife which the slaughterer uses to cut the animal's throat be perfectly smooth. The slightest notch on the knife's blade makes the knife unfit for the kosher slaughter of animals. Thus, the training of a *shochet* entailed, in addition to his familiarity with all the laws of *shechitah*, also the skill of preparing the knife to make it perfectly smooth and sharp, and to develop a sensitivity for testing its smoothness (namely by going over the sharp end of the blade with the tip of his fingernail to detect even the slightest notch or imperfection).

The slaughterer's knife in general use at that time, as from olden days, was made of wrought or cast iron. The preparation, i.e. sharpening and smoothing, of the knife entailed a lengthy process, requiring both skill and patience on the part of each individual shochet, and even then it was difficult to attain perfection in both smoothness and keenness. Consequently, most shochetim concentrated on the keenness of the knife. During the time of the Maggid of Miezricz, especially later, on the insistence of Rabbi Schneur Zalman, the honed steel knife was introduced for exclusive use by the Chasidic shochetim, since this knife had the advantage of being more pliable and practical, and could more quickly and with less effort be made both smooth and sharp to perfection. Eventually, more precisely in the following generation, the honed steel knife was universally accepted by all Jews, as it is still used to this day. However, in the early days of the controversy, the innovation by the Chasidim was strenuously opposed, as in the case of all other "innovations," regardless of their merit. The fact that these innovations were conceived for the more meticulous observance of the law was ignored in the heat of the opposition to the Chasidic movement in its totality.[7]

With all his insistence upon the use of the honed steel knife, Rabbi Schneur Zalman did not rule out the older practice as no longer valid. Indeed, when he learned that some of his Chasidim refused to eat meat at weddings, or similar repasts, where the meat was of animals slaughtered by the old method, he urged his Chasidim not to embarrass their hosts and other guests in public, since the meat was kosher. Thus, in a letter (of uncertain date) he wrote to his Chasidim in Vilna:

> The shechitah with honed knives is a great and profound *mitzvah* which our rabbis, the heavenly saints, adopted, and were verily prepared to make the supreme sacrifice for it. There can be no financial consideration in having a permanent shochet [of our own]. However, if you sometimes participate in a *seudat-mitzvah* (religious repast) with other Jews of your community, heaven forfend that you should separate yourselves from them, to regard them as if they were eating from a [non-kosher] carcass, G-d forbid and forfend. I have never myself taken exception to the cooking utensils [in which such meat was cooked]. . . .[8]

The controversy on this issue continued all through the lifetime of Rabbi Schneur Zalman. In Vilna, where the Chasidim eventually succeeded in obtaining a predominating influence in the community council, the leading non-Chasidic rabbis complained to Rabbi Schneur Zalman as late as 5571 (1811) that they were placed in a position where they had to use meat of Chasidic shochetim using honed knives, much to their dismay!

In reply, Rabbi Schneur Zalman wrote to them a lengthy epistle, with an erudite discussion on the Halachic points involved, to prove that not only is shechitah with a honed knife in order, but that it in fact reflects a more stringent compliance with the Halachah. He also pointed out that when the out-standing *gaon* Rabbi Chaim of Volozhin visited White Russia in 5563 (1803) he had declared in the house of his saintly rabbi, the Gaon of Vilna, that, from the viewpoint of the Halachah, according to the Talmud and *poskim*, there was no prohibition against the use of honed knives. The reason for the ban against the practice was the same that served as the basis for the entire ban against the Chasidim which was issued in 5532 (1772), namely, the erroneous belief that the Chasidim constituted a heretical sect, and consequently merited all the stringent and punitive measures issued against the Chasidim at that time. Even that reason no longer existed.

Rabbi Schneur Zalman pointed out, moreover, that the use of honed knives had become a common practice throughout the Ukraine, Galicia and Podolia, in much of Wolhynia, as well as in the large cities of Dubno, Ostrog, Kremenitz and Lutzk, all of which were predominantly non-Chasidic; also in the Holy Land, and by the Sephardim. To invalidate the Chasidic use of honed knives for shechitah would mean to invalidate a practice which had already been accepted by tens of thousands of Jews, both Chasidim and non-Chasidim.[9]

Thus, at the time when the said letter was written, nearly thirty years after the ban against the Chasidim of 1772, the use of honed knives was already widespread even among the Mitnagdim. But in the period under discussion, the issue of the shechitah as well as the other issues in the controversy, provided sufficient fuel for a sustained attack against the new "sect."

Being mostly on the defensive, the Chasidic community assumed the characteristics of a brotherhood, with its members voluntarily pledged to mutual assistance, aid and comfort. Yet Rabbi Schneur Zalman was not content with merely strengthen-ing the Chasidic ranks. He was bent on peaceful expansion of the movement. His disciples, men of Talmudic as well as Chasidic learning, after years of study and training in his

Chadarim, were strategically placed in various Jewish communities, to propagate the Chasidic teachings and way of life. In debates with their opponents they could more than hold their own. Rabbi Schneur Zalman himself sometimes visited various Mitnagdic strongholds and, being a gifted preacher, won many new adherents.

In the year 5543 (1783) an important disputation took place in Minsk between leading Mitnagdic *gaonim* from Vilna, Shklov, Brisk, Minsk and Slutzk on one side, and Rabbi Schneur Zalman on the other. The disputation was to be conducted on two levels.

There was, first of all, to be a test of the Talmudic scholarship of the Chasidic protagonist. The Mitnagdim took the position that they would not debate with any Chasidic leader unless they were satisfied with the latter's proficiency in Talmudic knowledge.

Rabbi Schneur Zalman agreed to these terms on condition that the Mitnagdim, too, would agree to be put to the same test. His counter-proposal was accepted.

The second phase of the disputation was to be centered on the doctrines of the Baal Shem Tov.

The *gaonim* of the Mitnagdic camp began to examine Rabbi Schneur Zalman by a series of questions in Talmud and Halachah. Rabbi Schneur Zalman's answers were precise, clear, and to the point. The simple and succinct manner in which he disposed of some rather involved questions amazed the audience. They were similarly impressed by the questions which he, in turn, put to his contestants. Rabbi Schneur Zalman obviously had the ability to present most intricate problems in a few words.

The venerable *gaon* Rabbi Aharon Yaakov, the head of the *yeshiva* of Slutzk, and the equally famed *gaon* Rabbi Zelmele Slutzker, the leading contestants of the Mitnagdim, failed to solve the problems which Rabbi Schneur Zalman put to them. They requested Rabbi Schneur Zalman to answer his own questions. This he did, with the exception of two, which remained unresolved.

Having satisfactorily disposed of the preliminary phase of the disputation, the antagonists of Chasidut began to outline their objections to the teachings of the Baal Shem Tov.

The main strictures which the Mitnagdim leveled against the Beshtian doctrines centered on two points:

Firstly, the teachings of the Baal Shem Tov accorded especial esteem to the prayers and *Tehillim* recital of the unlearned and untutored Jew, even though he did not know what he was saying. This attitude, the Mitnagdim contended, tended to give the *am-ha'aretz* and ignoramus a sense of undeserved self-importance, and lowered the prestige of the *talmidei-chachamim*. It seemed to ignore the Talmudic saying that "all calamities that occur in the world are due to the *amei-ha'aretz*."[10]

Secondly, according to the doctrine of the Baal Shem Tov, even a *gaon* and *tzaddik* have to serve G-d in the way of *teshuvah*. The Mitnagdim took strong exception to this doctrine, arguing that it placed the saint and scholar in the category of ordinary sinners and repenters. Such a notion surely undermined the honor of the Torah and the dignity of the *talmidei-chachamim*. The Mitnagdim further concluded that this notion was in contradiction to the view of the Torah, Written and Oral, which described the *tzaddik* as the "foundation of the world"[11] and the *talmidei-chachamim* as those who "increase peace in the world" and as the true "builders" of the Jewish nation.[12] The Beshtian notion of requiring them, too, to do penance was humiliating, and most objectionable.

Rabbi Schneur Zalman replied to the said two main contentions of the Mitnagdim as follows:

"The basis of the doctrine of the Baal Shem Tov and of the teachings of his successor, my teacher and master the Maggid of Miezricz, which illuminate the way of Divine service, followed by all the disciples of our master the Maggid, is to be found in the first Divine revelation to Moshe Rabbeinu.

"My teacher, the Maggid of Miezricz, taught me the following doctrine, which he had received from the Baal Shem Tov:

It is written, "And the angel of G-d appeared (*vayyera*) to him in a flame of fire from the midst of the bush. And he saw that the bush was burning with fire, but the bush was not consumed. Then said Moshe, 'I will turn aside and see this great sight'" (Exod. 3:2-3).

The Targum renders the word *vayyera* ("appeared") by *v'itgali* ("revealed himself"). The meaning of "revelation" is that it comes within the perception of everyone, to each one according to one's capacity, down to the lowest levels. Thus, the Targum also renders the word *vayyered* in Exod. 19:20 ("And G-d *came down* on Mount Sinai") by *v'it-gali*("revealed himself"), though elsewhere, e.g. Gen. 38:1 ("And Judah *came down*"), the word *vayyered is* rendered by *v'nahat* ("descended"). Similarly in Gen. 11:5 the Targum gives a corresponding rendition in the sense of "revelation," as in the case of the revelation at Mt. Sinai.

Now, just as the revelation at Sinai was intended for *all* the people, from Moshe down to the Jew of the most humble station, so must "revelation" be understood in the other instances, including the first revelation to Moshe out of the Burning Bush. Here, too, we must assume a revelation which can be perceived on all levels, down to the lowest, as already mentioned.

The words *b'labat esh* are rendered by Rashi by *b'shalhevet shel esh, libo shel esh* ("in a flame of fire; the heart of fire"). Thus, the message of G-d (i.e. "G-dliness") is to be found in the "heart of fire," i.e. in the earnest and sincere inwardness of the heart, where the fiery embers of G-dliness abide.

The words "from the midst of the bush" elicit Rashi's further commentary: "But not from another [more stately] tree, alluding to the verse, 'I am with him in distress (*tzarah*)'"(Ps. 91:15). *Tzarah* (literally "narrow place") alludes to this material world, which is so called because it is limited in space; and also because the Light of the *En Sof* is concealed therein in Nature, and is thus "confined" and "constricted," as it were. By contrast, the supernal worlds, where the Light of the *En Sof* shines forth manifestly, are called "wide, open spaces."

However, the design and purpose of the creation of this physical world is to illuminate it and convert it from צרה to צהר—"light"—by means of the light of the Torah and the

Mitzvot, to be studied and observed in the daily life.

It is written, "Man is like a tree of the field" (Deut. 20: 19). There are fruit-bearing trees, to which, according to Rabbi Yochanan, the *talmidei-chachamim* are likened (*Taanit* 7a); and there is the *sneh*, a humble bush that bears no fruit. Yet, the "fiery flame" was manifest in the *Sneh*. To be sure, the *talmidei-chachamim*, the students of the Torah, are filled with fire, since the Torah is called "fire" (Deut. 33:2), but it is not the inextinguishable kind of fire which burned in the *sneh*. The *talmidei-chachamim*, can, and do, quench their inner fire by the intellectual gratification which they derive from their Torah studies, from the new insights which they discover, and from original innovations in the interpretation and exposition of the wisdom of the Talmud.

Not so the ordinary and unlearned Jew, the *sneh*—in whom burns an inextinguishable fire, and unquenchable longing for attachment to G-d. The only spiritual expression that the simple and untutored Jew can find is in prayer and the recital of *Tehillim*. And though he may not know the exact meaning of the sacred words he intones, they contain the full force of his sincerity and wholeheartedness.

The only motivation of these humble Jews is their simple faith in G-d, which creates in them the burning and insatiable desire for Torah and. Mitzvot, a desire which, of necessity, remains unsatisfied and unquenched.

This is why the eternal "fiery flame" (*labat esh*) is to be found precisely in the hearts of these simple, sincere folk.

It is written, "And Moshe said, 'I will turn and see this great sight'" (Exod. 3:3), which, according to Rashi means, "I will turn from here, to come closer to there." This indicates that Moshe Rabbeinu understood the Divine message of the Burning Bush which emphasized the unique quality of the ordinary Jew—the *labat esh* being found precisely in the *sneh*, rather than in the cedars of Lebanon. The realization of this evoked a sense of *teshuvah* in him, and a change of outlook and direction ("I will turn [*ashuva*] from here to come closer there").

Now, Moshe Rabbeinu was a perfect *tzaddik*. The course

of *teshuvah* of the perfect *tzaddik* is quite different from that of the ordinary repenter. It is effected in the manner of "I will turn from here to come closer there." In other words, no one, not even the greatest *tzaddik*, should be static in his Divine service, however perfect it may seem at any time. There must be a constant striving toward ever greater heights, turning from one high level to a still higher one, with a constant desire to get closer to G-d. In this progression, which is essentially an infinite process, each higher level attained leaves the previous level, however satisfactory it seemed previously, deficient by comparison. Hence there is room for *teshuvah* even for the perfect *tzaddik*."

Rabbi Schneur Zalman emphasized that the said fundamental tenets of the Baal Shem Tov were based on the *first* Divine revelation to Moshe Rabbeinu, whom G-d had chosen to be the *first* deliverer and leader of the Jewish nation, and he went on to explain the precedental nature of that revelation:

The Divine revelation to Moshe Rabbeinu was quite different from the Divine revelation to Noah, or even to Abraham. For, the Divine revelation to Noah was a personal one, due to special Divine grace. Whether Noah was singled out for this Divine love because "Noah found favor in the eyes of G-d" (Gen. 6:8), or because he actually merited it, as it is written, "For I have found you righteous before Me in this generation" (ibid. 7: 1), it was, nevertheless, a personal revelation, confined to him only.

The Divine revelation to Abraham was quite different. It contained certain instructions as to Divine service, and was attended by extraordinary tests and trials. It was, obviously, on an altogether higher level, though it, too, came as a result of special Divine love, as it is written, "For I know him (Rashi: *love him*) that he will command his children and his household after him, that they observe the way of G-d, to do righteousness and justice," (Gen. 18:19). In the *Midrash*, Abraham was also called the "Supreme King's favorite" (B.R. ch. 42). Be it as it may, G-d's revelation to Abraham was also, essentially, a personal one.

However, the Divine revelation to Moshe Rabbeinu—

48

Rabbi Schneur Zalman explained—was not merely a personal one, but rather a general one, serving as a guideline for all future leaders of our people. This revelation showed that a Jewish leader should look for the *labat esh* in the *sneh*—among the ordinary people. The leader must try to discover this spark in the heart of the simple folk and fan it into an all-consuming flame.

Rabbi Schneur Zalman spoke with much feeling and conviction, concluding with the challenge:

In truth, the higher one's standing as a Torah scholar, the more humble must be one's submission to G-d; otherwise one is guilty of rebelliousness against the King of the Universe Himself. In that case one must indeed do repentance from the depth of a contrite heart, and eradicate the "Amalekite" from within[13] that cools the religious ardor of the Divine service.

According to eyewitness accounts, Rabbi Schneur Zalman's exposition of the basic doctrines of the Baal Shem Tov, and his concluding remarks, spoken with profound feeling and inspiration, left a tremendous impression on all present. Many who had come to witness the disputation in order to scoff at the head of the *Kat* (Sect), had been so inspired by his extraordinary erudition of the entire Talmudic literature, and his brilliant defense of the Besht's teachings, that they were at once "converted."

It was said that four hundred followers, all of them distinguished Talmudic scholars, both young adults and elderly men, joined the Chasidic community, as a direct result of that disputation. Scores of young scholars followed Rabbi Schneur Zalman to Liozna.[14]

There is reason to believe that as a result of the public debate in Minsk in 1783, the Chasidic community in that city received numerous adherents. Indeed, it grew sufficiently strong to force the *Kahal* to come to terms with it on certain communal matters.[15]

On his return from Minsk, Rabbi Schneur Zalman stopped for a week in Smilian, which was also a center of Torah study in those days. Here, too, Rabbi Schneur Zalman gained many new adherents to Chasidut. All these adherents, in turn, helped further to disseminate the teachings of the Baal Shem Tov and to increase the Chasidic ranks.

CHAPTER V

ENTRENCHMENT UNDER FIRE

A renewed attempt to curb the Chasidim was made in 1784 in Mohilev, but it likewise bore little fruit, except to create agitation, strife, and bitterness among the two sections of the Jewish population. On his part, however, Rabbi Schneur Zalman repeatedly urged his followers to exercise the utmost restraint in their relationship with their opponents, or complete passivity where the occasion demanded it. "Wait patiently until the storm blows over," he wrote to his Chasidim in the town of Oushatz. On that occasion, he even called upon his followers to refrain from holding separate congregational worship in order to avoid provocation.[1]

Some of the Chasidic leaders in other parts of the country attempted to persuade Rabbi Schneur Zalman to take a militant attitude against the extreme elements among the Mitnagdim. However, Rabbi Schneur Zalman resolutely refused to be drawn into any move that could only widen the gulf between the two camps and make it well-nigh impossible to heal the breach. The following eye-witness account, related by Pinchas Reizes,[2] one of Rabbi Schneur Zalman's prominent Chasidim, describes the confrontation between Rabbi Schneur Zalman and his militant colleagues on the crucial issue of self-defense:

One day, early in the summer of 1785 (during the month of *Sivan*, 5545), a plain, horse-drawn wagon pulled up near the house of Rabbi Schneur Zalman. Two Jews alighted. One was an elderly person of short stature; the other was younger and taller.[3] Speaking with a pronounced Polish-Wolhynian-Podolian accent, they inquired if that was the house of Rabbi "Zalmena Litvak."[4]

At first, we could not quite make out what they were saying. However, two other Chasidim, Simcha Zissel of Horodok and Shmuel of Kalisk (better known as Shmuel Munkis)[5] immediately recognized the strangers' request and pointed to the residence of the Rebbe (Rabbi Schneur Zalman), while I—Pinchas Reizes continued—and another young Chasid, Zalman Chienes of Beshenkowitz, a seminarian of Cheder Gimmel, accompanied them to show them the way.

We led the strangers through the Small *Beit HaMidrash* to the room where the Rebbe received visitors in private audience. The Chasidim reverently called this "Small Synagogue"—the "Lower *Gan Eden*." At that moment two young men were engaged in ardent study in the Small *Beit HaMidrash*. They were Arke Assayer (later known as the saintly Rabbi Aharon of Strashelia),[6] and the older son of Rabbi Schneur Zalman, Rabbi Dov Ber. The latter rose to greet and shake hands with the visitors, extending to them the traditional greeting of "*Shalom Aleichem*." The older one of the strangers said a few words to the Rebbe's son, but they were unintelligible to me because of his accent. The Rebbe's son, however, obviously understood him and answered briefly. From the answer I gathered that the older man had inquired about the subject matter which the two had been studying. Then the older man asked again, "Which is the residence of Rabbi Zalmena Litvak?" This brought a smile to the lips of the Rebbe's son who knew that this was the name by which his father was affectionately called when he first came to Miezricz.

Before he had a chance to reply to the question, the door to the adjoining private room of the Rebbe opened, and the strangers' faces lit up with delight as they saw the Rebbe in the doorway. The Rebbe extended his hand to them with the traditional greeting, and they followed him into his private chamber.

For several hours the visitors remained secluded with the Rebbe. Moshele, the Rebbe's youngest son, who still could not speak properly, came running to us into the courtyard, saying excitedly that the visitors were arguing with his father, and his father kept on repeating, "It is *assur*" (forbidden).

None of us knew who the visitors were, nor what they had come to discuss with the Rebbe—Rabbi Pinchas Reizes continued. The seminarians, as well as the older Chasidim, attracted by the news of the arrival of the mysterious visitors, and forming small groups near the Rebbe's house, were most curious to know the identity of these visitors, and the nature of their business with the Rebbe. Some of the older seminarians of *Cheder Aleph* were visibly excited. Suddenly, Arke Assayer came rushing out of the house, calling out loudly, "Berel (Dov Ber, Rabbi Schneur Zalman's son) has fainted!"

Chaim Elia of Druya, Avraham Zalman of Beshenkowitz and Nachman Velvel of Babinowitz were the first to rush into the Small *Beit HaMidrash*, where they found the Rebbe's son sprawled on the floor near the door of the Rebbe's private study.

The first two, somewhat excitable and impetuous by nature, began calling out, "Rebbe, Rebbe!" which brought the Rebbe out of his room.

When I came into the *Beit HaMidrash*, together with others, the Rebbe was bent over his son who now lay stretched out on a couch, his face pale, and his eyes closed. His father held his hand to Berel's head.

The Rebbe requested cold water. When it was brought to him, be sprinkled some drops on his son's face. The latter opened his eyes and emitted a deep sigh.

The Rebbe's son developed a high fever. Zalman Baruch and I moved him from the Small *Beit HaMidrash* into the Rebbe's living quarters and placed him in his bed, where he immediately fell asleep.

Zalman Baruch remained at his bedside while I returned to the Small *Beit HaMidrash*. I found Arke still there, and I begged him to tell me what he knew about the mysterious visitors, and what had transpired. At first he declined to tell me anything, and I suspected that he knew more than he cared to admit. When I continued to press him he began to weep. This filled me with profound grief and increased my anxiety to know what had actually taken place to cause the Rebbe's son to faint. However, all my pleadings with Arke Assayer to take me into his confidence were to no avail. Finally, I promised him a reward: I would divulge to him several Chasidic insights which the Rebbe had revealed to me on the occasion of my private audience with him. Arke knew that I was one of the senior students of *Cheder Beit* and particularly close to the Rebbe.

The tempting reward swayed him, and he told me what had happened: "Soon after the door closed behind the Rebbe and his visitors, we heard the latter's raised voices. We, the Rebbe's son and I, continued our study. As the hours passed, and the discussion behind the closed door became more animated, at times quite heated, we decided to get close to the door in order to overhear what the discussion was about. For a time it seemed to center on some Talmudic point, then it dawned on me that the subject was a proposed *cherem* (excommunication) against the leading opponents of Chasidut. The emissaries told the Rebbe that a *minyan* (ten, constituting a quorum) of senior disciples of the late Maggid of Miezricz, members of the Holy Society, had decided to fight back against the Mitnagdim with their own weapon—the *cherem*, and they wished their colleague, Rabbi Schneur Zalman, to join them in this. The Rebbe argued that this was *assur* (forbidden), because the effect of such an anathema is to cut a person off from the source of his soul, which might lead the anathematized person into heresy, thus creating a *Chilul HaShem* (profanation of G-d's Name).

"The older one of the emissaries declared that they had considered this possibility and had decided that, in view of the danger threatening the teachings of the Baal Shem Tov and the Maggid, placing the whole future of the Chasidic movement in dire jeopardy, there was no other recourse but to fight back with the same weapon.

"The Rebbe insisted that the law of the Torah forbade such a step, and that not only would he not be a party to it, but he most strongly disapproved of it. This stand provoked the older emissary to utter an imprecation, and it was this malediction which so shocked the Rebbe's son that he fainted!"

Continuing the story, Rabbi Pinchas Reizes went on:

After hearing from Arke what had transpired, I became more intrigued than ever. I stationed myself near the door, and strained my ears to hear the discussion inside the Rebbe's room. I could clearly hear the animated debate that was being carried on by the Rebbe and his visitors, on the laws pertaining to the three forms of excommunication (*nidduy, cherem,* and *shamta*).

Presently, the Rebbe's youngest son Moshele bounced into the Small *Beit HaMidrash*, and ran around the *shulchan* (table, or pulpit, used for the reading of the Torah).

A little while later, the door of the Rebbe's room opened, and the visitors appeared, accompanied by the Rebbe. They halted at the door, still continuing the Halachic debate. Moshele, seeing his father, ran up to him, and the Rebbe affectionately placed his hand on the boy's head.

"Well, Reb Zalmena?" the older emissary said. "Do you still refuse to join us? Consider it earnestly!" The Rebbe reiterated, however, that, according to the law of the Torah, it would be flagrantly sinful to cause such a *Chilul HaShem*, whereupon the older emissary again repeated the imprecation, and the two of them walked out briskly.

With extraordinary composure the Rebbe accompanied the two emissaries to their carriage. All of us seminarians present were profoundly impressed by the Rebbe's composure, and we realized that the emissaries were prominent Chasidic leaders in their native land.

The Rebbe's son, Dov Ber, was confined to bed with a

high fever for several weeks, but finally recovered.[7]

Having refused to join his colleagues on the warpath, even though they recognized it as a desperate step for self-defense and survival, Rabbi Schneur Zalman redoubled his efforts to fortify the Chasidic movement by persuasion and penetration.

Soon after the ill-fated visit of the two mysterious emissaries, Rabbi Yehuda Leib, the Rebbe's brother and dean of the seminaries, summoned several young men of *Cheder Beit*. He told them that the Rebbe requested them to volunteer their services during the summer months as his emissaries. They were to visit certain communities in Lithuania, with a view to disseminating in those places the Chasidic doctrine and way of Divine service, in an unobtrusive and secret manner. Rabbi Pinchas Reizes was one of them, and, as he later recounted his experiences, all the selected young men carried out their secret mission with complete dedication and with great success.

New faces began to appear in Liozna; they were scholarly young men who had been "converted" to Chasidut by Rabbi Schneur Zalman's emissaries.

Seeing that the effort had succeeded so well, it was repeated again during the next summer (1786). This time a new team of disciples were sent to spread the teachings of Chasidut and win new adherents. A concerted effort was made to penetrate the city of Vilna and its environs, and the initial success indicated that the time was ripe for a personal visit by Rabbi Schneur Zalman in one of the towns in the vicinity of Vilna.

After Rosh Hashanah it became known that the Rebbe would visit Swintzan, near Vilna, soon after Succot. Hundreds of Chasidim and non-committed young Talmudic scholars, as well as many from the entire district, prepared to go to Swintzan.

The autumn of that year (5547/1786), as Pinchas Reizes recounted, was an unusually severe one. The first snow fell in Liozna as early as *Chol-HaMoed* Succot. It was so cold that one had to put on one's fur coat and wintry felt boots when sitting in the *succah*. Many times it was necessary to clear the snow from the roof of the *succah*, as was also the case on the eighth day of

Succot—Shemini Atzeret—which happened that year to be on Shabbat.

All night long it had snowed heavily, and the Rebbe's *succah* had a thick cover of snow. Kuzma, the gentile janitor, was apprised of the fact that, so long as the snow was on the roof, it was not permissible to eat in the *succah*. Kuzma, dull-witted as he sometimes was, was quick this time to grasp the hint, and he cleared away the snow from the roof of the *succah*. Whereupon Rabbi Schneur Zalman made *kiddush* and ate the Shabbat and Yom-Tov repast in the *succah*.

Many of the visitors, who had come to spend the last festive days of Succot in Liozna, arrived chilled to the bone. Many came with frost-bitten fingers and toes.

It was the Rebbe's custom—Pinchas Reizes related—to have the scrolls of the Torah prepared for the *hakafot* (dancing with the Torah) which were to be held on the night of Shemini Atzeret, as well as on the following night and morning of Simchat Torah. Because of the jostling and hustling of the exuberant crowd during the *hakafot*, the holy scrolls were considerably jolted, and there was danger of some of the parchments receiving violent breaks. Hence, by order of the Rebbe, all the scrolls were taken out of the Holy Ark, rewound and tied up again at the seam, according to the requirement of the law, so that if a break did occur, it would be at the seam, which could be easily repaired.

The inspection and preparation of the scrolls was done by Michel the *shamash* (beadle), with the assistance of several seminarians, on Hoshana Rabba (the day before Shemini Atzeret).

A special supervisor was appointed to supervise the proceedings and then report to the Rebbe that the task had been properly executed.

That year—Pinchas Reizes related further—it was my great privilege to be the appointed supervisor for this task. When I came in to report to the Rebbe about the completion of the assignment, he was in a festive and elated frame of mind. I mentioned to him that many of the Chasidim who had come for Yom Tov had caught severe colds, and some of them were confined to bed with high fevers.

The Rebbe became engrossed in thought, with his head resting on his hands, as he was sitting at his desk. For some time he appeared to be in a saintly reverie. Then he raised his head, opened his eyes and declared:

"The Torah says of itself, 'At His Right Hand, there was a Fiery Law' (Deut. 33:2). We are rejoicing now with the Torah. Let all the sick men be brought to *hakafot*. Fire consumes fire. The fire of the rejoicing with the Torah will do away with the fever brought on by the colds and the chills!"

Now in Liozna there were two elderly Jews, noted Talmudists, who were obstinate Mitnagdim. They had, of course, the highest respect for the Rebbe, but they could not rid themselves of their anti-Chasidic prejudice. They were known as Rabbi Eizik *Mechadesh* ("the Discoverer") and Rabbi Naftali *Zahir* ("the Scrupulous One"). Both were men of outstanding Talmudic learning and of great piety. Their appellations were characteristic. Reb Eizik often used to say: "Today, I have—praise G-d—discovered a new insight in the Talmud," while Reb Naftali used to say: "I am scrupulous in my food," or "I am scrupulous in my speech," or "I am scrupulous in my views." He was always "scrupulous" in something or other.

Rabbi Eizik and Rabbi Naftali had studied at the famed *yeshiva* in Smilewitz, under the tutelage of the saintly *gaon* and *tzaddik* Rabbi Shilem Yudel, of whom it was said that Elijah appeared to him frequently. Many of his disciples were noted Talmudic scholars. At the time that Eizik and Naftali studied in Smilewitz, Rabbi Shilem Yudel was already a venerable sage, and was sightless. The lectures were delivered by his second son-in-law Rabbi Shimon Elia, the "*Iluy*" (prodigy) of Drutzen (a village in the vicinity of Kochanow, in the district of Mohilev).

My father—continued Pinchas Reizes—was, in his youth, a student of the *Iluy* of Drutzen when the latter had already been the senior *Rosh Yeshiva* of Smilewitz for twenty years. My father related that when the *gaon*, Rabbi Shimon Elia, gave a Torah-talk, it was so sweet and enchanting that the audience lost all sense of time. But when he delivered a *pilpul* (intricate Talmudic discourse), one felt as if the arguments pro and con hovered in the air, and one's head began to ache from the profundity of concentration. Subsequently, when my father inevitably became an intellectual admirer of the Rebbe (Rabbi Schneur Zalman), he said that if the *gaon* Rabbi Shimon Elia, the *Iluy* of Drutzen, had occasion to listen to the profound depth of the Divine wisdom of Chasidut, he would, undoubtedly, have become a Chasid. Moreover, if he had applied his brilliant mind and eloquence to the exposition of the Chasidic teachings, he would have converted the greatest of the great of Israel to the Chasidic doctrine.

Rabbi Eizik "Mechadesh" was a native of Aptzug, and Rabbi Naftali "Zahir" was a native of Kochanow. Both had arrived in Liozna fifty years previously as sons-in-law of well-to-do *baalei-battim*, and, being adequately provided for, devoted all their time to the study of Torah.

Eye-witnesses had related that when Rabbi Schneur Zalman came to Liozna as the newly-elected Maggid and delivered a *pilpul*, Rabbi Eizik was excitedly impressed. Both he and Rabbi Naftali declared that it was the first time they had heard such a *pilpul* since the day they had left the *yeshiva* of Smilewitz, where the *gaon* Rabbi Shimon Elia used to deliver a *pilpul* to an exclusive group of Talmudic scholars, twice a week.

In those days, the inhabitants of Liozna, like those in the surrounding towns, were Mitnagdim, whose religious life did not differ from that of their fellow-Jews elsewhere. Yet, they were not militantly antagonistic, like those of Vilna, Pinsk, Brisk and Slutzk.

The hoary old Jews of Vitebsk used to tell that they had frequently met itinerant wayfarers who stopped at the local synagogues and spoke of a wondrous *gaon* and *tzaddik* who lived in the province of Podolia. They spoke in glowing terms of his efforts to improve the lot of his brethren, and of his supernatural powers.

Some of these itinerants were obviously men of extraordinary Talmudic learning, and they could cite parallels in the Talmud of the kind of wonders performed by certain *Tanaim* and *Amoraim* in whose category they placed those performed by the Miracle-Worker of Podolia.

In those days—Pinchas Reizes continued—little was known about those itinerant wayfarers. But since we became followers of the Rebbe we learned that the passing wayfarers were colleagues or disciples of the Baal Shem Tov; they were his secret emissaries, who roamed the country to spread the teaching of the Besht and his mode of Divine service among the Jewish masses.

In due course the Rabbinic Council (*Vaad Ha'aratzot*) became alarmed at the spread of the Chasidic movement. At the annual fairs in Vilna and Slutzk bans were pronounced against the dissemination of the Besht's teachings. But the Jew in the street failed to comprehend the attitude of the Rabbinic Council. He loved to hear the wonderful stories which inspired him with new faith and warmth. Many Jews living in the districts of Vitebsk and Mohilev, the unlearned as well as the learned, all being sincere and dedicated in their faith and piety, were quickly attracted to the new movement. Even those who did not identify themselves with Chasidim in these provinces, at least did not become militantly hostile to the Chasidic movement.

When Rabbi Schneur Zalman began to disseminate the teachings of the Baal Shem Tov and of the Maggid of Miezricz, the two elderly Mitnagdim kept their distance from him, but observed an attitude of strict respect for him. Subsequently, when Rabbi Schneur Zalman's brothers, the saintly *gaonim* Rabbi Yehuda Leib, Rabbi Mordechai and Rabbi Moshe, came to live in Liozna, and Rabbi Schneur Zalman gave them in-depth lectures in the study of the Talmud three times a week, Rabbi Eizik and Rabbi Naftali were the only outsiders who participated in these sessions. Later on, when Rabbi Schneur Zalman established his first Seminar (*Cheder Aleph*) in 5536 (1776) and placed it under the tutelage of his brother Rabbi Yehuda Leib, both Rabbi Eizik and Rabbi Naftali frequented the "White *Beit HaMidrash*" to engage the young men in Talmudic discussion. However, when Rabbi Schneur Zalman began to deliver periodic lectures in Chasidut, the two Mitnagdim again became conspicuous by their absence.

Yet, when the Regional Rabbinic Council (*Vaad Ha'aratzot*) of Slutzk pronounced a ban against Rabbi Schneur Zalman and the teachings of Chasidut in the year 5539 (1779), Rabbi Eizik and Rabbi Naftali sent their written protest against the ban, testifying from personal knowledge to the inordinate learning and piety of Rabbi Schneur Zalman. Nevertheless, they obstinately refused to become Chasidim of Rabbi Schneur Zalman, or to believe any of the wonders which were current among the Chasidim about their Rebbe.

To get back to our story—Pinchas Reizes continued— a nephew of the said Rabbi Eizik, whose name was Moshe Aptzuger, was a Chasid of Rabbi Schneur Zalman. He was among the many Chasidim who came to spend the latter part of Succot in Liozna. He was accompanied by his two sons and his son-in-law, and they were staying with Rabbi Eizik.

The stress of the journey and the unusually inclement weather had visibly undermined Rabbi Moshe's health, and, being a person of delicate health to begin with, he became severely ill with a high fever, and was confined to bed. His two sons and his son-in-law also took ill. Abraham the *Rofeh* (doctor) declared that, insofar as the younger men were concerned, he was confident, with G-d's help, that they would recover. However, he was quite pessimistic about Rabbi Moshe's condition, in view of his age and the severity of the attack.

When the Rebbe told me—Pinchas Reizes continued—that "the fire of the Torah will cure all the chills and colds," I enlisted the help of several fellow-seminarians, among them Ephraim Michel of Shklov and Chaim Elia of Dubrovna, and we went around town to all the bed-ridden

Chasidim to take them to *hakafot* on the night of Shemini Atzeret. The Rebbe's promise that "the fire of the Torah will cure all the colds," had already reached all the ailing Chasidim. For, when I had come out of the Rebbe's room, I spread the word in the synagogue, whence it was quickly transmitted throughout the town. Wherever we came to help the ailing Chasidim to come to *hakafot*, we found great excitement.

Everywhere I was asked to repeat the Rebbe's words verbatim, which I gladly did, and it was heartwarming to see the instantaneous impact of the Rebbe's words. Not only the invalids, but all the households where they were staying, were elated, being absolutely confident that the sick would be cured, with G-d's help.

To add to the inclemency of the weather that evening, snow, mixed with rain, began to fall, and an icy wind sent chills down the spine. The slush in the unpaved streets was ankle-deep. Yet none of these discomforts kept anyone at home. Those who could walk aided by others, walked to the synagogue; others were carried.

Arriving in the house of Rabbi Eizik, we found him engaged in a heated debate with Moshe's sons and son-in-law. The latter three had asked that word be sent to the synagogue to come and help them, and also help carry their father to the synagogue. Rabbi Eizik argued that it would be folly for them to go to the synagogue in their condition. As for their father, it would undoubtedly be fatal for him to be taken outside in that frigid weather. Besides, he was in any case delirious with fever and completely oblivious to *hakafot*, or anything else.

As we came into the house—our group included Chaim Elia of Dubrovna, two other young men and me— Rabbi Moshe's sons welcomed us with a cry of triumph: "Praise G-d, our father and we are saved!"

Rabbi Eizik countered with an equally vehement cry, of dismay: "Murderers! Assassins! It's a travesty of the holy Torah!"

I went up to Moshe's bed, and was appalled at the sight

that met my eyes. He lay still as a log, his color a mixture of blue and black, his eyes shut, his fever at a climactic height. For a moment I was at a loss what to do.

Rabbi Eizik continued to press his argument, citing a passage in Talmud where it is expressly stated that the lame and the sick were exempt from making the three annual pilgrimages to the Sanctuary in Jerusalem.[8] Surely, he contended, our sick may be excused from *hakafot*. If Rabbi Moshe is taken outside, it will be a plain case of manslaughter!

On the other hand, Chaim and Baruch, Moshe's sons, insisted that, in view of the Rebbe's statement, which they trusted with perfect faith, their father should be taken to *shul* (synagogue) and should not be denied the promised cure!

I must admit—continued Pinchas Reizes—that I was at a loss what to say or do. I could see the logic of Rabbi Eizik's position. Moshe's condition was such that it was doubtful if he could survive the trip to *shul*; the shock might easily kill him. Yet I was even more impressed by the unwavering faith of the two brothers. They were, after all, only plain laymen, yet they accepted the Rebbe's words without question, to the point of taking their lives, and their father's life, in their own hands.

The more I thought of their extraordinary faith, the more ashamed I became of my own wavering. I thought to myself: "Shame on you, Pinnie (Pinchas), the son of Rabbi Henoch Shklover, and student of the *gaonim* of Shklov. With all your knowledge of the Talmud, Responsa and religious philosophy, and with all your recognition of the Rebbe's greatness (being closely associated with him for eight years already), you have not yet mastered yourself, letting your common-sense rule over the Divine intelligence of your soul, whereas these plain young men who come to visit the Rebbe out of piety and simple faith, knowing little of the Rebbe's profundity, have attained a higher degree of self-mastery!"

I resolved there and then that I would have to seek a

personal audience with the Rebbe to help me strengthen my faltering faith.

I was so engrossed in my own thoughts that I became quite oblivious to my surroundings, until Chaim Elia of Dubrovna brought me out of my reverie by nudging me. He told me that Abraham the *Rofeh* (Doctor) had declared that Rabbi Moshe had but a few hours to live. From Rabbi Moshe's room came sounds of commotion, and I heard Baruch's voice trying to rouse his father.

"Father, the Rebbe has sent messengers to take you to *hakafot!*"

When I came into Rabbi Moshe's room, I found him wide awake, his face all smiles, in eager anticipation.

Finally we managed to bring Moshe to shul. The shul was crowded and hot. Quite a number of the congregants were obviously much the worse for their colds. Coughs and sighs punctuated the otherwise quiet atmosphere. One of the most serious invalids was Yeshaya of Chatimsk, a man in his early sixties. He was a Torah scholar and a devout worshipper. He was an innkeeper, and a *melamed* (teacher) on the side. Yeshaya was known as a charitable and hospitable man. He was tall, broad-shouldered, and strong. Many times he walked to Miezricz, and later to Horodok. After Rabbi Mendel of Horodok emigrated to the Holy Land he began to make regular pilgrimages to Rabbi Schneur Zalman. He was respected as one of the senior Chasidim, and as a man of higher intelligence and mental grasp. Because of his superior physique, the illness struck him with especial violence, Abraham the Rofeh declared, adding, however, that his hardy constitution would help him ward off the Angel of Death. This prediction seemed optimistic, for at that moment Rabbi Yeshaya was a wreck of a man, pitiful to behold.

Now, the customary procedure of the Rebbe in connection with Shemini Atzeret was as follows: *Minchah* on Hoshana Rabba (the day preceding Shemini Atzeret) was recited earlier than usual, in the Small *Beit HaMidrash* (the so-called "*Gan Eden HaTachton*"—"Lower Paradise"), at about the same time that *minchah* was recited on the day before Yom Kippur. Immediately after *minchah*, the atmosphere became charged with pleasurable anticipation. A feeling of joy filled every heart. Frequently the Rebbe's voice could be heard studying aloud in his room. In the evening, the Rebbe gave a Torah discourse for the seminarians and a few select visitors. Several hours later *Maariv* was recited in the Rebbe's Small Synagogue, whereupon the Rebbe joined in *hakafot* with a select group of seminarians and visitors. The Rebbe himself recited *Atah Hareita* (the verses recited before *hakafot*). He marched at the head of each of the seven circuitous Torah processions, carrying a scroll in his right hand, and reciting the verses which accompanied each *hakafah*. Halfway, he stopped, transferred the scroll to his left hand, then, placing his right hand on the shoulder of the Chasid nearest to him, he began a *rikud* (Chasidic dance). Everyone joined in the dancing to the strains of a lively melody, and with every moment the ecstasy grew, the heart overflowing with love and yearning for G-d. Whoever was privileged to witness and participate in the Rebbe's *hakafot* could never forget that mystic experience of soulful rapture which overwhelmed everyone present in the Rebbe's Small Synagogue. One had the feeling of being in the Holy of Holies, in communion with the ineffable Divine Presence. This was the moment when the innermost core of the soul seemed to manifest itself. It was a rare opportunity of attaining the sublimest heights of repentance and edification, or, in Chasidic terminology, the moment of "convergence of the flame and the spark."

Chasidim firmly believed that the Rebbe's conduct reflected the celestial state at any particular moment. It was a propitious time of Heavenly grace and radiating Divine Countenance; hence the radiance of the Rebbe's face and his inner delight. The Rebbe's *Yechidut-hakafot* ("private *hakafot*") could transform a Chasid. I remember the first time I was privileged to participate in these *hakafot*—Rabbi Pinchas Reizes recalled. The effect was traumatic. I became a changed man. For the first time I could well imagine how a Jew must have felt when he made the pilgrimage to Jerusalem of old, and entered the Sanctuary, in the presence of the Divine *Shechinah* that was manifest there.

Each bodily organ has its function and particular gratification: the head has the pleasure of intellectual activity; the eyes—the pleasure of sight; the ear—the pleasure of sound; the heart—the pleasure of emotions; the hand—the pleasure of creative action; the legs—the pleasure of locomotion, etc. There is, however, the kind of pleasure which pervades all the faculties and organs of the mind and body, when all the senses are submerged in this all-pervasive pleasure. Such was the pleasure that a Chasid felt during the "*Yechidut-hakafot*" of the Rebbe.

All the Rebbe's actions and practices were premeditated and regulated in time and place. The Chasidim were always aware of the *Takanot* (special regulations) which the Rebbe had instituted, and which they observed meticulously, for the Chasidim were devoted to the Rebbe with all their heart and soul. All the Chasidim knew that only those who were explicitly mentioned by the Rebbe's appointee were to attend the Rebbe's *hakafot*. It was the fervent hope of every Chasid to be privileged with an invitation to these *hakafot*. Without it, no Chasid dared to show himself at the Rebbe's *hakafot*. Having been once privileged to be invited to these *hakafot*, he was not to attend them again. There were very few exceptions, as in the case of the Rebbe's immediate circle and some of the closest Chasidim.

After the *Yechidut-hakafot*, the Rebbe made *kiddush* in the succah, and immediately thereafter went into the Large *Beit HaMidrash* for the congregational *hakafot*.

That year—Pinchas Reizes continued—there was an innovation in the Rebbe's routine. When the Rebbe entered the Succah for *kiddush*, he sent for three Chasidim—Micha'el Aharon of Vitebsk, Shabse Meir of Beshenkowitz, and Yaakov of Smilian.

When the three appeared, the Rebbe addressed each one in turn. To Micha'el Aharon he said: "You are a *Kohen*." To Shabse Meir he said: "You are a *Levi*," and to Yaakov he said: "You are a *Yisrael*." Then the Rebbe explained: "I require a *Beit-Din* of three, consisting of a *Kohen, Levi* and *Yisrael*. I have selected the three of you to constitute such a *Beit-Din*. You will hear me recite *kiddush* and you will respond with *Amen*, and attune your minds to mine." The Rebbe then requested a substantial quantity of wine.

Having made *kiddush* and partaken of the wine in the cup, the Rebbe poured the remainder of the wine from his cup into one of the bottles of wine which had been brought to him at his request. Then he told the *Beit Din* which he had appointed that they were to act as his emissaries on a "healing-mission." They were to mix the wine (in which he had poured the remainder of his *kiddush* cup) with other wine, and give some of this wine to each and every sick man to drink as a healing potion. The Rebbe also ordered that an announcement be made in the women's section to the effect that bereaved mothers and childless women would also be given of this wine to drink, so that they would be blessed with healthy offspring.

The said *Beit-Din* lost no time in carrying out this mission. They selected a number of young men to assist them in dispensing the "healing potion." Among them were: Ephraim Michel's, Shmaye Berel's, Zalman Motel's, Elia Avraham's, Yeshaya Nota's—all of Shklov; Chaim Elia, Shimon Baruch's, Avraham Zalman's and Leib Yitzchak— all of Dubrovna; Avraham Abba of Rudnia, Yehoshua of Horodok, Zelig of Kochanov, Gedalia of Kalisk, Berel Meir, Yosef Avraham, Tuvia Meilech's and Moshe Hirsh—of Vitebsk; Aharon Yosef, Shmuel Moshe and Yisrael—of Liozna. They were brawny young men who could cope with crowds.

The three-membered *Beit-Din*, accompanied by their assistants, ascended the *bimah* in the Large Synagogue from where Rabbi Yaakov of Smilian repeated aloud the Rebbe's words, word for word. Then he added: "What I just told you, are the Rebbe's words. Now I want to add a few words of explanation of my own. It has been transmitted from generation to generation that, in order that a blessing be effective, in other words, in order that the person receiving the blessing should merit its realization, two conditions are required on the part of the recipient:

(a) The recipient of the blessing must have implicit faith in the efficacy of the blessing bestowed by the giver, and

(b) the recipient must be willing to abide by the will and instructions of the giver in matters pertaining to the service of G-d, the Source of all blessings, namely, in the area of Torah-study, prayer and good conduct.

To make sure that everyone heard what Rabbi Yaakov of Smilian said, his own words were repeated by Rabbi Micha'el Aharon *HaKohen*, who possessed a powerful voice. When he concluded, the aides began to dispense the wine to the needy in an orderly fashion.

Silence fell on all in the synagogue when the Rebbe appeared for *hakafot*. Here, the Rebbe recited only the first and last verse of *Atah Hareita*, and led the procession of the first and last *hakafah*.

The following day the topic of conversation was the miracle of the recovery of the sick. Abraham the Rofeh declared that, insofar as the elderly were concerned, it was a case of the "Resurrection of the Dead," for, in the natural order of things they could not have survived.

The wonderful recovery of Rabbi Moshe finally "converted" Rabbi Eizik into a Chasid. The simple faith of his nephews, Rabbi Moshe's sons, had also left an indelible impact on him. Being by nature an ardent student who delved deeply into his studies, Rabbi Eizik immersed himself in the study of Chasidut, and before long, became proficient in all the Chasidic discourses which Rabbi Schneur Zalman had delivered in public."[9]

On the third day of the week, on the morrow of *Rosh Chodesh Cheshvan*, Rabbi Schneur Zalman set out for Swintzan in a hansom, accompanied by some twenty of his closest Chasidim and disciples. The Chasidic leader stayed there for three weeks. During that time he gave many public discourses in Talmud and Chasidut to a highly appreciative audience, which included outstanding Talmudists from Vilna and from the surrounding towns and townlets. Many scholars who had come armed with complicated queries relating to difficult passages in the Talmud, had them easily resolved by Rabbi Schneur Zalman, and they were deeply impressed by his extraordinary erudition. Hundreds of them joined the ranks of his followers and became ardent Chasidim.

On the third Shabbat of Rabbi Schneur Zalman's stay in Swintzan, an episode took place which had far-reaching reverberations. In the center of it was the venerable Rabbi Shlomo Refaels, a renowned figure throughout the province of Lithuania.

A native of Kaidan, Shlomo Refaels acquired fame as a great Talmudist, and as a man of unusual piety and good deeds. It was said that the *Rav* of Vilna, Rabbi Shaul, had been a student of his. For fifty years he sat in the *Beit Midrash* of the *Prushim*, studying in seclusion. He was a man of considerable means. Many prominent families from far and wide considered it an honor to establish matrimonial ties with his family, since he was also blessed with very eligible sons and daughters, six and four respectively. His sons and sons-in-law conducted his extensive business affairs, while he completely retired to a life of study and piety, and the practice of philanthropy. It goes without saying that Rabbi Shlomo Refaels commanded considerable authority and enjoyed immense influence.

Rabbi Shlomo Refaels was one of the most outspoken and militant opponents of the Baal Shem Tov and his successor the Maggid of Miezricz. He was an active participant in the earliest bans and proscriptions proclaimed against the Besht in Vilna, Slutzk and Shklov in the year 5517 (1757). He was 63 years old when he joined other leading opponents in their war against the new Chasidic movement, or *Kat* ("sect"), as they called it.

Needless to say, his children were brought up in the same

spirit of militant opposition to the Chasidim and, because of the tremendous influence and power of this widespread family, no Chasid had dared set foot in Swintzan for many years.

In the course of the thirty years—Rabbi Shlomo Refaels was well over ninety when Rabbi Schneur Zalman visited Swintzan in 5547—his descendants had multiplied and spread. Though only three sons and one son-in-law had survived, Rabbi Shlomo's children and grandchildren were well-established family-men, mostly well-to-do and of scholarly background, carrying on the tradition of their ancestor's opposition to the "sect." They, too, like their forebear, spent large sums subsidizing special messengers and preachers to carry the bans and proclamations throughout the land, and financing other expenses of the war against the Chasidim.

However, in Rabbi Shlomo Refaels himself a radical change took place when he reached the age of seventy. After being the driving force in the various anti-Chasidic campaigns which emanated from Vilna, Brisk, Slutzk, Minsk, and Shklov over a period of seven years, he suddenly, and without explanation, informed the leading Rabbis in the said cities that he was withdrawing from the campaign against the Chasidim. He also informed his children and grandchildren that the subject of the Chasidim was no longer to be broached to him.

This unexpected turn of events threw the anti-Chasidic camp into consternation. Feverish conferences took place, and urgent letters were exchanged among the leading spirits of the opposition. Finally, a general conclave was convened in Vilna. Two opinions were expressed at this gathering; one calling for the replacement of Rabbi Shlomo Refaels by someone else as the driving force of the anti-Chasidic campaign, and the second expressing a more moderate view, namely, to send a delegation to Rabbi Shlomo Refaels to find out why he had withdrawn from the "holy war" against the Chasidim. For, if his reasons were valid, they should be known.

The latter view prevailed, and a delegation was duly dispatched to Swintzan. The messengers stayed for three days, but could not elicit the reason that prompted Rabbi Shlomo Refaels to lay down his arms against the Chasidim.

"Have you discovered them to be observant and pious Jews?" he was asked.

"This can no longer be doubted," he replied.

The first Chasid to come to Swintzan to speak openly in favor of Chasidim was the famed *gaon* of Shklov, Rabbi Yosef Kolbo, who enjoyed an unquestioned reputation as a brilliant Talmudist and man of wisdom and saintliness. This was in 5537 (1777).

During the next decade many scholarly young men, among them some of Rabbi Refael's own grandchildren, were attracted to the movement and began to practice the Chasidic customs. Two of the latter, Moshe Gedalia of Swintzan and Pinchas Eliyahu of Ilukst, even became students of *Cheder Aleph* of Rabbi Schneur Zalman, under the influence of Rabbi Yosef Kolbo.

Before leaving Liozna to return to Swintzan, Moshe Gedalia, taking leave of his Rebbe, was requested by him to tell his grandfather that, in the merit of his keeping his promise for seventeen years, he would be blessed with long life and success in his Torah learning. This brief message of the Rebbe greatly delighted Rabbi Shlomo Refaels.

Now that Rabbi Schneur Zalman was in Swintzan, the aged patriarch came to listen to him and to ask him to resolve various Talmudic questions. Rabbi Shlomo Refaels was excitedly happy to hear Rabbi Schneur Zalman's incisive replies, which removed all his doubts and problems.

On the third Shabbat of Rabbi Schneur Zalman's stay in Swintzan, after the Rebbe concluded his Torah address in the unheated *Beit HaMidrash*, prior to the *minchah* service, the aged Rabbi Shlomo Refaels requested permission to say a few words. He then ascended the *bimah* and began to speak in a weak voice which was, however, quite audible in the hushed silence.

"My friends," he began, "I must confess my sins this day. About thirty years ago I participated in the conference of the geonim who issued a ban against the *tzaddik* Rabbi Israel Baal Shem Tov. Standing now in this holy place, I declare that our intention was for the sake of Heaven.

"My friends, on the day I became, with G-d's grace, seventy years old, I was learning the Tractate *Menachot*. I

71

became drowsy and dozed off. I dreamed that a man appeared to me and said: 'I am Israel Baal Shem Tov. You and your colleagues declared a ban against me and my disciples seven years ago. You did it without due process of the law of the Torah; without full and proper investigation. Reverse yourself!'

"I awoke greatly distressed, for it was a just argument. Did we fulfill the injunction of the Torah, 'You shall search and investigate well' (Deut. 13:15)? I began to investigate and scrutinize, and arrived at the conclusion that the Chasidim were Torah-true Jews, meticulous in their observance of the Divine precepts. Thereupon I withdrew from any further persecution of them.

"Since then more than twenty years have elapsed. All this time I continued my investigation and scrutiny of the teachings of Chasidut and the way of life of Chasidim, especially since the *gaon* and *tzaddik*, Rabbi Yossele (Yosef Kolbo) of Shklov, was here.

"I am now ninety-three years old. And, my friends, standing here in the sanctuary of G-d, I declare with all my heart, 'Blessed art Thou, O L-rd our G-d, King of the Universe, Who has preserved us alive, has sustained us and has enabled us to reach this season'—to see face to face the great leader of Israel, the *gaon* and *tzaddik*, who has brought thousands upon thousands of our brethren closer to true *Yirat Shamayim*, and has brought glory to our Torah. In the merit of this, may the Redeemer come to Zion, speedily in our time."

Rabbi Shlomo Refaels' words, publicly acclaiming Rabbi Schneur Zalman and the teachings of Chasidut, had a tremendous impact upon all present in the synagogue, and became the talk of the town.

Throughout the night following the termination of that Shabbat, Rabbi Schneur Zalman received visitors in private audience. On the following morning, after the service, Rabbi Schneur Zalman set out for Vitebsk, where he arrived on Tuesday afternoon. The following day (*Cheshvan* 24) Rabbi Schneur Zalman returned to Liozna.[10]

CHAPTER VI

INTERNAL CRISIS

Rabbi Schneur Zalman's fame continued to spread rapidly. His disciples, the students of the seminaries, branched out into various towns and townlets, establishing spearheads for further expansion. Wherever the scholarly disciples of Rabbi Schneur Zalman were actively disseminating the teachings of Chasidut, the ranks of Rabbi Schneur Zalman's followers swelled with new followers.

The new class of Chasidim—Chabad Chasidim—were no longer simple followers recruited from the unlearned masses. They were scholars of note who commanded respect for their learning and piety.

To the irascible and contentious among the Mitnagdim, the continued growth of the Chasidic movement constituted an ever-growing challenge. The agitation against the Chasidim in many a Jewish community flared up into violence from time to time. However, under the strict discipline which Rabbi Schneur Zalman imposed on his followers, the latter exercised considerable restraint, so that the strife was successfully confined to relatively small proportions. Yet, precisely at this time of external Chasidic expansion and personal celebrity, Rabbi Schneur Zalman found himself in the midst of an inner crisis brought about by rivaling Chasidic groups of Wolhynia, involving also the Chasidic leaders in the Holy Land. Jealousy reared its ugly head. Some rivaling Chasidim dipped their pens in slander, and cast aspersions on Rabbi Schneur Zalman's leadership, arousing suspicion among the Chasidic leaders in the Holy Land towards

Rabbi Schneur Zalman. This turn of events was more painful to Rabbi Schneur Zalman than all the opposition of the Mitnagdim, but the combined effect brought Rabbi Schneur Zalman to the verge of a critical emergency.

The unhappy situation was aggravated by Rabbi Schneur Zalman's personal misfortune in the loss of his beloved daughter Dvorah Leah, a woman of saintly character, who had always been very devoted to her father. She was the mother of a two-year old son, Menachem Mendel (who was destined to succeed Rabbi Schneur Zalman's son, Rabbi Dov Ber, to the third-generation leadership of the Chabad movement).

The tradition preserved in the family directly links her passing with Rabbi Schneur Zalman's critical situation, just mentioned. According to this tradition, the events unfolded themselves as follows:

Rabbi Schneur Zalman was deeply disturbed by the intrigues and dissention which jeopardized his activities, particularly those relating to the Chasidic community in the Holy Land. He knew that the jealousy which his successful work had aroused in certain Chasidic circles was only the result of the work of the Adversary on High, which threatened the very future of the Chasidic movement. He had a premonition that his own eclipse was at hand. One day,[1] Rabbi Schneur Zalman confided in his daughter Dvorah Leah, and expressed his utmost apprehension in regard to the future of the Chasidim and of the Baal Shem Tov's teachings.

Dvorah Leah realized the gravity of the situation and sensed that her father's life was linked with it. For several days she kept her anxiety to herself. Then she decided that it was her duty to divulge her secret to some of the senior Chasidim. She also resolved that she would give her life for the life of her father.

Thereupon Dvorah Leah asked three senior Chasidim, Moshe Meisels, Pinchas Reizes and Moshe Wilenker,[2] to meet with her. She asked them to promise on oath that they would act according to her request and instructions, whatever they might be, and would keep in strictest confidence all that she was about to tell them, until such time as it would be fitting to keep the matter secret no longer.

74

The three Chasidic sages requested time to consider her conditions. They realized that something was amiss. They had noticed that the Rebbe had secluded himself in his private room (which Chasidim reverently called "*Gan Eden HaElyon*"—the "Upper Paradise"), and not even Chasidim of the Rebbe's inner circle were admitted. This change in the Rebbe's routine was ominous, but what exactly was wrong they had no idea. Undoubtedly, the Rebbe's daughter knew something which was of extreme gravity. Several times during that day and during the night the three Chasidim conferred, and finally came to the conclusion that they had to accept Dvorah Leah's conditions.

The following day they presented themselves to Dvorah Leah with their resolution. She began by saying:

"We are all Chasidim of my father, our Rebbe, and each one of us must be ready and willing to give his or her life for him, and for the future of Chasidut." Then she was overcome by emotion, and gave vent to her feelings in a flood of tears.

At the sight of her distress the three Chasidim were deeply moved. Moshe rose to his feet and impulsively exclaimed: "Why are you crying? What is wrong? I will be the first to give my life for the Rebbe and for the perpetuation of the Baal Shem Tov's teachings. Tell us what we are to do. I will gladly go through fire or water. . . ."

"First," Dvorah Leah interrupted, "you must all swear to me by the most stringent Torah-oath which has no absolution, that you will do what I ask of you, without any mental reservation whatever, even if it be a matter of life."

Hearing these ominous words, even Moshe Wilenker, who was known for his extraordinary sedateness and presence of mind under all circumstances, lost his equanimity and, visibly disturbed, declared that such a matter must be reconsidered in a calm atmosphere and with due deliberation. The other two, however, brushed aside his objections, saying that they had already carefully weighed the matter and had agreed to abide by Dvorah Leah's conditions, come what may. Thereupon the three of them gave their solemn oath as requested.

"Now I make the three of you a *Beit-Din*, and you will agree to act as a *Beit-Din*, and to rule on the situation in accordance with the law of the Torah," Dvorah Leah said, continuing:

"The present situation, in the wake of the intrigue which has cast a shadow over the relationship between the Chasidic leaders in the Holy Land and in Wolhynia on the one hand, and my saintly father on the other, is grave in the extreme. From what I have heard from my father, the consequences could be frightful, G-d forbid. These were his words:

For thirty years a good fruit-bearing tree requires cultivation and care in order to bring it to its optimum fruitfulness. It is now thirty years since the teachings of our Master, Rabbi Israel Baal Shem Tov, were firmly planted by my Master, the Maggid of Miezricz, and grew into a Tree of Life. Now, the Adversary threatens to destroy it all. I do want to live, for this is the duty of every man, according to the Torah. Yet, more precious to me than life is my desire to cultivate this tree so that it continues to give its fruit until the coming of our Redeemer.

My teacher, the Maggid of Miezricz, had forewarned me of difficult times, and had promised to come to my aid. I saw my teacher and master, but his face was overcast, an ill-omen. . . .

Recalling that conversation, Moshe Wilenker related how they were all overcome by a fit of weeping, in utter distress. Presently, Dvorah Leah concluded: "In view of the situation, I resolved to put my life in lieu of my father's. I wish to be his atonement; I bequeath my life to him; I am going to die so that he may live a good and long life, in order to cultivate the Tree of Life. In this way I will also have a share in it."

Apparently unaware of his daughter's self-sacrifice for him, Rabbi Schneur Zalman sent a *pidyon* (a request for a prayer) to Rabbi Nachum of Czernobil,[3] in the early part of *Elul* 5550 (1790). The *pidyon*, in his own behalf and in behalf of Chasidut in general, was sent through the above mentioned Yaakov of Smilian.

On the first night of Rosh Hashanah, after the services, Rabbi Schneur Zalman, breaking his custom not to speak to anyone on that night, asked: "Where is Dvorah Leah? When she appeared, he began to wish her the customary blessing to "be inscribed unto a happy year." But she interrupted him immediately, and wished him, instead, to "be inscribed unto a happy year."

On the second day of Rosh Hashanah 5551 (1790), Rabbi Schneur Zalman gave a discourse on the teachings of Chasidut, as was his custom to do on both afternoons of Rosh Hashanah. After *Havdalah* he called his daughter Dvorah Leah and her husband Rabbi Shalom Shachna into his room. What was spoken there and then is not known, but Rabbi Shalom Shachna was heard saying amid tears: "What is to happen to the two-year old boy?"

The following day (the Fast of Gedaliah) Dvorah Leah passed away. Rabbi Schneur Zalman took the young orphan into his room and took personal charge of his upbringing.[4] (The boy grew up to be the famed and saintly Rabbi Menachem Mendel of Lubavitch, author of the monumental *Responsa Tzemach Tzedek*, and third generation head of the Chabad-Lubavitch movement).

The year 5552 (1791/1792) saw an intensification of intolerance on the part of the Mitnagdim in certain communities towards their Chasidic co-religionists. Rabbi Schneur Zalman realized that his hopes for a reconciliation were still premature, which greatly distressed him. The extent of his suffering became apparent on the festival of Shavuot, the anniversary of the Baal Shem Tov's demise. As usual on this festival, Rabbi Schneur Zalman spoke a great deal about the Besht, but his melodies had a tinge of bitterness. He was soon immersed in a state of profound *devekut* (soulful reverie), his eyes closed, his lips moving inaudibly. Tears trickled down his saintly face. It was an awesome sight. Those who were present surmised that the Rebbe was invoking Divine mercy, and felt as though the spirits of the Baal Shem Tov and of the Maggid of Miezricz were present.

Suddenly, Rabbi Schneur Zalman rose to his feet and tearfully exclaimed: "*Zaida* (Grandfather)!"—this is how he often referred to the Besht—"invoke Divine mercy upon me, and upon all your disciples and followers, and upon the survival of your teachings! Oy, oy, gvald, gvald![5] Our Heavenly Father, have mercy upon us!" Saying which, Rabbi Schneur Zalman collapsed in a deep, fainting spell.

Turmoil broke loose in the room. The Rebbe's wife and daughters rushed into the room. A messenger was quickly dispatched to summon Yonah, the physician.

In the midst of the commotion, little Menachem Mendel (the future "Tzemach Tzedek"), then two years and nine months old, came running into the room. Seeing his grandfather lying on the floor, he threw himself upon him, crying: "*Zaida! Zaida!*" ("Grandpa! Grandpa!"). Rabbi Schneur Zalman opened his eyes. He saw the proffered little hand of his grandson, who kept on saying: "*Zaida*, take hold of my hand and get up!" Reaching for the little hand, Rabbi Schneur Zalman said: "Give me your hand! and he stood up, adding, "This one will comfort us!

Rabbi Baruch Mordechai of Bobroysk,[6] son-in-law of the *Av-Beit-Din* of Vilna, Rabbi Shmuel, related how he became a Chasid, and his first experience of a private audience (*yechidut*) with Rabbi Schneur Zalman. This was his story:

Rabbi Schneur Zalman's visit to Vilna, in the company of Rabbi Menachem Mendel of Vitebsk, when they came to confront the Gaon of Vilna, had left a lasting impression on the Talmudic scholars in the city. They often quoted Rabbi Schneur Zalman's incisive exposition of certain difficult passages in the Talmud which they were privileged to hear from him on that occasion. This aroused my interest, and I began to study some of Rabbi Schneur Zalman's Chasidic discourses which were made available to me by local Chasidim. Subsequently, I met young scholars of note, who rehearsed various new insights of Rabbi Schneur Zalman, which singularly clarified complicated areas in the Talmud. I gained a profound respect for the Rebbe's erudition, but I was not sufficiently convinced to become a Chasid of his.

It was not until the year 5553 (1793) that I made my first visit to Liozna. My trip was not the pilgrimage of a Chasid; rather, it was prompted by scholastic curiosity to take a closer look at the teachings of Chasidut, as expounded by the Rebbe.

Arriving in Liozna, I discovered that there was a strict

routine to be followed by young men desirous of a private audience with the Rebbe. It was first necessary to be interviewed by Rabbi Yehuda Leib, the Rebbe's brother, who was in charge of admissions and arrangements for providing full board for the applicant. If he was satisfied with the applicant, he would recommend him for an examination in Talmudic proficiency. Then followed a period of two or three weeks of intensive Chasidic and Talmudic study, upon the completion of which the candidate would be admitted to a private audience with the Rebbe.

The examiners were the Rebbe's other brothers, Rabbi Mordechai and Rabbi Moshe. Rabbi Mordechai excelled himself especially in the Talmud *Bavli* and the *Rishonim* (Early Codifiers), while his brother's specialty was the Talmud *Yerushalmi* and the *Rambam*. Sometimes one of them was the sole examiner; sometimes both of them gave the examination.

My first Talmudic discussion with these two *gaonim* left me completely overwhelmed. I had passed the test, however, and after two weeks' preparation, I was admitted into private audience with the Rebbe.

I had prepared a number of questions pertaining to devoutness, which the Rebbe chose not to answer. Instead, he asked me if I had any questions in the area of Talmudic study.

It so happened that for over a year I had been wrestling with two problems, one in the Talmud *Yerushalmi* and the other in the *Rambam*. I had discussed them with the Gaon of Vilna, who helped me analyze the problems and thus greatly elucidated them, but actually gave me no answer to resolve them.

Now, standing before the Rebbe, I put these two questions before him, and I was amazed to receive a clear answer to them, which at once resolved them beyond a doubt.

Upon leaving the Rebbe's room and entering the "Lower *Gan Eden*" (as the Chasidim called the Small Synagogue in the Rebbe's house), I was drawn into the tra-

79

ditional "*Yechidut* Dance." This was a lively whirling dance which was introduced by the early Chasidim to celebrate a private audience with the Rebbe. I whirled around with the older Chasidim and younger seminarians, oblivious to what was going on, for I was excited beyond measure by the brilliance of the Rebbe's mind. For years afterward, the impressions of his awe-inspiring countenance and his profound wisdom remained vivid in my mind.

My association with the Rebbe's three illustrious brothers, though only of a few weeks' duration, opened new horizons for me in my Talmudic studies. My conceptual capacity was substantially enhanced. I began to apply myself more assiduously than ever before to the study of both Chasidut and Talmud, and with all the concentration I could muster.

Back home, I had to wait several months for my brother-in-law, Rabbi Shlomo's, return before I could share with him the excitement of having resolved my two problems. He, too, became very excited, and insisted that I go to the Gaon forthwith to hear his opinion about the answers. I agreed, and, accompanied by my brother-in-law, went to the Gaon.

As soon as I began to speak about the two problems, the Gaon reviewed them in a concise manner, adding that he frequently pondered over them, but as yet had found no satisfactory clue to the solution. I then advanced the answers without identifying the source of my information. The Gaon was visibly moved. Wrapped as he was in his tallit and tefillin, he rose to his full height and said reverently: "Such answers could issue only from the Head of the Heavenly Academy. Whoever the *gaon* and *tzaddik* was who gave these answers, he could only have known the solution by prophetic inspiration. Had I heard it from his mouth, I would have said as Rabbi Yochanan said: 'I would carry his bathing apparel for him to the bathhouse.'"

Later on I greatly regretted not having disclosed to the Gaon that it was the Rebbe of the Chasidim who had given me those answers, as it might have elicited a better attitude towards the Chasidim, and might have brought the two "giants" together.

Though, in due course, my affiliation with the Chasidim of Rabbi Schneur Zalman was no secret, I still had access to the Gaon of Vilna. On one such occasion, soon after the *Tanya* was publicly burnt in Vilna, I mentioned to the Gaon that the author of this book was the one who had told me the answers to those intricate problems, and I reminded the Gaon of his reaction at that time and what he had said, quoting Rabbi Yochanan. Unfortunately, the Gaon rejected my defense, stating that, according to the law of the Torah, I was an interested party, and consequently my testimony was not trustworthy.[7]

Chapter VII

Liozna, The Center Of Chabad

Rabbi Schneur Zalman's conciliatory policy towards the opposition, based as it was on the principle that it takes two adversaries to make a fight, went a long way towards calming the contentious spirits on both sides. Besides, the stringent measures which had been decreed against the Chasidim by the leading Rabbinates were not very effective insofar as the general public was concerned. The rank and file of the Mitnagdim were in closer touch with the Chasidim than some of their leaders, and they could not see anything so radically dangerous about the Chasidim as to warrant the extreme penalties imposed on them. Finally, external factors, connected with the political situation, which led to the partition of Poland in 1793, and again in 1795, called for a greater measure of solidarity within the Jewish community. These combined circumstances produced a period of relative peace between the two camps during the years 1788-1795. Needless to say, this was a most welcome intermission for Rabbi Schneur Zalman, who was now able to devote more time to his literary activities. He re-edited his *Shulchan Aruch* and completed his *Tanya*. Many of his Chasidic discourses and lectures, some of which were eventually published in book form, were at that time copied and re-copied, and eagerly studied by his followers. His following rapidly increased, especially after the second and third partitions of Poland, in 1793 and 1795 respectively, when Russia annexed large territories densely populated by Jews. By this time Rabbi Schneur Zalman was credited with a personal following of some 100,000 Chasidim.[1]

During these years Rabbi Schneur Zalman also strengthened the internal organization of the Chasidic movement. After the death (in 1788) of his senior colleague, Rabbi Menachem Mendel of Vitebsk, in Palestine, Rabbi Schneur Zalman was recognized as the chief leader of the Chasidim not only *de facto* but also *de jure*, as it were. Rabbi Schneur Zalman expanded the vast fund-raising apparatus which he had set up for the support of the Chasidic community in Palestine. He also took care of the support of individual Chasidim, including some prominent Chasidic rabbis and their families.[2]

The burden of leadership began to weigh heavily on Rabbi Schneur Zalman. With the increasing number of followers there came an ever-growing demand on his time and personal attention. He was constantly besieged by an endless stream of Chasidim, who came to Liozna to seek his advice, guidance and help, in spiritual as well as temporal matters. He appointed his brother Rabbi Yehuda Leib, his son Rabbi Dov Ber and his senior disciple Rabbi Aharon HaLevi Hurwitz, to assist him in his manifold duties. He also drew up a set of regulations, known as the *Takanot* of Liozna, whereby he laid down a discipline of conduct for his Chasidim, and the rules governing their visits to Liozna. These *Takanot*, among other things, called for the observance of strict decorum in the Chasidic congregational services and the submission of copied Chasidic discourses and lectures for perusal and correction. *Gabbaim* (wardens) were appointed in every Chasidic community to see to it that the *Takanot* were complied with. Visits to Liozna were permitted only once a year. Nevertheless the pressure of leadership of so vast a following became go overwhelming that he often contemplated escaping from it all and emigrating to Palestine.[3] However, his sense of duty and loyalty to his followers ruled out such a step. Rabbi Schneur Zalman had to resign himself to a life that was no longer his own.

Liozna was one of three small towns, all in White Russia, which are very closely associated with Chabad. The other two were Liadi and Lubavitch. Liozna was the cradle of Chabad. Here the founder of Chabad was born, and here he spent most of his life. In Liadi, as we shall see later, Rabbi Schneur Zalman spent the last twelve years of his life, when his fame was at its height. That is when Liadi became renowned. It gained its fame from the illustrious Chabad leader whose residence it was, and the two names became linked together, for Rabbi Schneur Zalman became known as the "*Rav* of Liadi." "Lubavitch" subsequently became synonymous with the Chabad-Chasidic movement, because it was the seat of the four succeeding generations of Chabad leaders, from Rabbi Dov Ber Schneuri,[4] the founder's oldest son and successor, to Rabbi Yosef Y. Schneersohn, the sixth "Lubavitcher Rebbe." For more than a century—102 years and two months, to be exact—Lubavitch was, without interruption, the center of the movement, and the Chabad Chasidim became more popularly known as "Lubavitcher" Chasidim. In Lubavitch, as we have noted,[5] Rabbi Schneur Zalman received his early Talmudic tutoring. His tutor, Rabbi Issachar Ber, later became one of Rabbi Schneur Zalman's most prominent senior Chasidim.

In the early history of the Chasidic movement, both Liozna and Lubavitch are mentioned, along with other neighboring towns and townlets.[6] They were the scene of quiet activity by secret mystics (*nistarim*) who spread the doctrines of the Baal Shem Tov before the latter revealed himself as the founder and leader of the Chasidic movement.[7] When Schneur Zalman was a small boy, the "ancients" of the town were able to relate some interesting facts about the development of the Jewish community of Liozna, whose Jewish population of some 35 families began to grow after Russia captured Vitebsk from the Poles in 1654. Many Jewish families from Vitebsk then settled in Liozna. Those "ancients" also knew to relate how Liozna twice narrowly escaped the consequences of blood-libels.[8]

Apart from those tales of the hoary past, Liozna was not distinguishable from any other similar small town in White Russia. It began to achieve distinction, however, when Rabbi Schneur Zalman was appointed as *maggid* in his native town, and more so when he took up residence in Liozna again, in mid-winter of 1788, after his frustrated migration to the Holy Land.

With the departure of Rabbi Schneur Zalman's senior colleagues for the Holy Land, and his own return to Liozna,[9] Rabbi

Schneur Zalman now remained the central figure in the Chasidic movement, with Liozna as its "capital." Chasidim from all parts of Russia began to make regular pilgrimages to Liozna, particularly for the festival seasons, in order to spend some time in the inspiring presence of their spiritual leader. It soon became necessary to introduce a strict system and calendar for such pilgrimages. These became known as the Liozna *"Takanot"* or "ordinances," to which brief reference was made a little earlier.

The first Takanot were instituted during the years 5540-3 (1780-3). The details were worked out by Rabbi Schneur Zalman's brothers with the other senior Chasidim, and approved by Rabbi Schneur Zalman. From time to time, over a period of fifteen years, the Takanot were amended. The last recorded Takanot bear the date of 5556 (1796).

The Takanot of Liozna began with a set of general rules regulating the manner and conduct of the daily services in the Chabad congregations everywhere. They were addressed particularly to the young adults.

These ordinances included the following:

All the young men are to assemble in their synagogues for daily congregational morning prayers at the same time when congregational services were held in the other local congregations, namely, in the summer not later than 6:30,[10] and in the winter at sunrise.

There is to be no talk or conversation whatever before the commencement of the service.

No young man will be admitted as a visitor to Liozna without a written testimonial, signed by two reliable witnesses, to the effect that the bearer had faithfully complied with the Takanot. If for some reason it is impossible for the visitor to furnish such a certificate, he has to make a solemn affirmation to the same effect....

With the commencement of the service, there should be no walking about in the synagogue....

Upon coming to Liozna, visitors have to report to Rabbi Aharon Halevi[11] and the Rebbe's son, to verify their admissibility.

Chasidic texts and copies of Chasidic discourses should be brought and submitted to Rabbi Yehuda Leib[12] to be checked for accuracy by himself and the other examiners working under him, because of the prevalence of copyists' errors. The material should be bound and bear the name of the owner.

Anyone failing to bring all his Chasidic writings for examination will not be admitted for an audience with the Rebbe....[13]

The above regulations clearly reflect Rabbi Schneur Zalman's concern for the proper decorum in the synagogue in compliance with Jewish Law, his emphasis on congregational service, and on the general adherence to orderly and disciplined conduct. These standards have come to characterize Chabad synagogues, often in conspicuous contrast to other Chasidic and non-Chasidic counterparts. His insistence upon ensuring correct study-texts is not less noteworthy.

Additional Takanot bear the date of the year 5553 (1793), and read as follows:

Whoever has already visited Liozna once, should not come again, except on a Shabbat when Rosh Chodesh is blessed. In the month of *Elul* only the last two Shabbatot before Rosh Hashanah are open to visits. In the month of *Tishrei* (visitors may come for) *Shabbat Shuvah*. During *Cheshvan* no one may come. In *Kislev*—only for the Shabbat when *Rosh Chodesh Tevet* is blessed. In *Tevet*—for the Shabbat when *Rosh Chodesh Shevat* is blessed. In *Shevat*—for the Shabbat when *Rosh Chodesh Adar* is blessed. In *Adar*—for the Shabbat when *Rosh Chodesh Nissan* is blessed. In *Nissan*—no visitors. In *Iyar*—for the Shabbat when *Rosh Chodesh Sivan* is blessed. Similarly in *Sivan*—for the Shabbat when *Rosh Chodesh Tammuz* is blessed, and similarly in *Tammuz*—for the Shabbat when *Rosh Chodesh Av* is blessed. During *Av*—only for *Shabbat-Nachamu*.

No one should come to Liozna more than once in the same year. . . . One should provide himself with board and lodging for two weeks at least.

One wishing to present a written petition to the Rebbe, should write the note at home, before leaving.[14]

It is clear from the above ordinances that the stream of visitors had so increased in the previous decade that it was necessary to limit admissions. Moreover, an audience with the Rebbe apparently entailed a waiting period of at least two weeks.

In the same year (1793) Rabbi Schneur Zalman felt impelled to send an encyclical to all his followers, and particularly to the *gabbaim* of the Chasidic communities, in which he implored them to stem the tide of the Chasidim streaming to Liozna.

The problems and sorrows which were incessantly laid before him by his Chasidim, deeply touched his sensitive nature and affected his daily life. He could only plead with his followers to spare him, at least, the anguish of listening to their material problems and plights, which he urged them to address to the merciful Father in Heaven. Thus he writes in his pastoral letter:

> . . . My soul is poured out with my request, and my plea is laid and spread before my loving friends, all our Chasidic fellowship in general, and particularly those active in holy work, the *gabbaim* for the Holy Land, may it be rebuilt speedily in our time. To them my plea is reiterated with all heart and soul, to watch with a watchful eye, in a matter concerning my very life, namely, to restrain the people from travelling here, and to earnestly admonish them not to cause me spiritual embitterment and soulful aggravation by an untimely trip, as will be explained below; and to request them—whether they be of the local city dwellers, or of the surrounding villages, or of other cities passing en route through your city, be they new or old Chasidim— with a redoubled and awesome warning, not to cause, by their said trip, an infringement of any of the hereunder mentioned conditions made in truth and justice, showing them a copy of this letter:
>
> First, those coming for the four well-known occasions[15] should not presume to request a private audience with me even in a very urgent matter concerning the service of G-d, not to mention any mundane matter however exceedingly important. For it is quite impossible that all those who

assemble here during the said four periods should come in to speak with me. Obviously all thirst to come in, and I cannot make distinctions between them, to arouse bitter jealousy of those that pressured their admittance. By my nature and inner sensitivity I cannot bear the anguish of those prevented from entry, who must return home with profound disappointment and, to their thinking, justified jealousy.

Besides . . . it is particularly painful to me that anyone of our new Chasidim wishing to come closer to the service of G-d should have to be firmly held back, since the need is great to speak to them personally and not in any other way. But what can I do, seeing that it is not at all opportune to speak personally with each and every one of the new [Chasidim] assembling during the said four periods.... Therefore the new ones should definitely not come during the four periods for an audience. They have ample time to come in any month of the year, for any of the first three Shabbatot, but they would have to remain for two or three days after Shabbat.

However, for the fourth Shabbat, when *Rosh Chodesh* is blessed, the new Chasidim should not come at all, inasmuch as this Shabbat is reserved for the old Chasidim to enable them to have an audience once a year and no more, as is well known . . . and in a very important matter where the individual cannot take counsel from any of the Chasidim in his town. This is further strictly conditioned on the circumstance that [in his problem] he has before him two alternatives and he does not know which to choose. But if there is only one way, which is inferior and it distresses him greatly, G-d forbid, and he feels impelled to inform me of his distress, G-d be merciful, then he should inform me by letter, or through my trusted *gabbai*, and he can rest assured that he will convey to me all his words fully . . . and if I will have anything to say in reply, I will also convey it through the said *[gabbai]*....

I cannot adequately describe in a letter the extent to which my very life is embittered by those who come in to me to pour out before me personally their sorrow in detail and at length, in order to infuse deep into my heart their sorrow and distress, G-d be merciful. Even if they seek counsel in matters free from sorrow and bitterness, I cannot bear the mental distraction and loss of time entailed in my having to concentrate my thought and mind upon the matter in order to give a proper answe r. . . Many times in this situation I deplore my very life, and many a time I resolved in my heart to uproot my tent from this country. But I look forward to G-d's help that He will open the eyes and hearts of all who hear these, my words. . . .

My beloved ones, my brothers and my friends![16] Out of a secret love to an open admonition. Come let us contend together. Remember the days of old, consider the years of former generations. Has there ever been such a thing since days immemorial? Where did you find such a custom in any one of the books of the sages of Israel . . . to seek counsel of a material nature . . . except in relation to the true prophets of old, as in the case of Samuel the Seer . . .[17] For truly all human affairs, except those pertaining to the Torah and the fear of Heaven, can only be grasped prophetically. . . . When a merciful, wise and righteous father strikes his son, the wise son does not turn his back [on him] to flee and seek help [elsewhere], or even [to seek] an intercessor [to intervene in his behalf] before his merciful, righteous and just father; but he will look up to his father, face to face, suffering his blows with love, for his lasting good. . . . Then G-d will also bestow the good and will cause His face to shine upon him with manifest love. . . .

This, too, I request that . . . whoever [of the old Chasidim] sometimes has an important matter in the service of G-d on which to consult me personally and not otherwise, then he must remain for about two weeks, perhaps there will be an opportune time to speak to him as he desires. . . .

Please, please, I appeal to your abundant mercies, do not drive me out of our land before the right and proper time, as it may please G-d. . . .

This is also to inform that in the months of *Nissan* and

89

Iyar, until the Shabbat before *Rosh Chodesh Sivan*, as well as after Simchat Torah until Shabbat Chanukah, there shall be no visitors, neither new nor old Chasidim.[18]

Clearly, Rabbi Schneur Zalman did not wish to assume the position of intercessor, whose blessings and prayers would bring miraculous help to those who believed in his supernatural powers. He wished to confine his role to that of teacher and spiritual counsellor, though he well knew that material stress was bound to affect one's spiritual well-being. However, he was too kind and sensitive a man to disregard the frailty of human nature, and he had to make concessions in extreme cases of material distress. It was related by those who were close to him, who knew his passionate desire for solitude and communion with G-d, that it was with supreme selflessness that he would tear himself away from his studies and worship in order to take time out to receive in private audience a man or woman in distress.

In 5555 (1795) a revised set of Takanot was issued, as follows:

1. Chasidim of long standing ("old Chasidim") can come to Liozna for the Shabbat preceding *Rosh Chodesh*. No more than one visit a year is permitted, without any exception whatever, even if one is prepared to rent his own [lodgings and] board, or bring food with him.

2. A "year" means a full year, not even one month sooner. It will be reckoned from the Shabbat preceding *Rosh Chodesh Sivan*. Except for the four periods when all are permitted to come. The four periods are: Simchat Torah, Shabbat-Chanukah, Purim, and *Shabbat-Shuvah*. Provided, however, that those coming for *Shabbat-Shuvah* who cannot afford to pay for their upkeep, should not come for Rosh Hashanah, even if it occurs on Thursday and Friday; in other words, they are permitted to come only when Rosh Hashanah occurs in the middle of the week, but only for the Shabbat [following, i.e. *Shabbat-Shuvah*], and immediately upon the termination of the Shabbat, should set out on their way.

3. If one feels he must make a second visit [in the same year], he should first write about the matter, and permission

may perhaps be granted. But without permission one is sternly forewarned. . . .

4. As for the Shabbat preceding *Rosh Chodesh*, permission is granted for once a year, except those preceding *Rosh Chodesh Nissan*, and *Iyar*, and *MarCheshvan* and *Kislev*. The others are permissible, namely, the Shabbat preceding *Rosh Chodesh Tevet*, also Shabbat-Chanukah in most years, the Shabbat preceding *Rosh Chodesh* of the months *Shevat*, *Adar* and *Adar* [*Sheni*], *Sivan*, *Tammuz*, *Menachem Av* and *Elul*; also for the Shabbat after the middle of *Elul*. But for Shavuot, *Shabbat-Nachamu*, and the Shabbat before Rosh Hashanah, no one should come under any circumstances.

5. Those arriving in Liozna, whether Chasidim of long standing or new ones, should never enter any house or courtyard of our town's *ba'alei-battim*, except two designated houses and courts as per bearer of this letter . . . This applies both to those coming by wagon as well as on foot. From the said courtyards our appointed will conduct each one to his place, to wit, those who can afford to pay [for their upkeep] will be conducted to lodgings suitable for them among the many houses in our town where payment is taken. The men who cannot afford, and only those who come on foot, will be assigned by our appointed to the upper *baalei-battim* in our town, each one according to his station, to the extent of the assessment with which everyone has been assessed in regard to providing free hospitality over the Shabbat days. During the weekdays free meals will be provided in the community dining-room, as will be explained by the bearer, during the period which the waiting for an audience necessitates, as for example in the case of new Chasidim.

6. Even if one is invited by a *Baal-habayit* in our town to eat with him on Shabbat or during the week, a strict ban is imposed upon the guest, except in the case of a parent, brother, brother-in-law or *mechutan*, and only for them alone, but not for the sons and sons-in-law who may be with them.

7. Anyone of the old Chasidim coming to our town for

any of the Shabbatot preceding *Rosh Chodesh* should not come without a written attestation by the *gabbaim* of his town to the effect that a complete year has passed since his previous visit. Whoever shall come without such written attestation will be denied any lodging, even if paid for, and certainly any food, even if paid for, not to mention *gratis* for the poor. The *gabbaim* must watch this constantly, as well as the general ordinances, to bring them to public attention and to remind the general public, including the new Chasidim, of this. Those living in rural areas should bring such a certificate from the *gabbai* in the nearby town to whom he gives his contributions for the Holy Land. The *gabbai*, on his part, should keep a register of all the visitors to our town, recording the names of the visitors and the month in which the visit was made, in order to avoid error.

8. All visitors for the said four periods shall return home immediately at the termination of the Shabbat or the Yom Tov; even one who is in very great need in spiritual matters, not to mention mundane matters, regardless how urgent. Let him imagine that I have already departed, etc. And there is no hindrance of G-d to send help, and He has many messengers besides me.

9. Anyone coming for any Shabbat preceding *Rosh Chodesh* mentioned above, who has a query in a matter of Torah, should write down his query, and I will reply to him in writing, or orally through my son[19] or my son-in-law.[20] Or he should provide himself with paid-for lodgings for an entire month, perchance after all I may find time to speak to him privately, inasmuch as there are very many new Chasidim who come daily, and for whom there is not sufficient time, as it is, to speak with them privately, except in public matters.

10. When one is in need in a very important mundane matter, if it is a matter wherein I am not in a position to be of practical help to him, such as writing a letter of recommendation for him, and the like, and his intention is only to acquaint me with his distress that I intercede in his behalf [On High] . . .[21]

Despite the ever growing restrictions and admonitions, the stream of visitors to Liozna continued unabated, and, in fact, grew steadily because of the numerical expansion of Rabbi Schneur Zalman's followers. Obviously, not all of them could hope to be received in private audience by the Rebbe. This was a physical impossibility. But many came just to be near him, if only for one Shabbat, and possibly to hear a Chasidic discourse delivered personally by the Rebbe. Many had various problems, economic or spiritual, health problems and family problems, and they believed implicitly in the Rebbe's intercession, and in his prayer and blessing. It is plain to see from the Takanot how great was the personal burden of Rabbi Schneur Zalman in shepherding his numerous and constantly growing flock.

In 5556 (1796) the regulations governing visits to Liozna were revised again. They were solemnly adopted at a large assembly of leading Chasidim from many communities, who met in Liozna. The document, which bears the date of Monday, 27th of *Adar* 1, 5556, was signed by 48 representatives from nearly as many different communities. It was approved and reaffirmed by a colophon over the signature of Rabbi Schneur Zalman himself, wherein he calls on all the Chasidic congregations to solemnly adopt the regulations and carry them out meticulously, declaring that they were designed for the public benefit.

These regulations contained the following main provisions:

1) No more than two visits to Liozna per year for old Chasidim.

2) No one should enter the Rebbe's study to speak to him privately, either in spiritual or mundane matters; nor submit any request in writing. One could, however, submit a written outline of the problem, without asking for advice, but only in order that the Rebbe remember him in prayer.

3) If there be a matter of extraordinary importance which may make it necessary to ask for the Rebbe's advice, the person must first submit it to a conclave of the three leading Chasidim in his community. Should they agree that the matter is indeed of extraordinary importance, that there could be more than one way of coping with it, and that they themselves cannot decide what course should be

taken—then the three were permitted to write to the Rebbe for advice. Under no circumstances was the person himself to come to Liozna to present his problem.

4) Whenever the Rebbe gave a public discourse or sermon, in the *Beit HaMidrash* or in the synagogue, no one is to press forward to ascend the *bimah*, except the members of the immediate family and special guests.

5) Certain provisions were made for collective visits in groups of 30 to 40 persons, to consult the Rebbe on Torah matters. For this purpose, the Rebbe volunteered two hours daily in the afternoon.

6) New Chasidim could come only during any of the first three Shabbatot of the month, but not for the Shabbat preceding *Rosh Chodesh*, which is reserved exclusively for old Chasidim.

7) The previous regulations governing board and lodgings were reaffirmed.

8) On three occasions in the year, visits to Liozna were liberalized for both old and new Chasidim. These were: Purim, *Shabbat-Shuvah* (the Shabbat between Rosh Hashanah and Yom Kippur) and the last days of the Succot festival. It was promised, however, that when the new building of the *Beit HaMidrash* would be completed, also Shabbat-Chanukah would be included in the special periods when visits to Liozna would be permitted to all.[22]

The frequent revisions and reaffirmations of the Takanot of Liozna graphically point to the fact that the Chasidic leader was wrestling with a serious problem of how to cope with the numerous visitors to Liozna. Vital issues at stake were not only humanitarian but also spiritual. Rabbi Schneur Zalman became, as it were, a captive of his own movement. His sensitive nature and his selfless dedication to each and every one of his Chasidim made him particularly vulnerable to *noblesse oblige*.

CHAPTER VIII

FIRST ENCOUNTER WITH THE HASKALAH

T he Haskalah movement, which was born in Germany, came to Eastern European Jewry almost at the same time as the Chasidic movement. The latter, as already mentioned,[1] began to spread in 1734. Barely twenty years later, in 1751, we find the first Haskalah polemic against the Chasidic movement in Solomon Helma's *Mirkevet HaMishneh*, followed by *Nezed HaDema* of Israel of Zamosc (1773) and *Toldot Chayyai* of Solomon Maimon (1792). The real confrontation came several decades later, with the launching of the aggressive literary campaign by the *Maskilim* of Galicia during the years 1815-1840.[2] In Lithuania and Russia the first open challenges by the Haskalah came even a little later, with the publication of Isaac Ber Lebensohn's *Te'udah b'Yisrael* (Vilna, 1828).[3]

Several factors helped to facilitate somewhat the introduction of the Haskalah into Eastern Europe.

Firstly, the dissolution of the Council of the Four Lands in 1764 weakened the communal organization in general, and rabbinic authority in particular. The previously centralized rabbinic authority gave way to localized rabbinic and lay leadership, with no unified body to deal with problems affecting religious Jewry as a whole.

In Lithuania the main rabbinic authority was vested in the hands of the Gaon of Vilna, of course. This extraordinarily brilliant Talmudic genius was favorably inclined towards the sciences. He believed that the natural as well as the exact sciences were rooted in the Torah, and that the sciences were a necessary aid to the understanding of the Torah. He was often quoted to the effect that a deficiency in the knowledge of the sciences meant a seven-fold deficiency in the knowledge of the Torah.[4] Himself a brilliant student of mathematics, astronomy, medicine and other branches of science, he encouraged the translation into Hebrew of scientific texts known in his time. In his mind there was such perfect harmony between the Torah and science, that he could not imagine that there could ever be a conflict between the two.

The Gaon's brother, Rabbi Yissachar, and his son Rabbi Abraham, outstanding Talmudic scholars, were also well versed in secular sciences and in languages. They read and spoke Polish, German and French, and thus had access to Western literature. There were others among the Gaon's disciples who studied foreign languages and were encouraged to study grammar, philosophy, mathematics, and so forth.

When the fame of Moses Mendelssohn[5] reached Vilna, especially the news of his translation of the Pentateuch into German, accompanied by a commentary ("*Biur*"), the Gaon became interested. Mendelssohn's reputation as a strictly observant Jew was untarnished. Moses was the son of a pious and learned *Sofer* (Scribe) in Dessau, whose name was Menachem Mendel. In his youth Moses absorbed a great deal of biblical and Talmudic learning in an atmosphere of piety. At the age of twelve his father died, and Moses was befriended by Rabbi David Frankel. The orphan became his diligent pupil. When Rabbi Frankel received a call from the Jewish community in Berlin, young Moses joined him there. In Berlin, Moses continued his Talmudic studies while he also devoted himself to the study of languages, ancient and modern, as well as philosophy and other secular subjects, under the tutelage of Israel of Zamosc and other *Maskilim*.

In due course, Mendelssohn translated the Pentateuch, the Book of Psalms, and Song of Songs into German, in cooperation with other *Maskilim* (Solomon Dubno, Naftali Hertz Wessely, Aharon of Yaroslav and Hertz Homberg), and produced the *Biur*

(Commentary) on the Pentateuch.

The *Translation* and *Commentary* fulfilled several objectives of the *Maskilim*:

To introduce the German language to the younger generation of students of Torah and Talmud, so as to give them access to German literature and philosophy. It was easy for a Jewish boy, who was familiar with the Hebrew text of the Pentateuch, to use the *Translation* as a vehicle to learn German by comparing the Hebrew text with the translation. The *Maskilim* also saw in the *Translation* a means of popularizing the German language among the masses of the Jewish people with a view to supplanting the "jargon" of Yiddish, which the new Jewish intelligentsia despised.

The *Commentary* was intended also to present a more "rational" and "scholarly" interpretation of the Pentateuch. While it was based on the classical commentaries of Rashi, Rashbam, Ibn Ezra and others, it omitted the *Midrashim* and *Aggadot*, and anything which had to do with the mystical and esoteric, concentrating on the plain sense of the words *(Pshat)*. Thus the *Biur* preserved the traditional character of the Pentateuch.

The *Biur* was designed also to encourage the study and understanding of Hebrew grammar and syntax, and to foster an appreciation of the aesthetic value of classical Hebrew and Hebrew poetry.

On the face of it, Mendelssohn's *Translation* and *Biur* appeared to be a positive contribution. In this light it was accepted by some well-meaning rabbis, who did not realize the inherent danger of the *Biur* in that it insidiously undermined simple faith in the Sages of the Talmud and *Midrash*, which had been so consistently fostered by Rashi.

Thus, when news of Mendelssohn's *Translation* and *Biur* reached Vilna, Rabbi Yissachar and Rabbi Abraham selected five of the Gaon's foremost disciples (among them was also Moshe Meisels, who later became an ardent Chasid of Rabbi Schneur Zalman) and sent them to Berlin. Their task was to become personally acquainted with the translator as well as with his work, and make a judgment as to their qualifications. They were particularly instructed to evaluate the merits of the *Biur* for wider dissemination. The five delegated students spent about a year in Berlin. They found Mendelssohn's adherence to Jewish traditions and religious observances beyond reproach. As for the *Translation* and *Biur*, they had copied sections from it and brought them back with them. The work was found satisfactory and was recommended as such to the Gaon, who gave his consent for its use.

A great deal of credit for the acceptance of the *Biur*, in certain rabbinic and *yeshiva* circles, was due to Solomon Dubno.[6] He was a disciple of the saintly *gaon* and Rabbi of Dubno, Rabbi Naftali, who was a disciple of the Baal Shem Tov. Later Solomon Dubno studied in Amsterdam, where he gained fame as an authority on the *T'NaCh* and Hebrew grammar. Subsequently he came to Berlin, where Mendelssohn engaged him as a teacher for his son, giving him room and board in his home. At Mendelssohn's suggestion, Solomon Dubno began writing a commentary on the Pentateuch. Indeed, his commentary on Genesis was eventually incorporated in the *Biur*.

During his stay in Berlin, it came to pass that his teacher Rabbi Naftali stopped over in Berlin for several days on his way from Offenbach (near Frankfurt am Main), where he went to receive medical treatment from a famous physician in that city. After his treatment, he visited the Jewish community at Frankfurt, at the invitation of its rabbi, Rabbi Pinchas Hurwitz (author of the *Haflaah*), and then returned home by way of Berlin. Solomon Dubno attended on his saintly teacher during his stay in Berlin. He told his teacher of his association with Mendelssohn and of their mutual endeavor. It is not known what the teacher said to his disciple in reply, but a few days later Solomon Dubno departed from the Mendelssohn home and went to Vilna. He was well received by the Gaon Rabbi Elijah and his disciples, and was offered hospitality by Joseph Peseles, a prominent and wealthy member of the Vilna community and a relative of the Gaon. Rabbi Chaim of Volozhin and his brother Rabbi Zelmele gave their approbation to Solomon Dubno's commentary on the Pentateuch, encouraging him also to write a commentary on the Books of the Prophets and Holy Writings.

The Maggid of Vilna, Rabbi Yechezkel Faivel, who was known for his learning and piety and was close to the Gaon of Vilna, often preached and admonished young Talmud scholars on the virtue of studying the Holy Scriptures with exegesis.

The Gaon's brother Rabbi Yissachar, himself the author of an exegetic work on the Pentateuch, convened periodic conferences for discussions on the Hebrew language and grammar to foster their study among the students. One of these conferences was attended by the venerable grammarian Rabbi Shlomo Zalman Hena, author of *Tzohar la'Tevah*, who was visiting in Vilna. His talks on the *T'NaCh* deeply touched all present and further stimulated the study of Hebrew and of the Scriptures among the *yeshiva* students.

Thus, the general climate in Vilna was conducive to the Haskalah spirit that breathed from Berlin. Scores of brilliant young men were induced to go to Berlin, Amsterdam, Padua and other centers of enlightenment, to study languages, medicine, astronomy, and mathematics. Some of them, like Baruch Schick and Benjamin Zalman Riveles of Shklov, Menashe of Ilya, Pinchas Eliyahu of Vilna (author of *Sefer HaBrit*) and Solomon Dubno, gained prominence, and served as forerunners of many others who sought to combine Talmudic knowledge with Western culture.

On the other hand, the Maggid of Miezricz and his disciples, the various Chasidic leaders. as well as some of the more influential rabbis such as the famed Rabbi Ezekiel Landau of Prague (an opponent of Chasidut), foreseeing the erosion which the Haskalah movement was bound to create in the foundations of traditional Judaism, fiercely opposed Mendelssohn's *Translation* and *Biur*, and thwarted all attempts of the Maskilim to disseminate Western culture among the Jewish masses in Eastern Europe.

The Maskilim, on their part, in order to captivate ever more young men and convert them to the Haskalah movement, tried to pierce through the defenses which the Chasidim set up in their communities. They sent secret emissaries to various Chasidic communities to recruit gifted young scholars for the Haskalah. Frequently, their efforts were successful and many a *yeshiva* student was persuaded to go to Berlin to join the ranks of the "seekers of enlightenment."

During the years 1791-1796, the secret emissaries of the Maskilim were particularly active among the Chasidic communities of Lithuania and the Ukraine. However, as soon as their mission was discovered, they were subjected to ridicule and abuse, and their further stay was made intolerable for them.

One such secret agent of the Maskilim was a certain Shimon of Zamut. He came to Vilna in 1792. With a good background in Talmudic studies and an extraordinary erudition in *T'NaCh*, coupled with proficiency in grammar (having been a disciple of a disciple of Zalman Hena) and in astronomy and geometry (a disciple of a disciple of Israel Lifschitz), Shimon of Zamut was eagerly welcomed by Rabbi Yissachar, the Gaon's brother, and Rabbi Abraham, the Gaon's son. They appointed him as a general supervisor over all the teachers in the *Talmud Torahs* of Vilna.

The Gaon, too, treated this seemingly pious and erudite scholar with deference and, moreover, requested him to peruse his own work *Dikduk Eliyahu*. It could not have occurred to anyone that this Shimon was one of the secret Maskilim, whose paramount interest was to recruit "converts" to the Haskalah.

In his capacity as supervisor over the *Talmud Torahs*, Shimon classified the students according to their mental capacities. Those who showed particular promise for admission to the *yeshiva* to study the Talmud intensively, were assigned by him to special studies in *T'NaCh*. Gradually he brought many of the brighter boys under his influence. When some of them were completely won over to his viewpoint, he persuaded them to go to centers of Haskalah in Germany and elsewhere, under the guise of going to study in the *yeshivot* of Minsk, Slutzk, Smargon, or Brest.

For about four years Shimon continued his undercover work with considerable success. It was a common practice in those days to follow the advice of the Sages of the Talmud (*Avot 4:14*) "Wander out to a place of Torah." Away from the distractions of one's home, a boy was expected to concentrate more fully on his studies. It aroused no one's suspicions, therefore, when some of the brighter boys left town ostensibly to go to any of the better known *yeshivot* elsewhere, but actually to enter any one of several schools of the Maskilim in Galicia, Poland and Germany. Only the aforementioned Joseph Peseles shared Shimon's secret. A secret Maskil himself, Peseles supported the work of the Maskilim with considerable sums of money.

During those years in Vilna, Shimon succeeded in winning the confidence also of the Chasidim. Taking no part in the quarrels and contests between the two factions of the Jewish community in Vilna, he was sometimes able to assume the role of an impartial arbitrator between the representatives of the two communities in the *Kehilah*, the *Parnassim*, of each side. He particularly curried the favor of the two leaders of the Chasidic community in Vilna, Baruch Mordechai and Moshe Meisels. Both were grammarians and lovers of the Holy Tongue. Moreover, Moshe Meisels liked to try his skill at Hebrew rhymes, and considered Shimon something of an expert on Hebrew poetry. All this served as the basis for an affinity between them and Shimon of Zamut.

At that time, the *nusach* of prayer which Rabbi Schneur Zalman had instituted, was already in use among the Chasidim. The Chabad Prayer Book had not yet been printed, but the Chasidim used to annotate the prayer books in use to conform to the *Nusach Chabad*. Where possible, they used the *siddur Sha'ar HaShamayim* of the Sheloh (Rabbi Isaiah Hurwitz) which was closest to the *Nusach Chabad*. But lacking that, any *siddur* could be made to harmonize with their *nusach* with the aid of annotations.

To be sure, the changes instituted in the *Nusach Chabad* presented another bone of contention for the Mitnagdim. However, those of them who had a knowledge of Hebrew grammar and syntax, had to admit that Rabbi Schneur Zalman meticulously embodied in his *nusach* the principles of the Hebrew language, so that the most erudite grammarians could find no fault with it.

Shimon of Zamut, who was not adverse to flattering the Chasidim to win their favor, could do so honestly in regard to their *nusach*. He often used to say that he was no authority on the esoteric significance of the *nusach*, or the essential differences between *Nusach Ashkenaz* and *Nusach Ari*, or the Kabbalistic reasons for the particular sequence of certain prayers. However, insofar as the grammatical rules were concerned, he could declare without hesitation that the *Nusach Chabad* was superior by far. Indeed, he would express his astonishment that, in view of the obvious erudition of their leader in the Hebrew language and grammar, the Chasidim generally did not make it their practice to study these subjects in a systematic way.

Like many of the other leading Maskilim, Shimon felt a certain respect for the Chabad Chasidim. They regarded the Chabad leader and his Chasidim as a class of their own among the Chasidim in general. Some of the leading Maskilim of the Berlin school had occasion to meet with leading Chabad Chasidim, such as Yosef Kolbo, Pinchas Schick, Binyamin of Kletzk, and others from Shklov and elsewhere, who came to the fairs in Leipzig. They found these Chabad Chasidim to be men of profound knowledge not only in the Talmud, but also in religious philosophy, whose piety was matched by their refinement of character. These could not be labeled as "fanatical ignoramuses" and "children of darkness" as the Maskilim were wont to refer to the Chasidim of Galicia and Poland. Consequently, it was the Galician, and later the Polish Chasidim, who were the first targets of the satirical and vituperous invectives of the Maskilim. As for the Chasidim of Lithuania and the Ukraine, these, the Maskilim realized, had to be drawn into the Haskalah movement by persuasion rather than by satire and ridicule. Consequently, a number of Haskalah protagonists were active among the Chasidic communities in Lithuania and the Ukraine during the years 1791-96 in an effort to persuade them of the need to study the Hebrew language and grammar, which the Maskilim considered as the first step towards a full-fledged Haskalah orientation. However, these Maskilim, some of whom might have been well intentioned, met with a firm rebuttal everywhere. At best, the Haskalah emissaries were ignored; but more often they were treated with contempt and simply told to get out. Sometimes these emissaries were even threatened with violence if they would not stop their insidious activity. Moreover, the

Mitnagdim, too, often joined the Chasidim in frustrating the efforts of the Haskalah emissaries.

The religious community was particularly incensed by a tragic incident which was said to have occurred in Ponieviezh at that time. The story, which gained widespread circulation, was as follows: A new *cheder* had been established in the town of Ponieviezh for intensive study of *Gemara*. A *melamed* (teacher), who hailed from Zolkiev, was engaged to teach the boys. He introduced into the curriculum the study of *T'NaCh* with various commentaries. After a while, the teacher urged the boys to obtain their parents' consent to attend certain classes in the local non-Jewish school. The school was headed by a priest, and the Jewish students fell under the influence of his missionary zeal. One of his methods was to exclude the Jewish children from the free meals which were given at the school for the Christian students. Two Jewish boys, unable to resist the priest's influence and temptation, converted to Christianity. According to the rumor, which spread throughout the entire region, the teacher from Zolkiev was blamed for the tragic conversion of the boys. Excitement and indignation ran high, and the dangers of the Haskalah were brought home to every Jewish family, Chasidic and Mitnagdic alike.[7]

In view of the reports coming in from the various Haskalah emissaries about the poor results of their efforts, the Haskalah leaders instructed Shimon of Zamut to visit the various Chasidic communities in Lithuania and the Ukraine, including also the very center of the Chabad Chasidim, and their leader—in Liozna. Shimon was to survey the situation and report his findings to the central committee of the Maskilim, together with recommendations as to how best to penetrate the Chasidic strongholds. Because of the excellent reputation which Shimon enjoyed in Vilna, both among the Mitnagdim and Chasidim, he seemed to be eminently suitable for this task. On the basis of family reasons, Shimon obtained leave of absence from his duties for several months, and set out on his tour of Chasidic communities, including Liozna.

Shimon was to return to Vilna before Rosh Hashanah. But several weeks prior to his return, the Chasidic leaders, Baruch

Mordechai and Moshe Meisels, received a letter from Liozna alerting them to the true identity of Shimon of Zamut. The letter, written in the name of Rabbi Schneur Zalman, informed them that Shimon, who had been held in such high esteem as a very pious Jew and admirer of the *Chabad Nusach*, was in reality a secret emissary of the Maskilim. The Chasidic leaders were to keep a watchful eye on him, gather evidence on his clandestine activities, and at the proper time, they were to expose him for what he really was.

In the meantime, the relation between the Mitnagdim and Chasidim of Vilna became more strained. The Chasidim had succeeded in gaining two more representatives on the community council. Though this strengthened the community and was beneficial also financially, since additional income poured into the community chest from the Chasidim who had previously boycotted the community council, some of the militant Mitnagdim were concerned about the growing strength of the Chasidim, and plotted to undermine the Chasidic influence. At the head of these plotters was the above-mentioned Joseph Peseles.

The Chasidim, on their part, took steps to thwart any new attacks against them, by infiltrating the very councils of the Mitnagdim. Of particular service to the Chasidim was a relative of Peseles' wife, a certain Betzalel Baruch. A physical monstrosity of a man—a hunchback, limping on one leg, seemingly half blind and deaf, with impaired speech—Betzalel Baruch made the impression of a half-wit. In reality, however, he was a clever and alert man, who missed nothing of what was going on in the Peseles' house, where he lived and performed odd jobs in return for his keep. Unobtrusively he was always around when some conference was taking place in this house. Open letters were never concealed from him, nor were any drawers locked for him. Betzalel Baruch kept his eyes and ears open, read the letters and memoranda which were within easy access, and copied some of them. All the information which he carefully gathered, he turned over to the Chasidim.

It was with the help of this Betzalel Baruch that the first clue was discovered to Shimon's true identity. For Betzalel Baruch was able to copy an informative and revealing letter which Shimon had written to Peseles.

In this letter, written from Cracow, Shimon reported on his visits to various Chasidic communities, including the very capital of the Chasidim. After spending about a week in Liozna, several days of which he was ill, he was received in private audience by the leader of the Chasidim. Before the audience was over, the Rebbe of the Chasidim recognized him for what he was—an emissary and spy of the Maskilim. Shimon could not account for this uncanny perceptiveness of the Rebbe—perhaps he sniffed that he, Shimon, had not put on tefillin that day, as in the case of the *yenuka*[8] mentioned in the *Zohar,* whose sensitive nostrils discovered a man's failure to read the Shema—Shimon added sarcastically. Be it as it might, he had to beat a hasty escape that very night.

Shimon went on to say that throughout the towns of White Russia through which he passed, he found the Chasidim firmly entrenched, and that it would not be easy to dislodge them. A well thought-out strategy would be required to enlighten those "fanatics," the Chasidim and non-Chasidim alike. "For, to all of us who do not believe that there ever was, or is, a G-d, both the followers of *nakdishach*[9] and *keter* as well as of *nekadesh* and *na'aritzach* beat the air and cling to an antiquated age," Shimon wrote. He concluded by saying that all the measures hitherto employed by the committee in Vilna in their fight against the Chasidim was like a drop in the bucket by comparison with what will have to be done, and that he would report in detail on his return to Vilna.

Now that Baruch Mordechai and Moshe Meisels had no more doubt about Shimon's identity, they resolved to gather further evidence about him. They decided on a bold step, namely to search Shimon's belongings before his return to Vilna. They recalled that Shimon had often spoken glowingly of a relative of his, a certain Aizik'l Frumeles, a prominent merchant who lived in Polotzk. According to Shimon, this man was an avid Hebrew grammarian, who had entered into matrimonial ties with Chasidic families and became one of them, praying in their *klaus*. Being a man of means, with business dealings in surrounding communities, Aizik'l Frumeles enjoyed considerable influence among the Chasidim of Polotzk and vicinity.

In the light of this information, the two Chasidic leaders of Vilna called upon one of the Chasidim of the town of Swintzan, whose name was Zalman Leib, to appear in Vilna on a visit to Shimon, as a relative of the said Aizik'l Frumeles. As such, he was admitted to Shimon's room and allowed to stay there for a few days, pending the latter's arrival.

Zalman Leib found bundles of letters and notes, received as well as written, by Shimon. Here was Shimon's entire correspondence with a number of leading Maskilim, including Naftali Hertz Wessely, Isaac Eichel, M. Bresslau, David Franco Mendes, Solomon Maimon, M. M. Levin, Baruch Linda, the brothers Friedlander, and other leading members of the "*Meassefim,*"[10] who had already become well-known for their apostasy and militantism against Jewish orthodoxy. It was evident from this correspondence that Shimon was no small peg in the campaign to spread the Haskalah movement among the *yeshiva* students in Lithuania. Zalman Leib also found among Shimon's notes a list of the boys whom he had sent away to Haskalah schools in Warsaw, Cracow, Vienna, Berlin, Breslau, Dessau, Koenigsberg, Hamburg and other centers of the Maskilim; copies of letters of introduction for each of the boys, their background, mental ability and past progress; financial accounts of moneys received and spent in his propaganda work; correspondence with the teachers of the boys on the latter's brain-washing to clear their minds of the "antiquated" beliefs and opinions which they had absorbed at home and at the *yeshiva*, in order to make them more receptive to the new spirit of the "enlightenment."

All this material left no doubt as to Shimon's character, his views and activities. It was quite clear that Shimon was an atheist, who had completely broken away from Jewish tradition, and in his heart ridiculed and despised the Sages of old and their teachings. Above all, he was an undercover-agent for the Maskilim, who shrewdly and successfully had already trapped many promising young Talmudic students in his missionary net.

Baruch Mordechai and Moshe Meisels carefully copied and documented the incriminating material for the proper use at the proper time.

On the Fast of Gedaliah (the day after Rosh Hashanah), Betzalel Baruch informed Baruch Mordechai that Shimon had returned on the day before Rosh Hashanah and that during the two days of the festival, he held frequent talks with Peseles. Betzalel Baruch related to him all that he had overheard of Shimon's account of his visit in the Chasidic capital, including all the details of Shimon's audience with the Rebbe, his talks with the Rebbe's brothers and sons, the Chasidic customs and conduct which he had observed, and so forth. Shimon made no secret of the fact that he had been greatly impressed by the extraordinary discipline which prevailed among the Chasidim, and by their general conduct.

The highlights of Shimon's report, as recounted by Betzalel Baruch were as follows:

Already on arrival in Vitebsk, some 25 miles distant from Liozna, Shimon noted how everybody spoke most reverently of the Rebbe, as well as of his brothers and sons. Members of the Rebbe's family were never referred to by their full names, but by their initials. Even the Rebbe's grandson Menachem Mendel, a boy of some six or seven years, was also called in this way— RaMaM, and he was highly praised as an unusually brilliant and knowledgeable boy, with extraordinary mental capacities.

During the three days Shimon spent in Vitebsk, he visited many synagogues and *Batei-Midrash*, and everywhere he found groups of men sitting at long tables and studying out of printed but unbound folios. Their prayers were as animated and as inspired as their learning.

Shimon discovered that what the Chasidim were studying so avidly were the newly printed sheets of a book by their Rebbe, which was coming off the printing-press in Slavita. So eager and impatient were the Chasidim to study this book, that they had arranged with the printer to send them the printed sheets as soon as they came off the press.

He had seen these printed and unbound folios in various towns on his route, as well as in Vilna before his departure.

Shimon described a Chasidic get-together which he had witnessed in one of the synagogues in a late afternoon, following the *Mincha* prayer. He, too, was invited to join in the *"Seudat-*

Mitzvah." The fare was simple: a loaf of bread, two herrings, watermelon and a bottle of liquor. But the spirits were high. They drank to the health of their Rebbe, and sang melodies. The talk around the table was animated, for the subject matter was the latest news emanating from Liozna, about the great strides which the Chasidim had made in various communities. One of the elders of the group related an episode about the Rebbe's early days in Miezricz, when he was a disciple of the Maggid. The Chasid used this episode as a text for his sermonette. It went something like this:

> When our master and teacher, the Rebbe, was about to leave Miezricz, the Maggid's son, Rabbi Abraham, known as the "Angel" because of his saintliness,[11] accompanied him to the wagon. Rabbi Abraham then said to the driver, "Whip the horses until they cease to be horses." Thereupon our Rebbe changed his mind and decided to stay a little longer. He declared that Rabbi Abraham's words, "Whip the horses until they cease to be horses," opened a new way of serving G-d, which he wished to explore.

> The elder of the group then went on to explain the meaning of the lesson. Referring to the Scriptural verse, "A whip for the horse, a bridle for the donkey, and a rod for the fool's back" (Prov. 26:3), he explained that the "horse," the "donkey," and the "fool" were metaphors for certain types of Jews who failed to live up to their function and purpose in life. Some Jews, like a blind or rebellious horse, refuse to go in the right direction. He identified them as the militant Mitnagdim, who refuse to see the good of the Chasidic way of life. Others, like the donkey (*chamor,* from the word *chomer,* clay, matter), simply are too much concerned with their material needs and bodily pleasures, albeit in the area of permitted things. These need a bridle to curb their appetites and refine their natures—precisely what Chasidut seeks to accomplish. Finally, there are the "fools" who consider themselves the wisest. These he identified as the Maskilim.

Relating this experience, Shimon said he was sorely provoked to take the speaker to task, but, remembering his mission and realizing also the futility of a debate with people who would not listen to reason, he repressed his feelings, and stayed on to see the affair conclude with a collection of donations to be sent to their Rebbe. Shimon was amazed at the magnanimous response of the Chasidim who raised a substantial sum of money in ready cash there and then. Lots were cast as to who would be the two lucky representatives to take the money to the Rebbe, together with the names of the contributors.

Of particular interest was Shimon's account of his adventure in the Chasidic capital:

I arrived in Liozna on a Monday afternoon, about two o'clock. I entered the synagogue in the Rebbe's court. In the adjoining vestry I found a number of men still wrapped in their praying shawls and phylacteries, praying individually in melodious tones, some of them snapping their fingers and swaying in rapt devotion.

In another room a group of young men were engaged in intensive Talmudic study, with the Rebbe's brother Maharil (Rabbi Yehuda Leib) at the head of the table, conducting the seminar.

In a third room a larger group of young men were busy studying those folios which I had seen in Vitebsk and elsewhere. Leading this group was a young man, who was reading from the text and explaining it at length. The subject matter was the eighth chapter of the Rebbe's book, which centered on the transgression of eating forbidden food, and the defilement of the body and soul caused thereby. He discussed the difference between the defilement caused by the transgressions of frivolity, arrogance and idle talk, which dull the heart and senses, and the defilement of the mind caused by the study of secular philosophy. The great philosophers Maimonides and Nachmanides were exceptions, however, because they sought this knowledge only as a tool in the service of G-d.

I had to admit to myself that his explanations were logical, and the subject was captivating. Later I learned that the young man was the Rebbe's older son Dov Ber, who gave a regular class twice a week to two groups of students, each of about 25 students.

That day I bought the first three printed sheets of the book, beginning with the first chapter and finishing with page twelve, at the beginning of the tenth chapter. For the next three days I studied the text with concentration, to the best of my mental capacity. I also enlisted the help of some of the older Chasidim to clarify some passages for me. I found the subject matter largely beyond my ken. Some topics, such as the Supernal *Sefirot*, the *yichudim* ("unions") achieved through Torah and prayer, the purgatories of fire and snow, I could only take with a goodly measure of salt, of course. But on the whole I was considerably impressed by the sweep of the author's imagination, his lucid style, and conciseness of expression, and the general adherence of the text to the laws and norms of the Hebrew language.

During these days I was able to observe also the other sons of the Rebbe. The middle one, Chaim Abraham, was fond of seclusion. He immersed himself in his studies with silent concentration, and was more contemplative than voluble. By contrast, the youngest, Moshe, a lad of about fourteen or fifteen, was a lively one. His sparkling eyes exuded intelligence and self confidence. He loved to talk and debate. I heard that he was thoroughly proficient in the entire Talmud and in religious philosophy. He is said to have the *Guide, Kuzari* and *Ikkarim* at his finger tips, for he was gifted with an extraordinary mental grasp and memory. I asked him if he had studied Hebrew grammar, and he replied, "It is an integral part of Torah; how can one not learn it? Without grammatical knowledge one cannot properly understand the words of *T'NaCh*, or the meaning of the prayers!"

The Chasidim have certain customs and rites of their own. A Chasid who is granted an audience with the Rebbe undergoes three days' preparation. Some even extend it over a week.

The preparation essentially takes the form of a spiritual stocktaking and the purification of the mind. On the day of the audience, for several hours before the appointed time, the candidates gather in one of the vestries of the synagogue to study Torah. Some of them also stay up the night before for *Tikun Chatzot* (midnight prayer), to recite supplications and *Tehillim* (Psalms), usually accompanied by tears and sighs, in contrition and penitence.

After the audience, which the Chasidim call *Yechidut* ("Alone" with the Rebbe), those who had this privilege do a special dance called the "*Yechidut* Dance," or "*Taharah* Dance," to the tune of a special melody. The dancing expresses their elated feelings at having been privileged to see the Rebbe face to face, and their absolute confidence that the problem about which they had petitioned the Rebbe will now be happily resolved. While the inspired petitioners dance in a circle, the other Chasidim present clap their hands and join in the lively melody.

The Chasidim love to sing, and they have special *nigunim* (tunes) for various occasions. There are the tunes which they hum during their prayers; those they sing during study; those at a *seudah* (festive meal), and those at a *hitvaadut* (get-together). In each case the *nigunim* are appropriate to the occasion, and are rather inspiring. Three *nigunim* made a particularly profound impression on me: The "*Hitvaadut* Melody" which they usually call the "Nigun of Brotherly Love"; the "Contemplation Nigun," also called "Nigun of *Teshuvah* (Repentance)," and the "Yechidut Nigun," also called the "Nigun of the *Mikdash* (Sanctuary)."

The Nigun of Brotherly Love I heard for the first time in Vitebsk. It consists of five stanzas, all harmoniously blended into one another, with a crescendo of tender and caressing strains, culminating in a rhapsody of tender passion.

The Nigun of *Teshuvah* consists of three stanzas. The first evoking a dematerialization of the self, and thought-concentration; the second appealing to the inner conscience, is profoundly nostalgic, while the third is designed to excite contrition, giving way to comforting solace and blissful reconciliation.

111

The Yechidut Nigun also consists of five stanzas. The first two, expressed in moderate tones, evoke contemplation and introspection. The third and fourth express gratitude and hope, in tender and reassuring strains. The fifth voices confidence, in cheerful and rhythmical tones, which stimulate the legs to dance, and the hands to rise upwards in accord with the temperament of the tune.

One further noteworthy custom of the Chasidim is to stay up two nights in the week, on Thursday night and on Saturday night. On these nights they study the Talmud and Codes until midnight, and sometimes they engage in a *farbrengen* (get-together), over glasses of liquor and refreshments. After *Tikun Chatzot*, they spend the rest of the night in the study of Chasidut.

The Rebbe's house, or, as the Chasidim call it—the "Sanctuary," is situated in a spacious courtyard, in which there is a garden lined with trees, a vegetable plot and various structures.

The house occupies an area of about twenty-five by twelve meters and has an upper structure. The living quarters are divided into two sections, separated by the entrance hall. On the right side of it are the Rebbe's private living quarters, while on the left is a small synagogue, which the Chasidim affectionately call the "Lower *Gan Eden*." It also serves as the waiting room for those who have been granted an interview with the Rebbe. The upper floor consists of two rooms, separated by the entrance room. One is the Rebbe's private study, and the second is the reception room for those received in audience. The Chasidim reverently refer to it as the "Upper *Gan Eden*."

During the first few days after my arrival in Liozna, I was unable to see the Rebbe. I was told that during weekdays he appears only for the reading of the Torah, and when he gives a Torah discourse in the "Lower *Gan Eden*." As a rule, the Rebbe himself reads the Torah. He could also be seen, I was told, on *erev* Shabbat, when he goes to the *mikvah* for immersion.

I had hoped to see him on *erev* Shabbat. However, I

awoke on Friday morning with a high temperature and was confined to my bed for three full days. Fortunately, my host took good care of me, gave me various medicines, a rub-down, and covered me with blankets, all of which made me perspire profusely. On the fourth day, a Monday, I was able to get out of bed, but I still felt very weak. On Wednesday it was my turn to be received in audience by the Rebbe.

As I entered the Rebbe's room, I was overcome with an overpowering sense of awe. His impressive face, penetrating eyes, and strong voice as he said to me, "What is your wish?" left me speechless for a moment. However, soon I was able to recover my composure, and I replied, "I am a *melamed* of small children in my town. I teach them *Chumash* with emphasis on the principles and laws of *dik-duk*. My fellow teachers oppose my method and criticize me for teaching them also the Hebrew language. In defense of my position I cited the grammatical punctiliousness of the Rebbe's new edition of the *siddur*. Nevertheless my colleagues are not convinced. It would be of general benefit if I could obtain a letter to commend the use of the grammatical method, to train the children to read correctly, as well as to teach them the *T'NaCh*."

For a few minutes the Rebbe seemed engrossed in concentrated thought. Then he raised his head, opened his eyes, and said, "True, the prayers, particularly the *Shema* and the *Shemone-Esrei*, should be recited carefully and correctly. However, the method of interpreting the Torah mainly on the basis of grammar and linguistics could come too dangerously close to misinterpretation."

The Rebbe again immersed himself in thought for a few moments, and then posed the question to me: "How do you explain to your pupils the verse, 'And Yitzchak trembled very exceedingly' (Gen. 27:33)?"

I replied, "According to the first interpretation of Rashi—in the sense of astonishment."

"And why not also tell your pupils of Rashi's second interpretation, in the name of the *Midrash*, that Yitzchak saw the *Gehinnom* open at Esau's feet?"

113

"In my opinion . . . I think that the tender minds of the children should not be crammed with *aggadic* material in general, particularly with such a horrifying subject as *Gehinnom* and the like, which are beyond a child's imagination. Moreover, the child would find it hard to believe that the great and fiery *Gehinnom* would suddenly blaze forth in Yitzchak's room, while both Yitzchak and Esau remained alive, and not even their clothes were singed!"

"But where did the *Midrash* get this idea?" he asked me again, to which I made no reply.

After a brief pause, during which he was again deeply immersed in thought, he raised one of the two candles which were burning on the table—for it was his custom, when he received people in audience, even during the day, to have two lighted candles on his table, on which were also a *Chumash* and a volume of the *Zohar*. He looked into my face with his deep and penetrating eyes, then solemnly and deliberately said to me: "When a man comes from Vilna and says he comes from Zamut; When he leads Jewish children to the *Moloch*[12] of the Haskalah and says that he is a *melamed*—Gehinnom opens before him. How many souls have you led to perdition? Yet you obstinately persist in your rebelliousness! You have gone the way of apostasy from which there is no return."

I hastily withdrew from the Rebbe's room, the "Upper *Gan Eden*," determined to return at once to my lodgings and to leave town forthwith. I realized that I had been caught, and I did not cherish the idea of being stretched out on a table, with my pants down, taking a lashing like a truant schoolboy—as has been done to some of my fellow-emissaries who had been discovered in certain Chasidic strongholds.

However, as I passed the small synagogue, the "Lower *Gan Eden*" as they called it, I was surrounded by some five or six young men, who dragged me into the synagogue. You can imagine my fright! To my great relief, however, I soon realized that all they wanted was to do the "Yechidut Dance" with me! Needless to say, I did not feel like dancing. I was badly shaken by my encounter with the Rebbe, and I had not fully recovered from my illness. Several times I tried in vain to wriggle myself out of their affectionate embrace, but they held on to me firmly and whirled around with me until I was well-nigh exhausted. Finally, the ordeal was over. I was barely able to walk—crawl would describe it more accurately—to my lodging. I waited for daybreak in fear and trembling, and at the crack of dawn, I took my belongings and walked out on my tiptoes. I walked to the nearby village, where I hired a horse-and-wagon driver for my speedy departure, blessing my stars that I was able to get away without a scratch.[13]

Shimon went on to report that he spent the following six weeks traveling through the districts of Mohilev, Minsk, and Tchernigov, and then went to Lvov, where he had arranged to meet with his colleagues. After hearing his account of the growing strength and rapid expansion of the Chasidic movement, the group decided that it was necessary to take stringent measures to combat the Chasidic expansion. Among the first steps to be taken in this direction was the renewal of the *cherem* (ban) against the Chasidim with redoubled vigor, so as to truly isolate them from the rest of the Jewish community. The next step was to denounce the Chasidic leader to the highest authorities as a traitor and seditionist. The charges were to be that he was collecting large sums of money and sending them to Turkey, with a view to eventually proclaiming himself the Jewish Messiah and King, as the false Messiahs Shabbatai Tzvi and Jacob Frank had done in the not-too-distant past.

Betzalel Baruch told Baruch Mordechai that insofar as he gathered, Shimon brought with him a ready text of the *cherem*, which required only the signature of the Gaon, and that Joseph Peseles was confident that he could obtain the Gaon's consent and signature.

At the termination of *Shabbat-Shuvah*, Baruch Mordechai and Moshe Meisels convened a meeting of the leaders of the Chasidic community and informed them of Shimon's machinations. It was then decided that a public meeting should be called by the Community Council during *Chol-HaMoed* Succot, when the evidence of Shimon's true character would be made public and he would be completely unmasked.

In the meantime, on Thursday, the day after Yom Kippur (5557/1796), news spread with lightning speed throughout the city that the Gaon had pronounced a strict *cherem* against the Chasidim and their Rebbe. According to this *cherem*, it was said, everybody was permitted, nay urged, to take all possible repressions against the Chasidim, without mercy or compassion, and anyone having any friendly dealings with them would be put to the pillory.

News of the *cherem* aroused not only the Chasidim, but also the moderates among the Mitnagdim. Later that day a new rumor sped around town that the *cherem* was issued without the Gaon's knowledge, for he was old (seventy-seven and a half years of age) and frail, and the fast of Yom Kippur had further weakened his condition. The ban was therefore issued by the militant anti-Chasidic committee headed by Peseles. For this reason it was pronounced during the early morning in the presence of only a few bystanders.[14]

On the following day, Friday, the 12th of *Tishrei*, Meir Refaels, a Chasidic member of the Community Council, who happened to be the *Parnass-Chodesh* (Monthly President), made a public announcement for the Jews of Vilna and its suburbs, to the effect that (a) the purported *cherem* against the Chasidim had not been approved by the *Beit-Din*, in the absence of a clear directive from the Gaon, and (b) that on Wednesday, the first day of *Chol-HaMoed* Succot there would be a mass meeting called by the Council, which everyone, men, women, and children over Bar Mitzvah age, were urged to attend.

Indeed, the meeting was overcrowded and tense with anticipation. Present were all the members of the Community Council, the *Beit Din*, and the most prominent members of the community. Two pious Jews then ascended the podium and solemnly gave testimony that the man known as Shimon the Grammarian is an emissary of the Maskilim, sent for the purpose of raiding the *yeshivot* and *talmud-Torahs*, with a view to inducing some of their most promising students to leave their Torah studies and secretly join the schools founded by Maskilim in

Galicia and Germany. The accusers substantiated their charge by the documents which had come into their possession, and which were there and then presented in evidence. These included a list of the students which Shimon succeeded to win over during the past four years (5552-5556), the account of the expenditures involved, and various documents written in Shimon's own hand, or received by him. The accusers further declared that they were ready to take a solemn oath on the veracity of their testimony, and demanded that Joseph Peseles should likewise be adjured to reveal all he knew of Shimon's treacherous deeds.

The unexpected revelations stunned all present, and most of all Shimon himself. There followed a tremendous uproar as the impact of the testimony struck home. The parents of the boys, who had been beguiled into believing that their sons would one day return home with attestations of excellence in Torah scholarship and certificates of rabbinic ordination, were ready to give vent to their violent feelings against the treacherous impostor. From the women's gallery there came a terrible wail. Shimon was trapped. Two beadles and several young Chasidim made sure that he would not escape, nor be set upon by the enraged people.

The scandal of Shimon's uncovered treachery completely eclipsed the *cherem,* which was all but forgotten in the new excitement. For the next three weeks the *Beit-Din* was engaged in studying the documents and papers which came to light at the public meeting, as well as the additional material which was uncovered by a search of Shimon's home, while Shimon was held in the community guardhouse. The investigation left no doubt as to Shimon's true character and misdeeds. The *Beit-Din* then pronounced their verdict. Three days at the pillory, followed by disgraceful expulsion. The sentence was duly carried out, and on the 23rd of *MarCheshvan,* Shimon and his family were led through a jeering crowd, and expelled from the city.[15]

The Shimon affair cast a shadow on many a prominent member of the community, who had been taken in by Shimon's deceptions. Most embarrassed was Rabbi Abraham, the son of the Gaon, and the Gaon's brother. As for Joseph Peseles, the wealthy and prominent communal leader, he could not easily remove the stigma of being a collaborator with the despised

Maskilim of Berlin.

If the Chasidim of Vilna had gained a moral victory over some of their most outspoken adversaries, it did not help to soften the attitude of their opponents towards them. The influential Joseph Peseles, in particular, could not forgive the Chasidim for the coup which they so neatly executed against him and his friends.

In the meantime, the Gaon's health steadily deteriorated. Already during the festival of Succot he was unable to sit in the Succah. He was confined to his bed a great deal, and his foremost disciples, headed by the celebrated *gaon*, Rabbi Chaim of Volozhin, took turns at attending on him all the time. Nevertheless, most of the day, the Gaon Rabbi Elijah was wrapped in his tallit and tefillin, and words of Torah incessantly flowed from his lips. His eyes dimmed, and with his concentration failing at times, he did not trust himself to recite the prayers alone, and he begged his disciple in attendance to read the prayers with him word for word.

The condition of the Gaon's health caused great concern to the *Beit-Din* and the Community Council. They ordered public prayers and the recitation of *Tehillim* for the Gaon's health. In all the synagogues of Vilna and its environs, including the Chasidic synagogues, Jews earnestly prayed for the recovery of the saintly and revered Gaon.

In the first days of *Tevet*, the Chasidim of Vilna received the first-printed copies of the *Likutei Amarim* (*Tanya*), which had come off the press in Slavita on the 20th of *Kislev*. This was a cause for great rejoicing among the Chasidim. It so happened that on the night of this Chasidic celebration, the Gaon had a relapse and fainted twice. The following day, on learning of the Gaon's condition during the night, Peseles and his friends stiffed up the tempest against the Chasidim by accusing them of rejoicing at the Gaon's illness. Not content with a virulent verbal campaign against the Chasidim, Joseph Peseles bought several copies of the *Likutei Amarim*, and in the presence of his friends and sympathizers, ceremoniously consigned them to the flames of a bonfire in the court of the synagogue, claiming to do so with the approval of the ailing Gaon.[16]

Despite the extreme provocation at seeing the sacred book trodden upon and burnt, the Chasidim exercised restraint, having been sternly admonished by their leaders not to allow themselves to be drawn into open hostilities. Though many prominent individuals in the Mitnagdic community dissociated themselves from the militant anti-Chasidic group, and some of them, particularly the *gaon*, Rabbi Chaim of Volozhin, even praised the Chasidim for their remarkable self-discipline, the irreconcilable opposition was steering towards a head-on collision.

CHAPTER IX

PUBLICATION OF THE TANYA

As early as 5552 (1792) handwritten copies of essays and discourses—which eventually made up the book of *Likutei Amarim* (*Tanya*) by Rabbi Schneur Zalman—began to circulate among the Chasidim. Word spread quickly among the Chasidim that their Rebbe had written a work on practical, religious ethics, as a "guide" for the seekers of religious devotion. There was a great demand for copies of this work. In various towns, such as Liadi, Haditch, Rudnia, Lubavitch, Dobromysl, Kalisk and Dubrovna, qualified copiers were busy copying the book.

In the course of several years, copies of the book found their way also to Rumania and Galicia. News of the appearance of a written work on Chasidut and its widespread distribution, also reached various rabbinic convocations which convened in Vitebsk, Minsk, and other White-Russian cities, as well as in the Ukraine.

In the Mitnagdic camp the news aroused renewed concern about the spread of Chasidic influence. A group of zealous opponents contrived to introduce certain passages into the book and make certain other forgeries, which would raise questions and doubts in fundamental matters of faith, and stamp the book as a work full of heretical tendencies. Such a forged copy was submitted to the Gaon of Vilna, in the year 5555 (1795) for his judgment.

At the time there lived in Slutzk a hoary sage, a centenarian, Rabbi Tanchum *Porush* ("The Hermit"). In his youth he had been one of the outstanding Talmudic prodigies of his time. A contemporary of Rabbi Elijah's grandfather, from whom he was said to have received a blessing for longevity, Rabbi Tanchum was a vehement opponent of the Baal Shem Tov. At the rabbinic convocations in Minsk and in his hometown Slutzk, Rabbi Tanchum was an outspoken foe of the Chasidim. He demanded that the most stringent *cherem* (excommunication) be imposed against the Chasidim, with all the paraphernalia of black candles and the sounding of the *shofar* (ram's horn), and that it should include, not only the members of the "*Kat*" (sect), but also their abettors and associates. He was supported in his views by the other Geonim of Slutzk, including his son Rabbi Yaakov Klonymos Kalmen, Rabbi Moshe Shmuel and Rabbi Betzalel Azriel, and their disciples.

The leading Mitnagdim of Shklov were headed by the famed *gaon* and preacher, Rabbi Pinchas Zeira, son of the *gaon* and preacher Rabbi Yehuda Porush; the venerable preacher Rabbi Tuvia Kalmen Faivush Porush, celebrated for his weekly fasts from one Shabbat to the next (breaking his fasts only at night); and famed preacher Rabbi Avraham Porush. They proposed that a new work on *Mussar* (religious ethics) be published that would compete with the book published by the head of the Chasidim. Indeed, a suitable work was found, entitled *Lekach Tov* ("Good Doctrine").[1]

Rabbi Yaakov Klonymos Kalmen republished it in the year 5556 (1796). It bore the imprimatur of the Geonim Chanoch Henoch, son of Rabbi Schmuel Schick; Tzvi Hirsch, the son of Rabbi Mahdam; and Pinchas the son of Rabbi Yehuda. The book aroused much interest and was distributed gratis in the thousands.

In the meantime, Rabbi Schneur Zalman had received inquiries from various places in Galicia and Rumania for elucidation of certain passages in the *Tanya*. It became apparent that the reason for the inquiries was the fact that many copyists' errors had crept into the copies, or that the copies had been forged by Mitnagdim in Brisk and Vilna.

Two Chasidim, Pinchas Schick and his brother-in-law Binyamin of Kletzk, attending the fair at Leipzig, were very pleased to see pamphlets of the *Tanya* being circulated there. They were soon dismayed, however, when they discovered that the text had been tampered with, and that the pamphlets were forgeries. Further inquiries led them to the distributor. The two Chasidim, presenting themselves as Mitnagdim, won the distributor's confidence. They learned that the man had brought with him six hundred forged copies, of which he had sold about one hundred and fifty. Pinchas and Binyamin bought all the remainder of his stock from him.

Seeing the danger inherent in the proliferous copying of the *Tanya*, and in order to forestall any further tampering with the text by unscrupulous opponents, Rabbi Schneur Zalman finally consented to have the *Tanya* printed. There were two conditions attached to his consent: (a) The printed edition must have the approbation *(haskamah)* of both Rabbi Meshulam Zusia of Anipoli[2] and Rabbi Yehuda Leib HaKohen,[3] both of them disciples of Rabbi Dov Ber of Miezricz and the author's senior colleagues. (b) The book must appear anonymously.

Towards the end of the year 5556 (1796) the written approbations arrived, and the printing of the *Tanya* was commissioned to the Slavita printers by Rabbi Shalom Shachna, Rabbi Schneur Zalman's son-in-law, and his partner Rabbi Shmuel HaLevi. On the 20th of *Kislev* (Tuesday, Dec. 20, 1796), the printing was completed. The first edition numbered 15,000 copies. In the following year a second printing, with 5,000 copies, and a year later a third printing, with 20,000 copies, came off the printing press. Thereafter new reprints of the latter edition appeared frequently, as the demand for this Chabad classic continued to grow.[4]

The first edition appeared under the title *Likutei Amarim* ("Collected Essays") and contained only the first part, entitled *Sefer Shel Benonim* ("Book of the Intermediate") and the second part, *Sha'ar HaYichud VehaEmunah* ("Portal of Unity and Belief").

A new edition of the book, bearing the title *Tanya* (after the initial word with which this work begins) appeared in 5559 (Aug. 9, 1798, according to the official stamp of the censor) in Zolkiev, which included also the third part *Iggeret HaTeshuvah*

("Epistle of Repentance"), as yet not divided into chapters. The second imprint of this edition appeared in 5565 (1805), also in Zolkiev. Subsequently it was reprinted twice again.

A similar edition, but bearing the title *Likutei Amarim* appeared in Shklov in 5566 (1806), and was reprinted in the same year.

In 5574 (1814) the first posthumous editions began to appear in Shklov and elsewhere, now with the name of the author printed on the title page, and with the approbation of the author's sons by way of an introduction.

The first complete editions of the *Tanya*, including also the last two sections, *Iggeret HaKodesh* ("Sacred Epistles") and *Kuntres Acharon* ("Latest Discourse"), came off the press in Koenigsberg, in 5571 (1811).

Altogether the *Tanya* has seen more than sixty editions in print to this day, of which at least eight were printed in the author's lifetime anonymously.

The sixth Lubavitcher Rebbe, Rabbi Yosef Yitzchak Schneersohn, in a letter about this work, makes the following observations:

> The *Book of Tanya* is the "Written Torah" of the teachings of Chabad Chasidut, in that not only has each sentence been carefully and concisely composed, but also each letter has been carefully chosen. The work is punctilious in every detail, so that each word and each letter is meaningful. Among the leaders of Chabad and the early generations of Chasidim the *Tanya* commanded a reverence second only to the *Chumash* (Pentateuch).[5]

The sixth Lubavitcher Rebbe records several traditions relating to the publications of the *Tanya*. One of them was transmitted by the Chasid Chanoch Henoch, as he received it from the Chasid Tzvi of Smilian, known among Chasidim as "Hershel *der Waremer*" (the "Warm One") and "Hershel *Bren*" (the "Firebrand"),[6] who, in turn, heard it in his youth from a contemporary Chasid of Rabbi Schneur Zalman, Yaakov of Smilian (of whom mention has already been made).

It was the Rebbe's custom—Yaakov of Smilian related—to lead in prayer on the *yahrzeit* day (19th of *Kislev*) of the Maggid of Miezricz. Rabbi Schneur Zalman acted as Reader during all three daily services. After the Evening Prayer he usually gave a Chasidic discourse in his own room to a select group, while after *Minchah* he gave a public discourse.

In the year 5557 (1796) the day of *yahrzeit* occurred on a Monday (Dec. 19th), and the Rebbe observed his annual custom. Some three months earlier, towards the end of the month of *Elul* (5556), the emissaries Moshe, Pinchas, and Yitzchak Moshe, whom the Rebbe had sent to the saintly Rabbis, Yehuda Leib HaKohen and Meshulam Zusia of Anipoli, returned with the written approbations of the two Chasidic leaders to be published with the *Tanya*. Thereupon the Rebbe informed the printers in Slavita to proceed with the printing of the book, requesting that the book come off the press not later than the beginning of *Kislev* (5557), and that the copies be delivered forthwith to Liozna. He was anxious that the printed copies of the book be in the hands of the Chasidim before the *yahrzeit* of the Maggid of Miezricz, so that it could be studied on that day.

Word of the Rebbe's consent to the printing of the *Tanya* spread quickly among the Chasidim and evoked jubilation in their circles.

However, when mid-*Cheshvan* came and it was learned that the last print-sheet could not be put into the press in time for the book to be completed on or before the specified date, the Rebbe was visibly upset.

During the Morning Prayers on the *yahrzeit* day, it being a Monday, when the first section of the weekly portion is read from a *Sefer-Torah*, the Rebbe read from the Torah scroll himself. The first *aliyah* (calling up to the reading) was given to the *Kohen*, Elimelech of Yanov; the second—to the *Levi*, Zelig of Ulla, and the third was taken by the Rebbe himself. He read the portion (dealing with Joseph's dreams) with especial fervor, emphasizing particularly the last verses, "*And he related* [the dream] *to his father and brothers . . . and his brothers envied him . . . but his father kept the matter* [in his mind]" (Gen. 37: 10-11).

Completing the reading, he sighed deeply, and as he recited the benediction after the Torah reading, followed by *Kaddish*, his voice shook with emotion. He remained at the *shulchan* (reading table) for quite a while, in deep contemplation. All of us present were overawed.

On the second day of Chanukah (26th of *Kislev*) a special messenger arrived from Slavita, bringing the first 200 copies of the printed *Tanya* which had come off the press on the previous Tuesday (*Kislev* 20th). When the first copy was handed to the Rebbe, he looked at it for a long time and then said, "'Many are the thoughts in a man's heart, but it is the counsel of G-d that prevails' (Prov. 19:21). It was my desire that the book be completed by the beginning of the month of *Kislev*, so that it could be studied on the day of my master's *yahrzeit*. But G-d willed it otherwise, and the printing was completed on the 20th of *Kislev* . . . the 20th of *Kislev* (he repeated again, and a third time). And all that the Merciful One does is for the good."

None of us, not even the Rebbe's sons, could understand why the Rebbe was so upset by the delay in the appearance of the printed *Tanya*, a delay of only some two weeks. Nor could we understand what was significant about the 20th of *Kislev* that the Rebbe meaningfully repeated the date several times.

In the beginning of the month of *Cheshvan*, in the following year 5558 (1797)—Yaakov Smilianer continued—I was to leave on my annual round trip to collect contributions for the support of the Jews in the Holy Land. The Rebbe instructed me to tell all the Chasidim they should study the book diligently, and on the 20th of *Kislev* (occurring on Shabbat that year) they were urged to learn at least two chapters of the first part, and one chapter of the second part; again, all of us were mystified. The mystery cleared up, however, the following year, when the Rebbe was released from prison on the 19th of *Kislev*, after being cleared of the slanderous charges made against him by his malicious opponents. On that occasion he was mistakenly taken into the house of one of the vicious Mitnagdim, and only late that night of the 20th of *Kislev* was he finally released from his predicament. That is when we realized the significance of the date of the 20th of *Kislev*.

Subsequently, we heard it explicitly from the Rebbe's son and successor, Rabbi Dov Ber, that the vitality which the printed *Tanya* had instilled into Torah study and religious conduct of the Chasidim in the two years since the book's appearance in print, had stood his father in good stead and saved him from certain death, and that the countless myriads of angels which had been created by the reading of the sacred words and letters of the *Tanya* had intervened for him On High to bring about his triumphant vindication.[7]

Another tradition was transmitted by the sixth Lubavitcher Rebbe's uncle Rabbi Zalman Aharon, as he heard it from his great uncle Rabbi Nachum, who in turn received it from his father Rabbi Dov Ber, Rabbi Schneur Zalman's son and successor. It gave the following account:

Rabbi Schneur Zalman worked on the *Tanya* for about twenty years. He wrote and rewrote it many times, perfecting its text to the last letter. Finally, he permitted it to be copied for wide distribution. However, being copied and recopied in the many thousands, by many different hands, copious errors had crept into the text. Then Rabbi Schneur Zalman sent emissaries to the saintly Rabbi Yehuda Leib HaKohen and Rabbi Zusia of Anipoli to consult with them as to whether to have the book printed. Obtaining their written approbation, the Rebbe consented to have the book printed. He wrote a letter to the printers in Slavita imploring them to be meticulous in setting up the type, spelling out each word exactly as written, since each word and letter had a particular significance.[8]

A third tradition was transmitted by the father of the sixth Lubavitcher Rebbe as it was conveyed to him by the Chasid Rabbi Shmuel Dov Ber (RaShDaM), the *mashpia* (teacher of Chasidut in the Lubavitcher *Yeshiva*), who had heard it from the saintly Rabbi Eizik of Homel:

Having heard the news that the Rebbe (Rabbi Schneur Zalman) was released from prison[9] and was on his way home, we set out for Liozna. Arriving in Liozna, we found there hundreds of Chasidim from near and far. When the Rebbe reached Liozna, we all went out to welcome His Holiness.

Several days later, the senior Chasidim gathered for a celebration. The Rebbe's son—Rabbi Dov Ber—joined the Chasidic get-together. He related that when the *Tanya* appeared in print, the Adversary On High raised a storm of protest against the Rebbe, which did not pass unheeded. Thereupon the Rebbe offered himself for whatever sanctions that lay in store for him, even mortal agony, provided his books would be well received among the Jewish people, to stimulate a higher degree of dedication and reverence in the service of G-d.

For two years, the agitation of the Adversary On High persisted, because the Rebbe had succeeded in disseminating the Baal Shem Tov's way of Divine worship among the masses, enabling every Jew to rise to a high level of devoutness, each according to his capacity. On the first day of Rosh Hashanah, at the time of the sounding of the *shofar*, came a critical moment, when the Rebbe and the entire Chasidic community faced the gravest of peril. Divine mercies were evoked which mitigated the Supreme Heavenly Court's sentence. The Rebbe was to be spared, but only after suffering mortal anguish. Indeed, as we have seen, he suffered the utmost mortification for fifty-three days (of imprisonment), a day for each chapter of the *Tanya*. However, in view of his self-sacrifice for the teachings of Chasidut, the Heavenly Court ruled that his adherents and followers should henceforth be successful in overcoming every obstacle in all matters of Torah, piety and good works.[10]

A fourth tradition was transmitted by the Chasid Dov Ze'ev Kazabnikov, who related what he had heard from the saintly Rabbi Hillel of Paritch, who in turn received it from his master

127

Rabbi Zalman Zezmer:

In my youth—Rabbi Zalman related—I studied at the feet of the venerable sage and *gaon*, Rabbi Elimelech Shaul of Polotzk. Some four years before his death—I was then about sixteen years old—he revealed to me that he had frequently visited the Baal Shem Tov and later his disciple and successor, the Maggid of Miezricz, and that he was an associate of the saintly Rabbi Yisrael and Rabbi Azriel of Polotzk. That is when he began to teach me the ways of Divine service as taught by the Besht.

In the year 5543 (1783) my teacher Rabbi Elimelech Shaul passed away. Before his passing, he instructed me to go to Liozna, to study under the wings of Rabbi Schneur Zalman. The following year I was accepted as a student in the Third *Cheder* of the Rebbe.

From time to time my departed teacher would appear to me in my dreams, when he would speak to me words of Torah and give me instructions in the practice of Divine Worship.

When the *Tanya* was published, my departed teacher appeared to me one night in my dream and said to me: "Know that the book of *Tanya* by your master is designed in its chapters to correspond to the number of *sidrahs* in the Five Books of the Torah. And just as the portion of *Bereishit* is a comprehensive one, so is the Introduction to the *Tanya*; and each subsequent chapter directly corresponds to the subsequent portions of the Torah." Awaking from my dream, I decided to study each week a chapter of the *Tanya* in the same way as I reviewed the weekly Torah portion.

When the Rebbe was released from prison, it became a widespread custom among the senior Chasidim to review each week a chapter of *Tanya*, following the custom of reviewing the weekly *sidrah* of the Torah.[11]

The next tradition was transmitted by Rabbi Yitzchak Isaac of Vitebsk to Rabbi Shmuel (great-grandson of Rabbi Schneur Zalman). It concerns an episode which took place on the 19th of *Kislev*, 5560 (Dec. 16, 1799), the first anniversary of Rabbi Schneur Zalman's acquittal. The Chasidim were gathered in the synagogue of their leader to celebrate the occasion. They were in an elated frame of mind. Suddenly the Rebbe's young grandson (the future Rabbi Menachem Mendel, author of *Tzemach Tzedek*) came in, banged on the *amud* for silence, and called out, "Prepare for *Atah Hareita!*[12] He continued, "It is Simchat Torah today!" and began to distribute the honors of reading the verses in the manner of Simchat Torah before *hakafot*.[13]

The above-cited traditions (and others[14]) surrounding the publication of the *Tanya*, provide a penetrating commentary as to the esteem and reverence in which this work is held among Chabad Chasidim. Indeed, its preeminent status as the "Bible" of Chasidut has never waned.[15]

CHAPTER X

IMPRISONMENT AND VINDICATION - THE NINETEENTH OF KISLEV

In 1796, the storm of opposition broke loose again. Two causes sparked the renewed attack. One was a rumor, said to have emanated from Chasidic quarters, that Rabbi Elijah had reversed himself in his attitude towards the Chasidim. When the rumor reached Vilna, Rabbi Elijah sent out two emissaries[1] with a letter reaffirming his unequivocal opposition to the "wicked sect." The Chasidim countered the move by denouncing the letter as a forgery, pointing to the fact that the two emissaries could produce only what purported to be a copy of an original letter. When the leaders of the Jewish community in Minsk turned to Rabbi Elijah for a verification of his letter, Rabbi Elijah replied with a manifesto to all the communities of Lithuania, White Russia, Podolia, Wolhyn and others, condemning the "heresies" of the movement in no uncertain terms and demanding the most stringent measures against its followers.[2]

The other cause, which added much fuel to the conflagration, was the publication of the first edition of the *Tanya* towards the end of the same year, as mentioned in the preceding chapter. In Vilna, the printed copies of the *Tanya* were received with jubilation by Rabbi Schneur Zalman's considerable following, among them some prominent members of the community. The opposition to the emboldened Chasidim flared up. The Chasidim were subjected to abuse and economic sanctions. They appealed to Rabbi Schneur Zalman to come again to Vilna in an effort to meet with Rabbi Elijah. However, Rabbi Schneur Zalman realized that a personal interview with Rabbi Elijah, even if it materialized, could no longer settle some fundamental differences which came to light in their respective interpretations of certain doctrines of the Kabbala.[3] Being much younger than his adversary (Rabbi Elijah was 25 years his senior), and well aware of the latter's inflexibility, Rabbi Schneur Zalman could not hope to convert him, nor even to arrive at a *modus vivendi*. The fact that Rabbi Elijah stipulated as a condition of his receiving Rabbi Schneur Zalman that the Chasidim place in escrow a huge amount of money for a charitable cause, "so that his time would not have been altogether wasted,"[4] further convinced Rabbi Schneur Zalman of the futility of attempting to sway Rabbi Elijah's opinion. Nevertheless, in an effort to exhaust every avenue of a peaceful solution, Rabbi Schneur Zalman proposed that both he and Rabbi Elijah submit their differences in writing to the leading Kabbalists in Turkey, Italy, Germany and Poland "since none in our country would dare contradict Rabbi Elijah," and let them decide who was right and who was wrong. But, as could have been expected, Rabbi Elijah would not agree to any terms but his own. And so the two spiritual giants of the age never met,[5] and the conflict widened and intensified.

In the autumn of 1797 (during the Festival of Tabernacles, 5558), Rabbi Elijah died. While the community was profoundly shaken, some Chasidim in Vilna were gathered at the *succah* (Tabernacle) of one of their members to celebrate the traditional *Simchat Beit Hasho'evah*.[6] The Mitnagdim accused them of rejoicing at the death of their great opponent.[7] Filled with rage, they raided the place of gathering, dispersing the Chasidim with violence.[8] News of this incident, undoubtedly somewhat colored to suit the purpose of the particular source of information, spread far and wide, and gave rise to further excesses in various communities. As the Mitnagdim generally outnumbered the Chasidim, the latter usually were the victims, but where the Chasidim were preponderant, the Mitnagdim had cause for complaint too.

Rabbi Schneur Zalman tried his utmost to calm the heated spirits. He exhorted his followers to avoid conflict at all costs and

to answer every provocation with peaceful and conciliatory ges-
tures. He strictly forbade them to make any disparaging remarks
about the late Rabbi Elijah (to whom he referred in most respectful terms, calling him "the saintly pious one"), and warned them
against provoking their opponents in any way.[9] However all
Rabbi Schneur Zalman's conciliatory efforts failed to appease the
opposition. The rapid growth of the movement was sufficient
provocation in itself.

While the conflict had previously been confined within the
Jewish community, some hot-heads of the opposition now resorted to a very desperate measure: to denounce the Chasidic movement before the Czarist government.

These militant opponents came to the conclusion that further attempts at slander and defamation on the local level would
no longer be effective. The Chasidim were, by and large, already
known to be pious and honest Jews, whose sincere adherence to
the Jewish orthodoxy could not be impugned. Nor were there
any grounds for inducing provincial governments, or local city
administrations, to adopt restrictive measures against the
Chasidim.

On the other hand, the central government in Petersburg
was far removed from Jewish life in the pale of Jewish settlement,
and its suspicion against any Jewish element could be more easily aroused. Besides, a "case" could be made against the leader of
the Chasidim at least in some areas of his activity as well as doctrinal preaching. Thus, it was common knowledge among the
Jews of Russia that Rabbi Schneur Zalman was collecting and
sending funds to Palestine. After the first Chasidic emigration to
the Holy Land,[10] Rabbi Schneur Zalman organized a special fund
for the support of the Chasidic rabbis and scholars who migrated
to the Holy Land, where they dedicated themselves to Torah
study and Divine worship. Rabbi Schneur Zalman had made it
the obligation of every Chasid to help support the many
Chasidic families in the Holy Land. His personal emissaries reg-
ularly visited Chasidic communities everywhere, with a dual
function: to stimulate their spiritual life through the dissemination of the Rebbe's teachings, while at the same time to collect
their contributions towards the maintenance of the Rebbe's

institutions, particularly that of the Holy Land Fund.

Now, it so happened that Palestine was under Turkish rule, and Russia had been at war with Turkey (1787-1792), and relentlessly continued to press towards the Mediterranean. Under the circumstances the opportunity presented itself of accusing the Chasidic leader of betraying his country by sending funds to a hostile foreign power.

This "inimical" political activity was coupled with the accusation of inimical doctrines, such as the concept of "royalty" (*malchut*) in Rabbi Schneur Zalman's teachings. His enemies charged him with preaching that the attribute of *malchut* is not an independent attribute *per se*, but rather an outlet for the higher attributes (*sefirot*);[11] consequently it was the last and least significant of the Ten *Sefirot*. In other words, it was charged, this doctrine tended to undermine the royal status and authority of the Czar, and was tantamount to high treason.

These were the crucial charges, though there were also other accusations and denunciations designed to place the whole Chasidic movement in disrepute.

At the same time it was subtly suggested that the government would be well advised to handle the matter directly in order to bypass the local authorities, since the latter might be favorably disposed towards the Chasidim.

In 1798 a formal denunciation was submitted before the authorities in Petersburg, accusing Rabbi Schneur Zalman and other leading Chasidim of activities inimical to the Czar and the country. Political conditions resulting from the strained Russo-Polish and Franco-Russian relations were conducive to lend some credence to the charges. The territory had not long since been annexed from Poland and the Czar was highly sensitive to any possible activities by Polish nationalists. It was also in that year (1798) that the governor of Vilna, Bulgakov, informed the palace about treasonous activities carried on in those provinces in favor of the French, whereupon Emperor Paul ordered the "rebels" captured and brought to Petersburg.[12] The denunciation of Rabbi Schneur Zalman and his movement as subversive elements was thus well timed. Czar Paul lost no time in ordering the governor of the White Russian province to arrest Rabbi Schneur

Zalman and send him under heavy guard to Petersburg. An order was also sent to the governor of Lithuania to investigate the charges, which had originated in Vilna, and to have the leaders of the conspirators brought to the capital under the most stringent precautionary measures.

One may conjecture, with some measure of plausibility, that had Rabbi Elijah lived he would not have permitted such a drastic step. The fact that throughout his years of opposition to the Chasidic movement, the conflict remained an internal Jewish affair, seems to support such an assumption. Indeed, as we have seen, the weapons used against the Chasidim were the *cherem* (excommunication) and the pressures which the autonomous *kahal* (community administration) could bring to bear against rebellious members of the community. However, the powers of the *kahal* had been greatly curtailed, especially in such communities as Minsk and Vilna, where prominent Chasidim succeeded in inducing the local governors to protect them against the *kahal*, which was dominated by the Mitnagdim. If the Chasidim could resort to outside help, albeit in self-defense, their opponents felt justified in going direct to the Czarist regime in the capital, since there seemed no other way of curbing the Chasidic movement.[13]

In the autumn of 1798 (on the day after the Festival of Simchat Torah, i.e., the 24th day of *Tishrei*), Rabbi Schneur Zalman was arrested and taken under heavy armed guard from Liozna to Petersburg. He was placed in the Peter-Paul fortress, pending an investigation by the Secret Imperial Council, which was to present its report to the Senate for judgment. At the same time twenty-two of Rabbi Schneur Zalman's followers in Vilna were also arrested, of whom seven were brought to Petersburg, to await trial on charges of conspiracy and high treason.

The arrest of the leader threw panic into the hearts of the Chasidim.

According to accounts which may be culled together from the family records, the new attack on the Chasidic leader did not take him by surprise. Whether he had learned of the impending peril through his own channels or had a premonition of it, it was evident from his manner during the services on Rosh Hashanah preceding his arrest that some deep concern weighed heavily on his mind. His close Chasidim did not fail to notice it.

One interesting vignette is provided by Rabbi Menachem Mendel, author of the *Tzemach Tzedek*, the grandson of Rabbi Schneur Zalman. As we had occasion to note in a previous chapter he was orphaned of his mother, Rabbi Schneur Zalman's daughter, at an early age, and was raised by his grandfather. As a result, there developed a very intimate relationship and spiritual affinity between grandfather and grandson. Rabbi Menachem Mendel once related to his son (and eventual successor) Rabbi Shmuel of his extraordinary experience on that Rosh Hashanah of the year 5559, when he was ten years old.

> It was my grandfather's custom to take me under his *tallit* for the blowing of the *shofar*, until I reached the age of nine years, and for the Benediction of the *Kohanim* until my marriage (at the age of fourteen). That year, in 5559, at the time of the blowing of the *shofar*, I sensed that a grave danger threatened my grandfather. Moreover, I could not see his escape from it. Maybe because the salvation was not a complete one (for two years later he faced a similar predicament).[14]

During the Intermediate Days of the Festival of Succot the shocking fact of the Rebbe's impending arrest was confirmed. An imperial officer accompanied by a detachment of armed soldiers had arrived in Liozna with orders to arrest the Chasidic leader and take him to Petersburg. Soon the officer presented himself at the Rebbe's house. The Rebbe, however, wished to consider the situation undisturbed, and left his house by a back door, to meditate in the field. Presumably, the family entreated the officer to return after the conclusion of the festival, so as not to disturb the celebration of the Festival of Rejoicing. The officer, undoubtedly assured also by the local authorities that the saintly rabbi was not a dangerous criminal, agreed to postpone the arrest for several days. Leaving a few of his agents to keep watch on the situation, he left town.

In the meantime Rabbi Schneur Zalman had decided on a course of action: Should the officer return, he would surrender himself and bear whatever was in store for him. He revealed his decision to his intimates, particularly his devoted Chasid, Shmuel Munkis, who was known for his great wisdom and wit.

According to a reliable source, Shmuel Munkis said to him: "If you are indeed a 'Rebbe,' you will come out none the worse for it; if you are not—by what right have you deprived tens of thousands of Jews of their worldly pleasures? . . ."[15]

The festivals of Shemini Atzeret and Simchat Torah were marred by the impending arrest. The Chasidim were understandably bitter and agitated. The spirit of rejoicing which usually came to a climax during *hakafot* was dampened. There was an undercurrent of sadness in everybody's heart as the Rebbe led the *hakafot*, as well as during his reading of the Torah (the Rebbe usually acted as Reader himself). There was no doubt in anyone's mind that the Rebbe was not worried about himself, but what would happen to the Chasidic movement. His readiness to suffer martyrdom for the sake of the cause was reflected in the choice of his text for his Chasidic discourse, namely, the verse, "You have been shown, to know, that G-d is the Almighty, and there is none beside Him" (Deut. 4:35). This he interpreted in his characteristically Chasidic manner: "*You*—Who are the True Essence, the *En Sof* (Infinite)—have been *revealed*, through man's *painful* experience (Jud. 8:16), *in order* to establish the true Unity of G-d (both transcending and immanent), so that there is nothing beside Him."[16] Rabbi Schneur Zalman made a pointed reference to Jud. 8:16 (where the verb ידע is used in the sense of punishment), emphasizing that every person should be ready to accept bodily suffering for the sake of true monotheism, as the concept is explained in Chasidut.

On *Isru-Chag* (the day after the Festival)—it was a Thursday—many of the Chasidim who had come from the neighboring towns of Vitebsk, Rudnia, Kalisk, Liadi, Yanowitz, Dubrovna, and others, to spend the festival in Liozna, returned to their respective communities, bringing the sad news of the Rebbe's impending arrest. Everywhere there was profound consternation among the Chasidim, and excitement ran high.

Rabbi Schneur Zalman, a strict disciplinarian and exceptional organizer, rose early that morning and addressed a pastoral letter to all Chabad-Chasidim, cautioning them against any retaliatory action. He urged them to be strong in their faith and trust in G-d, and to have confidence in the merits of the saintly founders of Chasidut, that their cause will be vindicated. As for himself he expressed his readiness to bear patiently whatever he might be called upon to suffer. He went on to say that now he understood the hint which his master Rabbi Dov Ber of Miezricz had once indicated to him that he was destined to suffer hardships and critical times. He admonished the Chasidim most strictly and emphatically to remain calm, and to conduct themselves with forbearance towards the Mitnagdim, come what may. He called upon the older Chasidim to watch and restrain the younger Chasidim, while the latter were ordered to obey their elders.

The epistle was copied immediately, and copies were dispatched by special messengers to all Chasidic communities near and far.

Later that night the news of the return of the arresting officer spread among the Chasidim in Liozna. The Chasidic leader calmly waited for him.

A black carriage, one usually reserved for dangerous rebels, pulled up in front of Rabbi Schneur Zalman's house. The prisoner was ordered into the carriage, and it pulled away under heavy armed guard. It headed for Petersburg, by way of Vitebsk and Nevel.

Rabbi Schneur Zalman's calm composure was extraordinary. It was not a passive resignation to overpowering forces that was reflected in his demeanor, but rather a firm determination to meet a challenge which would put his leadership and all that he stood for to the supreme test. He was determined to pave the road of self-sacrifice for the Chasidic ideals and way of life, a road which, he knew, his successors and followers would have to tread time and again.

On the following day, it being a Friday, when six hours were left to the time of lighting the Shabbat candles, the prisoner requested the officer in charge to halt the journey until after the termination of the Shabbat. The officer refused to accede to the request. The next moment an axle of the carriage broke. Undismayed, the officer sent for repairmen who were brought from the nearest village. The axle was repaired, but when they were ready to proceed, one of the horses collapsed and died. The dead horse was replaced by a fresh horse from the village. However, strangely enough, the horses could not budge the carriage. The officer was now convinced that this was no ordinary situation. In a more conciliatory mood, the officer suggested to his prisoner that they proceed only as far as the nearby village and rest there. The Rebbe refused to proceed any further. However, he permitted the carriage to be turned off the highway into the adjacent field. There he spent the Shabbat.

The resting place of the Rebbe on that Shabbat, which was about two miles distant from the village of Saliba-Rudnia, on the outskirts of the town of Nevel, in the county of Vitebsk, became a landmark for the Chasidim of Nevel. They used to point out the place where the Rebbe observed the Shabbat on that fateful journey.[17]

Years later, a hoary Chasid, Micha'el of Nevel, used to relate that he had known elder Chasidim in his town who could point out the spot where the Rebbe had spent that Shabbat, and that he went to see it with his own eyes. According to his description, the highway led through lines of old and broken trees on both sides, but that near the place where the carriage was parked grew a majestic and vigorous shade-tree. Whenever the said Chasid related of his visit to that spot, he would fall into a state of ecstasy and reverence, as he vividly recalled his sensation when standing there, which in turn greatly infected his listeners.[18]

On the very night of the Rebbe's arrest, a group of dedicated and active Chasidim, former seminarians of the Rebbe's *chadarim*, gathered to take counsel on a course of action. The conferees decided that all of them, together with a number of other prominent Chasidim there and then named, would withdraw from all personal and family affairs, in order to dedicate themselves wholly and exclusively to a concerted effort of saving the Rebbe and the Chasidic movement. They pledged their total support to this effort, with body and soul and all material possessions.

Thereupon an executive committee was selected to direct all

activities concerned with the saving of the leader and the preservation of the Chasidic establishments throughout the country. Compliance with the directives of this committee was made obligatory upon all the Chasidim, young and old, on the penalty of exclusion from the Chasidic community.

An "order of the day" was then drawn up, signed, and sent out to all the Chasidic communities. It included the following directives and resolutions:

I. For the duration of the Rebbe's imprisonment—

I. All adult Chasidim should observe a fast on Mondays and Thursdays, excepting those who would normally be excused on grounds of health.

II. During the entire week only bread and boiled water were to be consumed, while at the Shabbat repasts only one cooked dish was to be eaten.

III. Throughout this period, no engagements or weddings were to be arranged. Weddings already arranged from before should take place on the pre-arranged dates, but without music, with no more than ten participating in a meatless wedding repast.

IV. Every *melamed* (teacher) should gather his pupils for a daily recital of *Tehillim* (Psalms), preceded by an explanation of the calamity that has befallen the sinful generation through a treacherous libel upon the *tzaddik hador* ("saint of the generation").

V. Each and every Chasid is to relate to his wife and children and other members of the household all that has happened. He is to explain to them how much the prisoner is suffering, how great is the sin of the slanderers, and the great reward awaiting those who share in the suffering of a *talmid-chacham* and *tzaddik*.

VI. Every one of the Chasidim must faithfully keep up his contributions toward the maintenance of the Rebbe's household and towards the funds for the poor in the Holy Land.

VII. Everyone of "*Anash*" (Chasidic fellowship) should

make a detailed list of all gold and silver objects and other valuables in his possession.

VIII. In every Chasidic community and settlement a trustee is to be selected to supervise the execution of all the above-mentioned directives, and to him are to be brought the contributions and valuables mentioned in articles vi and vii, above.

IX. In case of a death, G-d forbid, during the entire period, the whole adult Chasidic community is to gather, undergo immersion and, following the preparation of the body for burial, they are to adjure the soul of the dead person . . . to ascend to the heavenly abodes of the Maggid and the Baal Shem Tov, and to inform them the Rebbe is imprisoned, and the future of Chasidut is in danger. This solemn oath is to be administered three times: after shrouding; at the cemetery; and before filling the grave. The whole congregation is to fast that day.

II. The committee appointed three groups for action:

A. Those who would concentrate their activities upon saving the Rebbe.

B. Those whose efforts would be directed towards the raising of funds for the Rebbe's release; for the maintenance of his household; and for the support of the poor in the Holy Land.

C. Those whose concern would be with the defense of Chasidut and strengthening the morale of the Chasidim.

III. The committee named the members who would comprise each of the said groups, and assigned to each its respective tasks.

Group A, whose task was the saving of the Rebbe, were divided into three sections:

One was to operate in Petersburg, to keep themselves informed of all developments, and to do all that might be necessary.

The second would be in Vilna, secretly to gather information as to what was doing among the Mitnagdim.

The third was to do the same as the second, but in Shklov.

The three groups were to maintain intercommunication by way of special messengers only, and never through the mail. All their activities were to be conducted in the utmost secrecy.

Group B were to travel throughout the country to raise the necessary funds for the Rebbe's release, including the expenses of the Chasidim stationed in Petersburg, Vilna and Shklov, as well as the upkeep of the Rebbe's household. They were also to collect the regular contributions for the support of the poor in the Holy Land.

The fund-raising was to be carried out by means of an assessment, in conjunction with the local trustee and two local senior Chasidim. In addition to collecting the ready cash, the representatives were to examine the lists of jewelry and valuables submitted by the local Chasidim to the trustee. The owners of these valuables were to give written authorizations to use the valuables as collateral, and should be informed that if circumstances required it—in the event of the Rebbe's arrest being prolonged, G-d forbid, they would make the said valuables available to the trustee, so that there would be no delay in raising the funds, if and when necessary.

At the same time, a list should be drawn up of all dowry-monies held in safe-keeping for newly-married young men of the Chasidic community, and written authorizations should be obtained from them, whereby those monies could be transferred to the trustee in case of need.

The lists and authorization notes were to be kept by the trustee, and a copy sent to the central committee.

Group C, whose task was the defense of Chasidut and the strengthening of the morale of the Chasidim, were to

travel from city to city, and from village to village and settlement, to disseminate the teachings of Chasidut among
the masses. They were to preach and lecture publicly on
the philosophy and way of life of the Rebbe, with a view
also to attract new adherents to the Chasidic ranks.

At the same meeting certain territories were designated and divided among the members of the group, to be visited by them in pairs, or in groups of three, with the suggestion that wherever necessary one should stay behind for
a while longer. These emissaries were also to visit places
known to be centers of opposition.[19]

In the meantime, Rabbi Schneur Zalman was brought to
Petersburg and incarcerated in the Peter-Paul fortress, a maxi-
mum security prison reserved for the most serious offenders
charged with rebellion or subversive activity against the Czar.
Subsequently he was transferred to a more comfortable cell in
the same fortress.[20]

Rabbi Schneur Zalman was curious to know if any prisoner
held in that fortress was ever found innocent and released. He
surmised that a direct question on that point would meet with a
rebuff, so he obtained his desired information in a more subtle
way. Having established a friendly relationship with the guard,
he engaged him once in a friendly conversation, inquiring as to
the length of his service and similar innocent questions, in the
course of which he also asked him if he ever received any gifts or
tokens from grateful prisoners following their release. The guard
answered in the affirmative, which was reassuring.[21]

Among the various episodes relating to Rabbi Schneur
Zalman's imprisonment, the following is of particular interest:

The chief investigator who visited Rabbi Schneur
Zalman in his cell to interrogate him, was greatly impressed
with the prisoner, who, obviously, was no ordinary rebel.
This high official was a man of higher education, who was
also well versed in the Bible. On one occasion the interrogator asked the prisoner the meaning of the biblical verse,
"And G-d called unto Adam, and said to him, 'Where are
you?'" (Gen. 3:9). Did not G-d know where Adam was?

Rabbi Schneur Zalman explained the text in the light of the biblical commentaries, particularly that of Rashi, that it was in a manner of opening the conversation, so as not to overwhelm the man who was cowering in fear of punishment.

The interrogator replied that he was aware of this explanation, but wondered if the prisoner had something more profound to say on this question.

Thereupon, Rabbi Schneur Zalman asked the official if he believed in the eternal truth of the Holy Scriptures, and that the contents of the Holy Book had a validity for all times and all individuals.

The official replied that he did so believe.

It was immensely gratifying to the prisoner to know that his investigator was a G-d-fearing man, and he proceeded to explain the text to him in the following terms:

The question which G-d asked the first man, "Where are you?" is an eternal Divine call to each and every man, demanding constantly, "Where do you stand?" Every man is allotted a certain number of years and days to live on this earth, in order that every day, and every year, the person fulfill his duty to G-d and to fellow-man. And so the Divine call goes out every day to each and every individual, demanding introspection and self-examination as to his standing and station in life. For example, you are so many years old (he mentioned the exact age of the official); ask yourself, what have you accomplished in all these years, how much good have you done. . . .

The official was amazed that the sage should have divined his exact age. He was deeply impressed also by the meaningful explanation. He questioned the sage further on various matters pertaining to the Jewish faith, to which Rabbi Schneur Zalman replied point by point with extraordinary wisdom and erudition. The amazed official exclaimed, "This is truly divine!"[22]

It is characteristic of Chabad to interpret didactically every experience and episode in the life of the founder, as well as in the lives of the succeeding generations of Chabad leaders. Any such experience or episode becomes part of the Chabad tradition, and therefore assumes a far-reaching implication for the Chabad flock on an individual level, as a practical lesson in the daily life.

The episode of the dialogue on the meaning of "Where are you?" is a case in point, as explained by the seventh Lubavitcher Rebbe, Rabbi Menachem Mendel[23] in the following terms:

The Alter Rebbe (as Rabbi Schneur Zalman is usually referred to by Chabad Chasidim) was given to mystic flights of the soul—*kelot hanefesh*. The thought of having been chosen by Divine Providence to suffer martyrdom in behalf of the truths revealed by the Baal Shem Tov and the Maggid of Miezricz entranced him with ecstatic bliss, and brought him dangerously close to *kelot hanefesh*. It was while in such a state of mystic rapture that the question was presented to him by the chief investigator, and this brought him back to earth. For, reflecting on the questions, "Where are you? Have you accomplished your soul's destiny on earth?" made him realize that his life on earth must go on.

What this means, in terms of moral instruction, is that every Jew should be aware of the question "Where are you?" on his own level.

To one individual, this call may be an admonition not to withdraw completely from the world, in order to fulfill his soul's mission on this earth: the task of helping to make this material world a fitting abode for the Divine Presence. To another, on the opposite side of the pole, this call may be an admonition not to permit himself to be submerged by the temptations and distractions of the material life, but to devote more time to the eternal values of the Torah and Mitzvot.

This very call, issuing as it does from the eternal spirit, in itself provides a source of strength upon which the sensitive individual may draw, in his effort to reestablish the balance which is essential to the attainment of one's destiny with joy and gladness of heart.

Another interesting episode in Rabbi Schneur Zalman's imprisonment is presumably connected with the one mentioned above. It is related that—

Czar Paul, sensitive to anything that smacked of rebellion, was personally intrigued by the Jewish rebel accused of high treason. He was even more intrigued by the account of the chief investigator, who reported to him on the progress of the investigation. According to this account, the prisoner was a man of exceptional wisdom and saintliness, a man of the spirit, who was not likely to be involved in a conspiracy against the Emperor. The Czar was very curious to meet this extraordinary person. He decided to visit him incognito in his cell.

Disguised as one of the investigators, the Czar entered the prisoner's cell, whereupon the prisoner rose to his feet and, with the respect accorded to royalty, greeted the visitor with a benediction.

Asked to explain his conduct, the Rebbe declared, "Our Sages state that kingship on earth is a replica of the Kingship in Heaven. When Your Imperial Majesty entered, I felt a sense of awe and trembling such as I have not experienced with any of the officials that have visited here. I knew you were the Czar in person."[24]

During his imprisonment Rabbi Schneur Zalman succeeded in establishing contact with his Chasidim in the capital. Of this we have the following account:

From the moment the Alter Rebbe was taken into custody, he was held incommunicado. The Chasidim knew only that he was taken to Petersburg, but where he was held was unknown to them. Nor did they know what had happened to him since.

Having won the good graces and sympathy of the chief investigator, it was not long before the latter was amenable to do the prisoner a personal favor. The Alter Rebbe asked the official to pass on a message to one of his Chasidim, in order to reassure his family that he was alive. Contact could be made, the Rebbe suggested, simply by meeting a Chasid in the street. However, in order to make sure that the right party be contacted, and not just any Jew, who might even be one of the Mitnagdim responsible for his predicament, the Rebbe told the official that if he met a strange-looking Jew, dressed in country-style, that would be the man. "His name," the Rebbe said, "is Israel Kosik, and he is my brother-in-law. He was present at the time of my arrest, and I told him to go at once to Petersburg. I am certain that he went the way he was."

The official took a ride through the main streets of the capital. In due course he saw a Jew that answered the description given him by the imprisoned Rabbi. The official stopped him and asked his name. The stranger gave him a name which was not Israel Kosik. The official looked at him suspiciously and said, "I think you are lying," and went on his way.

When the official told the Rebbe that he had met the individual whom he had described, but that the name he mentioned was not Israel Kosik, the Rabbi was not surprised. He surmised that his brother-in-law had traveled to the capital on a borrowed passport. He begged the official to go out again into the street the following day, and to accost the same man again when he met him.

In the meantime Israel Kosik excitedly informed his colleagues of his encounter with a high official. They realized that their Rebbe was trying to pass on a message and they agreed that Israel Kosik was to go out again the following day, but this time tell his true name.

The following day the two met again. This time Israel Kosik replied truthfully to the official's question. The official said nothing further, but moved on leisurely. Israel Kosik followed him, at a distance, to his house. The official entered into his house, while Israel Kosik remained outside. Presently something was tossed out of the window. Israel Kosik picked up the object and put it in his pocket. He returned to his colleagues and they were delighted to find a note, on which was written, in the Rebbe's handwriting, the verse of *Shema*—"Hear O Israel, the L-rd is our G-d, the L-rd is One." Israel Kosik and his colleagues realized that the verse was well chosen. It proved to them that their Rebbe was alive, and also gave them an indication that there was hope for his eventual vindication.[25]

It is related also that the prisoner succeeded in obtaining food from one of his prominent followers in Petersburg, again by means of the friendly investigator. It came about several days after his imprisonment. The prisoner consistently refused to eat the prison fare, as he would not eat non-kosher food. The warden of the prison assumed that the prisoner was bent on suicide in fear of the outcome of his trial, and ordered that the prisoner be fed forcibly. The Rebbe clenched his teeth tight, and the prison guards attempted, unsuccessfully, to force the prisoner to open his mouth. During the ensuing commotion, the chief investigator arrived on the scene. He dismissed the guards and tried to persuade the Rebbe to eat, adding that his situation was far from hopeless, but it would take time, and there was no sense in placing his life in jeopardy by his own hand.

When the Rebbe explained the reason for his abstinence and that on no account would he eat non-kosher food, the chief investigator offered to procure kosher food for him. The Rebbe then said that since his stomach had been weakened, the only food he would eat would be a fruit preserve, or jam, if prepared by a Jew.

In the capital there lived a prominent Jewish purveyor who had dealings with government officials and was well known in their circle. His name was Mordechai, a native of the small town of Liepla, and he was one of the Rebbe's earliest and most devoted Chasidim. It is from the kitchen of this Mordechai Liepler that the preserves were procured for an unnamed Jewish prisoner. Mordechai had no doubt, of course, as to the identity of the prisoner, and a clandestine communication was established between the two.[26]

The investigation of the charges against Rabbi Schneur Zalman was carried out by a special commission of the Secret Council (*Tainy Soviet*)—whose headquarters were in another part of the city. In addition to studying the material involved in this case, the commission also required the prisoner to make a number of personal appearances before it. In such a case, the prisoner was taken from the Peter-Paul fortress and ferried across the Neva River. In this connection, the following interesting episode has been related by the sixth Lubavitcher Rabbi, Rabbi Yosef Yitzchak Schneersohn:

> One night, as the Rebbe was being ferried across the river, he requested the accompanying officer to stop the boat in order to permit him to recite the prayer for the Sanctification of the New Moon. The official refused the request, whereupon the boat stopped suddenly, and the Rebbe recited the introductory Psalm (Ps. 148). The boat then moved on. Again the Rabbi requested the officer in charge to halt the boat, to permit him to recite the main prayer. Convinced that his prisoner was a saintly man, the officer agreed to halt the boat on condition that the Rabbi give him a blessing. The Rebbe wrote a blessing on a piece of paper and gave it to the officer. The officer halted the boat and the Rebbe recited the prayer.
>
> That officer was subsequently promoted and rose to a high rank. He lived to a ripe old age, in honor and riches. He cherished the note which he had received from the Rabbi, and which was preserved by him under glass in a golden frame.
>
> The prominent Chasid, Dov Ze'ev of Yekaterinoslav related that he had occasion to see the Rebbe's note, then in possession of the officer's son.
>
> When the sixth Lubavitcher Rebbe told this story, he added that he first heard it when he was a young boy, and he wondered why it was necessary for the Alter Rebbe to ask the officer to halt the boat a second time, since he could have completed the prayer when it stopped for the first time. When he grew up, however—Rabbi Yosef Yitzchak continued—and was more deeply versed in Chasidic teachings, he realized that the Divine precepts had to be fulfilled in the natural order of things, and not by means of supernatural miracles. Hence, the Alter Rebbe acted the way he did. But that a sacred manuscript, written by the Alter Rebbe's own hand, should have fallen into the hands of a gentile—this is one of the inscrutable mysteries of Divine Providence, Rabbi Yosef Yitzchak concluded.[27]

Confronting the investigating commission, Rabbi Schneur

Zalman was asked, first of all, whether he was a follower of the Baal Shem Tov. All he had to do, Rabbi Schneur Zalman related subsequently, was to deny his connection with the Baal Shem Tov and his Chasidic movement, and his position would have been much easier. But he did not wish to dissociate himself from the Baal Shem Tov even for a moment, and even if only by word of mouth. So he replied that he was indeed a follower of the Baal Shem Tov.

He could also have stated that if anyone was to defend the teachings of the Besht, it should be the Besht's grandson who was then alive and the head of a large following.[28]

It is related that one day he had unexpected visitors, his teacher and master, the Maggid of Miezricz, and the Baal Shem Tov.

The Alter Rebbe asked them, "Why is this happening to me? What is demanded of me? What wrong have I done?"

"You have incurred displeasure in Heaven for teaching and revealing too much of the esoteric wisdom of Chasidut," they replied.

"Shall I then refrain from spreading Chasidut when I am released from this imprisonment?"

"Since you have started, do not terminate it. On the contrary, when you will be freed, continue with increased vigor."[29]

The Baal Shem Tov then asked the Alter Rebbe to deliver before them a Chasidic discourse. Thereupon the Alter Rebbe delivered the Chasidic discourse beginning with the words *Mar'ehem u'Ma'asehem* (published in *Torah Or*, p. 69 f.). When he concluded, the Besht remarked to the Maggid, "Indeed, it is a meticulously faithful transmission of the teaching you had received from me!"

Before leaving, the visitors from the Other World told the Alter Rebbe that when he would be brought before the judges, he should answer all their questions, and assured him that his answers would, with G-d's help, be well received. Finally, they blessed him to regain his liberty.[30]

During the interrogation the Rebbe was requested to answer many questions on the Jewish faith and religious practices. Included among them were questions about the innovations which he allegedly introduced into the religious life of his followers, such as certain changes in the order of the daily prayers; substituting steel knives for wrought-iron knives for ritual slaughter; encouraging to spend much time in prayer at the expense of study; about his Chasidic doctrines, particularly about the sphere of Royalty, which allegedly was degraded to the lowest of the spheres. He was also required to explain the meaning of the words *haf, af, af* which he interpolated in his prayers, something which the Baal Shem Tov also used to do, and which the denunciation alleged to mean that he was invoking G-d's anger (*af*, in Hebrew, means anger) against the government. The question of his alleged sending large sums of money to the Turkish Sultan also figured prominently in the interrogation. The last question was on the statement at the end of the first chapter of his work, the *Tanya*, quoting the Talmud, to the effect that the souls of the gentiles derived from the "unclean *kelipot*" ("shells") devoid of good, and that all their benevolent acts were tainted with selfishness.

Rabbi Schneur Zalman replied to each question in terms which would be within the grasp of his interrogators, whose minds were far removed from the subtle and profound subjects under question. He pointed out to them that the Chasidic doctrine and way of life did not constitute a radical and schismatic movement among the Jewish people, but that it was well within the mainstream of Jewish tradition; that the innovations were more a matter of emphasis than radical changes.

Thus, in reply to the question why the Chasidim devote "excessive" time to prayer, leaving for themselves less time for the study of Torah, Rabbi Schneur Zalman explained that there have always been among the Jews those who were predominantly men of scholarship, while others spent most of their time in prayer and devotion. He cited Talmud sources by way of illustration, attributing this diversity to the psychic make-up of Jewish souls, and their particular destinies.[31]

The question concerning the meaning of *Haf, af, af* presented a painful predicament for Rabbi Schneur Zalman, for it compelled him to reveal certain mystic aspects of the Baal Shem Tov's ways and ideas, too abstruse for his gentile interrogators. He could have invented some other explanation which would have satisfied them, but this he would not do.[32]

In one of his talks relating to the imprisonment of his ancestor, the sixth Lubavitcher Rebbe, Rabbi Yosef Y. Schneersohn, stated:

> It is well known that the last twelve days of the Alter Rebbe's imprisonment were the most trying for him. During those days it was sheer torture for him to be compelled to explain many questions of a theological and intimate nature, such as, What is a Jew? What is G-d? What are the ties that bind Jews to G-d and G-d to the Jews? To have to listen to these and similar questions, couched as they were, moreover, in crude terms, was acutely painful to him, and often brought tears to his eyes. Not less painful for him was the necessity to answer all such questions in simple and lucid language, to make the subject comprehensible even to the obtuse minds of his inquisitors.[33]

In reply to the question why he preached that the category of Royalty (*malchut*) is the last of the ten Divine attributes, thus denigrating the concept of kingship, Rabbi Schneur Zalman said that this question required an elaborate answer which he would prefer to give in writing. He was given time to prepare his written reply. Upon completion, the Hebrew text was sent to two different translators, one of them in Vilna, to be translated into Russian.

When the last question about the statement at the end of the first chapter of the *Tanya* came up, Rabbi Schneur Zalman offered no defense. He merely smiled knowingly, and the interrogators apparently accepted his meaningful smile in lieu of an answer, and did not press him further.

Later, when freed, Rabbi Schneur Zalman, while telling his closest Chasidim about his experiences, explained to them why he chose to remain silent on the last question. He felt his answers to the preceding twenty-one questions had been well received, and that he had convinced his interrogators of the truth of his words. In responding to the last question with merely a smile, the Rabbi indicated to his judges that, just as he had convincingly explained his position on all the previous questions, so he could give them irrefutable proof of the truth of the Talmudic statement which he had quoted in the *Tanya*. If that be so, it was surely better that this question remained unanswered. . . .

Rabbi Schneur Zalman added that he felt certain that the judges had fully grasped the message which he meant to convey to them, and that they had taken it in good grace.

By that time Rabbi Schneur Zalman was already quite confident that he would be vindicated and released.[34]

Back in Liozna, the family of Rabbi Schneur Zalman was in great distress, unaware of his fate. His wife, sons and daughters fasted and prayed daily. Particularly distressed was the grandson, nine-year-old Menachem Mendel, who was very much attached to his grandfather. He, too, young as he was, participated in the prayers and fasting. As he related years later, a *Beit-Din* of ten Chasidim daily went to the grave of his mother Dvorah Leah, who had given her life for her father.[35] There, at her grave, the whole Book of Psalms was read by this visiting congregation. It was followed by the reading of a declaration, the text of which had been prepared by Rabbi Schneur Zalman's oldest son, Rabbi Dov Ber. It outlined the circumstances of the Alter Rebbe's arrest, and concluded with a plea that read:

We, the Beit-Din (the names were mentioned aloud, though not written in the text), enjoin you to make our distress known to his teacher and master, the Maggid, and to the Baal Shem Tov, that they beseech On High in his behalf, that the imprisonment have no ill-effect on his health and that he be freed triumphantly.

Of the various members of the family, the old lady Rivkah, Rabbi Schneur Zalman's mother,[36] seemed to bear the tragedy most stoically. Her confidence and serene manner were a source of inspiration and strength for all. On one occasion (it was the

Shabbat of the weekly portion of *Vayyishlach*), when Rabbi Dov Ber fainted twice from anguish and exhaustion, she declared, "I swear that it will come to pass exactly as my father[37] had told me, namely, that during this coming week your father will be freed."

The most excited and impatient member of the family was Rabbi Moshe, the youngest son of Rabbi Schneur Zalman. A wise and handsome youth, and an eloquent speaker in both Russian and French which he had mastered to perfection,[38] he pleaded to be permitted to go to Petersburg to defend his father. He felt confident that he would be a successful advocate of his father's innocence; that he could even win an audience with the Czar, if need be, to obtain his father's release. However, they had their father's express orders that no member of the family should go to Petersburg except his brother-in-law Israel Kosik, and that neither should any other Chasidim go there except the members of the special committee. There was nothing the family could do except wait and hope.

The final phase of the investigation entailed the translation of Rabbi Schneur Zalman's replies to the questions put to him by his interrogators, which Rabbi Schneur Zalman had put down in writing in Hebrew. The Hebrew text was therefore sent to Vilna, to be translated there by the official government censor. In this connection we have the following account:

> One of the Chasidim sent to Vilna secretly to follow any developments there, spent most of his time in the synagogue which was the center of the militant Mitnagdim. There he overheard the news of the arrival of the document for translation by the censor. He also discovered that the plotters of the Rebbe's arrest were now determined to bribe the translator to slant his translation so as to put the Rebbe in an unfavorable light. The Chasid went to the translator and pleaded with him to make a faithful translation of the text. The translator assured him that he would do so—regardless of pressure, since his conscience and his duty compelled him to render a correct and faithful translation. Indeed, all the attempts of the plotters to persuade the translator to join in the conspiracy failed.[39]

With the return of the French translation of the document, (Nov. 1, 1798), the investigating commission completed their investigation and turned over the material with their recommendations to the Senate, for final disposition by a panel of judges.

On Friday, 15th of *Kislev* (November 23rd), Mordechai Liepler learned, through his friends in the higher spheres of the government, that the Senate investigation was completed, and that a favorable verdict was to be expected within a few days. Indeed, the following Tuesday, 19th of *Kislev*,[40] 5559 (Nov. 27, 1798), fifty-three days[41] after his arrest, Rabbi Schneur Zalman was informed that he had been found innocent of the charges, and he was released. Moreover, the Chasidic movement was officially sanctioned by the authorities and permitted to carry on its practices as before. Simultaneously an order was sent to Governor Bulgakov of Lithuania to release all the twenty-two Jews who had been imprisoned in Vilna, as leading collaborators with Rabbi Schneur Zalman, and had been held there pending the outcome of the investigation of their leader. By order of Czar Paul they were to be released at once, "Since nothing was found in the conduct of the Jews belonging to the Chasidic movement that was inimical to the State, nor anything that might be considered as depravity, or disturbance to the general peace." The release was conditioned on the provision that the future conduct of these people would remain above suspicion.

The official sanction of the Chasidic movement was contained in a special directive from the Governor of White Russia, Simon Zhegulin, to the chief of the Vitebsk district, dated December 15, 1798, stating that: "By order of his Imperial Majesty, directed to me by the most honorable privy counsellor and attorney general, Cavalier Peter Vasilyevitch Lapuchin, freedom was granted to Rabbi Zalman Boruchovitch, who had been arrested in Liozna, after the investigation of the circumstances. The Jewish sect, called Karlinist, retains its former status."[42]

Upon his release from prison in the late afternoon, Rabbi Schneur Zalman was asked where he wished to be taken. Rabbi Schneur Zalman replied that he wished to be taken to the house of Mordechai Liepler.

It so happened that on a lower floor in the same apartment house there lived one of the bitter opponents of the Chasidic leader, and by error Rabbi Schneur Zalman was brought to this apartment. It was a painfully embarrassing situation for both the surprised host and the unexpected visitor. Nevertheless, the host prepared the *samovar* (tea urn) and offered refreshments to the visitor. This did not, however, restrain the host from giving vent to his feelings of disappointment at the outcome of the trial. He warned the Chasidic leader that the opposition would not rest until the Chasidic movement was crushed. "Chasidim, indeed!" the host ranted derisively. "By what right have you assumed the title *Chasidim?*"

"We have not assumed it; it has been bestowed upon us by the Mitnagdim themselves," Rabbi Schneur Zalman replied, continuing, "You can see that it is, like everything else, a matter of Divine Providence. For, indeed, it should have been expected that the Mitnagdim would call us *Mitnagdim*, since they accuse us of opposition to the established order. Yet, Divine Providence has bestowed upon the Mitnagdim a glimmer of truth in that they themselves called us *Chasidim* and themselves *Mitnagdim.*"

The host continued to berate the Chasidic leader, attacking the innovations which he had introduced in the order of the prayers and in other aspects of Jewish life. In the meantime, the Chasidim, who had gathered at Mordechai Liepler's house, were anxiously awaiting their Rebbe's arrival. As the hours passed and the Rebbe did not appear, it occurred to Mordechai Liepler to look into the home of his downstairs neighbor. Accompanied by another Chasid, he entered his neighbor's apartment, where he found the Rebbe being abused by his ungracious host. The two Chasidim were ready to pounce upon the Mitnagid, but the Rebbe motioned to them to calm down. "Let us do honor to our host," he said. He finished his glass of tea and then accompanied Mordechai Liepler to his home. Later he told Mordechai, "What a relief it is to be out of that man's house. Believe me, throughout my imprisonment in the *Tainy Soviet*, I never felt so bad as during those three hours which I spent in the house of that Mitnagid.[43]

The news of the Rebbe's release electrified the Jewish community in the capital. The jubilation of the Chasidim was boundless. There was dancing in the streets, and some of the Chasidim even rolled in the snow. Towards evening of the following day, many Chasidim gathered in the house of Mordechai Liepler, and filled the courtyard outside. Despite the bitter cold, they waited for the Rebbe to come out. He did so, and delivered a discourse, beginning with the verse, "As water reflects the face, so does a man's heart respond to another's" (Prov. 27:19).

When Rabbi Schneur Zalman set out on his journey homeward, he was accompanied by many Chasidim. Their number continued to grow as they were joined by others on the way. By the time he reached Vitebsk (on the following Tuesday, 2nd day of Chanukah), his entourage numbered several thousand Chasidim. Here he spent the rest of Chanukah, and then went on to Liozna, where hundreds of Chasidim awaited his arrival, and many more were flocking from the surrounding communities. Everywhere there was great jubilation among the Chasidim.

Immediately after his return, Rabbi Schneur Zalman wrote a letter to Rabbi Levi Yitzchak of Berditchev in which, after acknowledging the latter's greetings, he writes:

> . . . It is beyond description to relate and recount all the wonders which G-d has wrought, which have magnified and sanctified His great and sacred Name in public, particularly among all the King's men . . . But who am I that G-d has brought me hither, and that the Name of Heaven should be magnified and sanctified through one so lowly among men, like myself. For the main battle was directed only against the teachings of the Baal Shem Tov and his disciples, and the latter's disciples. But G-d willed it to bestow upon us this distinction in the merit of the Holy Land and its inhabitants. It is this that stood us in good stead, and will continue to protect us in any emergency in the future, to deliver us from distress and uphold our honor for the honor of G-d, Who delights in His creatures.
>
> Indeed, this merits to be known, namely, that the day on which G-d dealt wondrously with us, is the day on which "it was good" is repeated twice,[44] [Tuesday], the 19th

day of *Kislev*, the *hillulo* and anniversary of the departure of our saintly master.[45] And as I was reading in the Book of *Tehillim*[46] the verse, "He has redeemed my soul in peace" (Ps. 55:19), before I began the next verse, I was liberated in peace. I conclude on this note of peace—from G-d Who is Peace.[47]

A similar letter was addressed by Rabbi Schneur Zalman to Rabbi Baruch,[48] the grandson of the Baal Shem Tov.

The agitation which the arrest of the Chasidic leader had evoked throughout the Jewish communities of Eastern Europe was not always unfavorable for the cause of the Chasidic movement. If the implacable opponents had hoped to put an end to the Chasidic movement by means of the denunciation to the Czarist government, this very drastic measure had the effect of eliciting sympathy for the martyred leader among the moderates and the non-committed. Many of them felt that the opposition had gone too far in resorting to calumny and denunciation to the government. The well-organized rescue campaign, on its part, kept alive the note of sympathy for their leader. As a result, new "converts" to Chasidut joined the ranks of Rabbi Schneur Zalman's followers. When, finally, the Chasidic leader was vindicated and, moreover, came out triumphant from his ordeal, many, who had been wavering in their attitude towards Chasidut, saw in it the "Hand of G-d," and became convinced of the justice of the Chasidic cause.

Rabbi Schneur Zalman was well aware of the cross-currents in the camp of the opposition. He did not delude himself that the militant opposition would give up their fight against Chasidut. Indeed, an allusion to this effect can be found in the above quoted letter when he expressed the prayerful hope in Divine protection "in any emergency in the future." Nevertheless, he resolved to try his best to bring about a rapprochement. Above all, he was determined to restrain his own followers.

Being apprehensive lest this triumph go to the heads of some excitable Chasidim, and in order to forestall any revengeful impulse, Rabbi Schneur Zalman, immediately upon his return from Petersburg, sent an encyclical to his followers. It was permeated with humility and love, and it appealed to his followers to exercise the utmost restraint and forbearance towards their opponents, and to seek a rapprochement with their fellow-Jews at all times.[49]

The encyclical begins with the biblical verse, "I am unworthy of all the kindnesses" (Gen. 32:11), and reads as follows:

"I am unworthy of all the kindness, etc." The meaning of these words is that each and every kindness which the Holy One, blessed be He, bestows upon a person should make him ever more humble. For "*chesed* (kindness) represents G-d's right arm,"[50] and it is written, "His right arm embraces me,"[51] indicating the very proximity of G-d, more closely than before. And the closer one is to G-d Above, the more humble one must feel here below, as it is written, "From afar—G-d appeared unto me."[52] It is also known that "all is like nothing in His presence,"[53] precisely [because of *His presence*]. Hence, the more one feels in *His presence*, the more one is like nothing and nought. This is the category of right (*dexter*) in the realm of holiness, *chesed of Abraham*[54] who said, "and I am but dust and ashes."[55] Such is also the quality of Jacob. This was the reason he feared Esau, notwithstanding the Divine promise, "Behold I am with you,"[56] etc. He considered himself entirely unworthy and undeserving of being rescued, etc., lest sin be a cause, as our Sages of blessed memory observe, since Jacob imagined that he had sinned.

On the other hand, in the *opposite order*[57] it is represented by Ishmael, *chesed of Kelipah*, where the more kindness received, the more swells the arrogance and pride.

Therefore, I came to inform publicly all our Chasidic fellowship about the abundant mercies which G-d has bestowed upon us, in order to follow the humble ways of Jacob, the "residue of His people, the remnant of Israel,"[58] who veritably considers himself as a useless "remnant" and "residue." Let not your hearts rise to scorn your brethren, nor let loosen your tongues, nor whistle at them, Heaven forbid and forfend, on awesome interdiction! Rather should you humble your spirit and heart, with the quality of the "truth of Jacob,"[59] in humility of spirit in the presence of all men; and "a soft answer turnes away wrath,"[60] and so forth. And after all this, perhaps G-d will enlighten the hearts of your brethren, for "as water reflects the face [so does a man's heart respond to another's]."[61]

Thus came into being the historic festival of *Yud-Tet* (19th) *Kislev*, the anniversary of the liberation of the founder of Chabad, the Alter Rebbe. The fortunate outcome of this crisis, which, as we have seen, the victim of the calumny considered as nothing less than miraculous, was not merely a personal triumph for himself. The future of the entire Chasidic movement had been in the balance. With the vindication of its leader, the Chasidic movement received a new lease on life; moreover, it came out stronger than before.

With historic insight, this day attained the status of "Rosh Hashanah (New Year) for Chasidut," indicating the measure of its significance in the Chasidic calendar. Indeed, the Chasidim claim, with a great deal of justification, that this day should be celebrated even more solemnly by the non-Chasidic community. For, had the outcome been different there would have been most serious consequences for Jewry as a whole, and an indelible blot upon the conscience of the non-Chasidic community.

It is related that some leading Chasidim desired to write a special "*Yud Tes Kislev Megilah*," to be read on that day, in a manner similar to that of the *Megilah* (Scroll) of Esther. Texts were prepared for such a scroll, and the Alter Rebbe was approached for his approval, but he did not permit them to do this. However, he did say, according to the tradition transmitted by the Chasid Abba Pearson, grandson of Ze'ev Wilenker, one of the leading Chasidim of Rabbi Schneur Zalman:

This day will be permanently instituted as a festival in Jewish life, an occasion for celebrating and sanctifying G-d's Name, when thousands of Jewish hearts will be inspired to repentance and prayer; for the event has been engraved upon the heart of Israel Above, and inscribed upon the heart of Israel below.[62]

For the first anniversary of the *Chag HaGeula* ("Festival of

Liberation") many Chasidim came to Liozna, to celebrate the occasion with their revered leader. There were also many new faces of new Chasidim, including erstwhile opponents, who had joined the Chasidic ranks. On that occasion Rabbi Schneur Zalman delivered a discourse, beginning with the text, "Blessed is He Who has wrought miracles for our forefathers."[63] In it he extolled the virtue of intellectual concentration in Divine worship over the emotional and ecstatic mode of worship. His deliberate emphasis on intellectual worship and de-emphasis of emotionalism was something of a temporary departure from his usual doctrine which calls for a harmonious blending of the two. It was obviously designed to counteract the exaggerated enthusiasm, and to tone down the excitement, which had held sway over his Chasidim during the entire year since his liberation.

CHAPTER XI

SECOND CRISIS

Rabbi Schneur Zalman's conciliatory action succeeded in reducing the tension between the Chasidim and Mitnagdim in most Jewish communities which came under his sphere of influence. In Vilna, however, the situation took its own course. As the Chasidim were gaining in strength and influence in this great Jewish center, they began to press more vigorously for representation in the Community Council, and the rivalry between the two sections of the Jewish community was on the ascendancy.

The Council consisted of seventeen members. Acting on the ban issued against the Chasidim on Hoshana Rabba, 5558 (Oct. 11, 1797),[1] the Council had passed a resolution barring any avowed Chasid from being elected to any office in the community administration. The Chasidim were nevertheless determined to obtain a foothold in the Community Council. Some of them were important tax-payers, and they demanded a voice in the Community administration.

The procedure of the elections to the Community Council was as follows:

Upon the expiration of the term of office of the elected community officials, a meeting was convened of the leading members of the community for the purpose of electing the succeeding administration. The slate of candidates comprised all those of the previous administration running for re-election, plus other prominent individuals. This made it possible for some names of prominent Chasidim to be included in the slate. From all these names, written down on pieces of paper, nine were drawn. These were the "electors" who selected five of their most outstanding members as "elders," and the latter chose from their ranks, by ballot or lottery, the *Parnass-Chodesh*, the monthly community chairman or president. The nine communal leaders constituted the administration of the community, who decided all communal affairs. In addition, eight other prominent members were elected, so that the community council consisted of seventeen members altogether.

The opportunity for the Chasidim of Vilna to capture some seats in the Community Council came in the early part of 1798 (5558), when the Chasidim discovered malfeasance in the handling of the community chest. This is how it came about:

One of the important functions of the Community Council was the supervision of the collection of the government tax. The tax assessment was made by the government, and the Council was responsible for its collection and payment to the government. The tax amounted to a very substantial sum. For 1798 (5558) the tax assessment for the Jews of Vilna and environs amounted to 22,000 golden rubles. However, the Community Council actually collected over 36,000 golden rubles, of which only 10,000 was paid into the government treasury.[2]

In view of the fact that the "Committee of Five" which had been organized in Vilna to combat the Chasidim included three members of the Community Council, the Chasidim had good reason to believe that the Council had been channeling large sums of community funds to that committee.[3] Consequently, the Chasidim informed the authorities of the misuse of the community funds by the council. This resulted in an official order by the authorities on the 26th of April, 1798 (*Iyar* 21, 5558), prohibiting the Community Council to collect, henceforth, taxes from the Jews over and above the official tax levy.

The Council, however, disregarded the order, and early in 1799 the Chasidim again informed the authorities of the continued violations of public trust and financial irregularities on the part of the Community Council. This time the authorities took more stringent action. On the 4th of February of that year (10th of *Adar* 1, 5559) all the members of the Community Council were arrested, and all the documents and books of the Council, as well as those of the Council members personally, were impounded.

After being in custody for one day, the Council members were released.

According to a complaint lodged by a Moshe Osherowitz, dated February 20, 1799, leading officials of the local government, accompanied by militiamen, as well as by some "Karlinists," burst into the synagogue that evening (it was Friday), disrupting the holy service. One of the officials, Councillor Eliashowitz, announced that the Community Council was dissolved. The complaint also charged that he distributed blows to some of the worshippers, with his fists and walking stick. Two days later, according to the said complaint, the City Commandant Falkin, with some "Karlinists . . . deviates from our faith," from Vilna and from the suburb of Antokol, appeared in the council chamber. Under his supervision a new election was carried out "contrary to our accepted customs, procedures, and established privileges," electing a new council. One of the leading members of the Karlinist sect, Meir Refaels, was appointed as president, while several relatives of his, and others, were elected, again contrary to law and custom, as elders. All this was carried out under the initiation of two Chasidim, Nachum Itzkovitz and Moshe Morduchovitz, "without the consent of the community," so the complaint charged.[4]

Thus, the Chasidim of Vilna gained eight seats on the Community Council. While this was one short of a majority, the Chasidim were now firmly entrenched in the Community Council.

The deposed communal leaders, with Moshe Osherowitz at their head, lodged a complaint with the chief public prosecutor against the local authorities, as already mentioned. They demanded, a) reinstatement, b) the removal of the eight newly elected Chasidim, c) the appointment of an impartial *Beit-Din* in the province of Lithuania to deal with disputes between them and the Karlinists, d) the appointment of an impartial committee to examine the financial records of the Community Council, and e) restraining the Karlinists from organizing spurious sects and inventing new customs.

At the same time, Itzik Milentowitz, another member of the Council, petitioned the highest authorities to grant the Community Council of Vilna the power of judging civil cases of local Jewish residents. This would have given the Community Council authority to curb the Chasidim.

The results of all these complaints and petitions were as follows:

The charge against Eliashowitz for his offensive conduct against the community was turned over to the Circuit Court of Vilna. The final disposition of this case, if there was one, could not be traced. Presumably, the desecration of the communal service, as charged, was somewhat exaggerated.[5]

The petition of Osherowitz to restrain the Karlinists from organizing new sects, as well as the petition of Milentowitz for communal authority to judge local civil cases resulted in an official declaration of January 1800 (5551) "to tolerate, by order of his Imperial Majesty, the Karlinist sect, and that the authority of the *Kahal* should be limited to matters of religious observance and worship, without interference in civil cases, for which there were appropriate legal agencies."[6]

Once again, the opponents of the Chasidim failed in their attempt to prevail over them. However, they were in no mood to give up their efforts to suppress the Chasidic movement, even if it required the intervention of the highest government authorities.

In the meantime, Rabbi Schneur Zalman's attention was concentrated on a new danger that threatened to bring about radical changes in the economic and cultural life of Russian Jewry. The threat became imminent when a powerful influence in the highest spheres of the government was about to assert itself in regard to the Jewish position. The person behind this influence was the famous Russian poet and statesman Gabriel R. Derzhavin.

Derzhavin, who was state-secretary and senator during the reign of Catherine II, member of the Supreme Council and state-treasurer under Paul, and finally Minister of Justice under Alexander, was a man of considerable influence at the Court. He was decidedly anti-Jewish, and when he was entrusted with the task of finding a solution to the "Jewish question" in Russia, the fate of Russian Jewry seemed quite precarious in his hands.

The son of a low-ranking officer and a mother who belonged to the lower nobility, Derzhavin was orphaned at the age of eleven years. His childhood was an unhappy one, with a goodly measure of poverty, misery and maltreatment. Part of his childhood he spent on an estate near Disna, and there he made the acquaintance of a Jew, Dov Ber Moshe, who was an ardent follower of Rabbi Schneur Zalman. In the house of this Jew the boy often found friendship and protection. Many years later, when the two met again in Petersburg, Derzhavin as the influential senator, and Dov Ber Moshe as a member of a twelve-man committee set up by Rabbi Schneur Zalman in the capital to protect the Jewish interests, Dov Ber Moshe tried to influence Derzhavin in his attitude towards the Jews. But Derzhavin's prejudice was deep-rooted. "If all Jews were like you, I would not hate them," he said to his only Jewish friend.[7] Derzhavin's prejudice undoubtedly sprang from his earliest teachers who were churchmen, and a German convict serving a lifeterm at hard labor.[8]

Derzhavin was first sent to White Russia by the Attorney General Lopukhin, to investigate complaints by the Jews of Shklov against their local overlord Zoritsch. He found nothing substantial in the charges and counter-charges, and he was recalled without completing the investigation. But the following year, in the summer, Derzhavin was again sent to White Russia, this time by order of Paul, to investigate the famine that ravaged that area.

Rabbi Schneur Zalman's committee in Petersburg, who were to work secretly and make connections with officials at the court in order to find out everything that was brewing in the high spheres relating to Jewish affairs, reported to Rabbi Schneur Zalman of Derzhavin's appointment as the one-man investigating committee, and the detailed itinerary of his tour.

Being well aware of Derzhavin's anti-Jewish prejudices, Rabbi Schneur Zalman was determined to see to it that

Derzhavin would find no excuse to justify these prejudices in the course of his investigation. Accordingly he mobilized his leading followers in the various areas lying on Derzhavin's route, with a view to securing promises from the local nobility and authorities that they would speak favorably about the Jews when the investigator arrived on the scene. Rabbi Schneur Zalman had also requested the above named Dov Ber Moshe to see Derzhavin before his departure and plead with him for an impartial report. It was then that Derzhavin replied in the terms quoted above, the kind of alibi behind which many an anti-Jewish bigot has sought refuge.

While Rabbi Schneur Zalman tried to do his utmost to safeguard the interests of the Jewish population as a whole, some Mitnagdim sought to take advantage of the situation to discredit the Chasidic leader and movement. This is evidenced from the unfavorable references to the Chasidic leader, which Derzhavin makes in his report, though he does not conceal the latter's great influence. Thus Derzhavin states:

A Jew, Zalman Boruchovitch, has gained fame as an arbitrator and enjoys authority even among foreign Jews. He lives in a small town, Liozna, where, under his very nose, I raided a still carried on by Jews on the basis of a privilege granted them by the nobility. In him believe especially the Chasidim, whose patriarch he is considered. His word is law for them—, they are sectarians with new ways and customs of their own. Some Jews complain about them that they alienate their children, also take away their gold and silver, which he is said to send to Palestine in expectation of the Messiah and the rebuilding of their temple in Jerusalem.[9]

Derzhavin returned to Petersburg in October of that year (1800) and presented his report, his so-called "Opinion" (Mnenie), consisting of two parts. The first part dealt with conditions in White Russia in general, and the second part outlined his opinion about the Jews, and his recommendations, which consisted of a number of economic restrictions. Derzhavin's report contained a mixture of truths, half-truths and fiction, and was obviously prejudiced and biased. There was at least one favorable view in it regarding the Jews, that of Prince Lubomirsky, a prominent nobleman and estate owner of White Russia, and highly influential at court, whose friendship Rabbi Schneur Zalman had cultivated through one of the latter's prominent followers. Lubomirsky stoutly defended the Jews and their importance to the economy of his estates. If there were more favorable opinions which were expressed by other noblemen and estate owners, Derzhavin passed over them in silence. We do know, however, that there was a concerted effort on the part of a number of estate owners to discredit Derzhavin by means of a complaint lodged against him with the Czar. However, being highly sensitive to the slightest suspicion of rebellion, Paul dismissed the complaint. Nevertheless, it is remarkable that Derzhavin's elaborate report was received unenthusiastically by the Czar. Derzhavin was not even granted an audience to present the report to the Czar in person, and Derzhavin, in his diary, complains bitterly about the intrigues at the Court.[10] Be it as it may, nothing radical came of Derzhavin's suggested reforms, thanks to the opposition of the local estate owners. For the next few years at least, the position of the Jews remained status quo. The events seem to indicate that Rabbi Schneur Zalman substantially contributed towards the frustration of Derzhavin's plans concerning the "Jewish question."[11]

These activities of Rabbi Schneur Zalman were not generally known even among his followers, except among those who were directly involved in them, since all his work was done in strict secrecy.[12]

While Rabbi Schneur Zalman was preoccupied with the Derzhavin affair, the leading Mitnagdim of Vilna were preparing for another attempt to deal a death blow to the movement by means of a second denunciation of Rabbi Schneur Zalman before the government in Petersburg. The initiative came from a certain Avigdor Chaimovitch (the son of Chaim), who had been the rabbi of Pinsk and its environs.

Avigdor Chaimovitch had a personal grievance of long standing against the Chasidim. He had bought the rabbinical position in Pinsk in the year 1772, and, as a further consideration, had advanced a substantial sum of money to the *kahal*, as he claimed later. Bitterly anti-Chasidic, he took a leading part in the efforts to suppress the movement, not only in his own community, but in Lithuania in general. It was he who in 1781 largely persuaded Rabbi Elijah of Vilna of the dangers of the movement, as a result of which a certain Chasidic book[13] was burnt publicly in Vilna by order of Rabbi Elijah. Avigdor's efforts to suppress the Chasidic movement in Pinsk and its environs proved futile. The Chasidim grew in number and in influence, so much so that about the year 1796 he was ousted from his post and driven from town. (There is reason to believe that Avigdor was behind the denunciation of Rabbi Schneur Zalman in 1798, which led to the latter's arrest, as mentioned earlier, although the signature of the informer was other than Avigdor's.)[14] Avigdor began a legal battle against the community of Pinsk for indemnification, taking his case to the highest spheres in Petersburg. He blamed the Chasidic sect in his community, whom he identified as "Karlinists,"[15] for his ouster. Four years later, in 1800, his claims had still produced no results. Now the Mitnagdim of Vilna found in him a convenient tool to spearhead another attack against the Chasidic movement. Avigdor was to lodge another appeal to Petersburg, ostensibly to obtain redress for the "injustice" done to him by the Pinsk community, but primarily to induce the Czar to suppress the Chasidic movement.

Armed with the published Chasidic works *Tzavaat HaRiBaSh*,[16] containing teachings of Rabbi Israel Baal Shem Tov; *Toldot Ya'akov Yosef* by Rabbi Jacob Joseph of Polonnoye; *Or HaTorah*, by Rabbi Dov Ber of Miezricz, and the *Tanya* by Rabbi Schneur Zalman—the latter being the surviving leader of the Chasidim—Avigdor arrived in Petersburg in the spring of 1800, where he lodged an appeal to the Czar to take up his claim against the "new sect" in Pinsk. His appeal was accompanied by a number of supporting documents and a lengthy polemic against the teachings of the sect.[17] He accused the above-named leaders of the sect of being followers of Shabbatai Tzvi and Jacob Frank, and charged them with spreading obnoxious doctrines which tended to undermine the morality of the Jewish people and their loyalty to the Czar. In support of his charges he "quotes" from the above-named works, often distorting the text through interpolations of his own, or taking them out of context and putting them in a bad light. Pedantically, and sometimes incoherently—features aggravated by the Russian translator, since the original text of the material was in Hebrew or Yiddish—Avigdor tries to show that the Chasidic teachings contradict the Holy Scriptures "hallowed by all the nations," and contain ideas which are harmful to the Jews, their Christian neighbors, and the Czar himself.

Thus, for example, Avigdor cites, among other excerpts, the following teachings of the Chasidim to illustrate his charges: a) It is incumbent upon a person to be always in a state of gaiety and cheerfulness; b) to believe with complete faith that G-d's benevolence hovers over him, and that G-d is his protector and shield; c) that man sees G-d as G-d sees him.[18]

Innocent as these doctrines appear, Avigdor provides a commentary of his own to each of them to distort their import. To the first citation Avigdor adds that in order to induce in themselves a feeling of joyfulness, the Chasidim arrange frequent gatherings. "At their gatherings they do nothing but eat and drink excessively, which leads them to licentiousness in particular, and to the establishment of secret orders, inspiring them to extraordinary brazenness and evil deeds."

The second quotation elicits Avigdor's observation that it teaches "to fear no human authority of law and order."

From the third, Avigdor deduces that "the members of the sect deny Mosaic Law, the very Bible in which all the nations of the world believe; hence they oppose all the nations."

Taking other statements from the teachings of the Baal Shem Tov and the Maggid of Miezricz out of their context, which he embellishes with his interpretations, Avigdor endeavors to "prove" that these condone murder and theft and similar immoral acts.

All these extracts, with his commentaries, Avigdor appended to his petition to the Czar.

One of the most serious charges which he leveled against the head of the sect was the sending of substantial sums of money to Palestine. Although admitting that it has been a custom of long standing for Jews to send financial support for their needy brethren in the Holy Land, Avigdor charged that only a small part of the funds sent by the Chasidim went for the support of the needy, while most of the vast sums went in support of their own fellow-sectarians in the Holy Land.

Included in the petition was also an appeal by Avigdor that the elections of *dayanim* (members of the Jewish ecclesiastical courts) be subject to official confirmation by His Majesty's government. This was a desperate and dangerous move on the part of the Mitnagdim, since it invited direct government intervention in Jewish religious affairs. However, the Mitnagdim, stung by their defeat in Vilna and Pinsk, were apparently fearful of losing out completely to the Chasidim in the religious and lay administration of community affairs. Hence they authorized Avigdor to include also the said appeal to the highest authorities. Had Czar Paul acceded to this petition, it would have deprived the Jews of their religious autonomy—

Fortunately, Paul was reluctant to act personally on the controversy within the Jewish community. Instead, he decided to turn over Avigdor's petition to the chief public prosecutor, to look into the charges of the plaintiff about "the pressure and persecution which he claims to have suffered from some new sect."[19]

On the 23rd of April (1800), the office of the Czar sent all the material to the Attorney General, Obolyaninov, suggesting an investigation through the local authority in the Lithuanian province. The Attorney General sent the material (June 7th) to the Military Governor of Lithuania, Golenishtschev-Kutuzov, with an accompanying request to investigate the complaint of the plaintiff, and to report on the sect. Kutuzov, having found no evidence in his territory to substantiate the charges, sent the material over to the Governor of Minsk, Kornev, since the town of Pinsk, the locale of the case, came under the latter's jurisdiction. At the same time Kutuzov informed the Attorney General of his action. Thereupon the Attorney General again wrote to the Governor of Lithuania, pointing out the fact that the complaint referred to a certain Elijah in Vilna, on whose instructions certain heretical books by the sect had been publicly burnt in front of the synagogue in Vilna. The Attorney General therefore suggested that the records of the previous Governor should contain some pertinent information on the subject.

In a dispatch dated July 12th (1800), Kutuzov conveyed to the Attorney General the information he had received from the Governor of Minsk. The latter's report referred to the sect in that area in favorable terms, describing its adherents as peaceful and law-abiding subjects, like the other Jews. As for the plaintiff's claim for damages, it recommended no action, since there were no documents to substantiate the claim. On his part, Kutuzov added that he fully concurred with the report of the Governor of Minsk. He, too, recommended that the suit be dismissed on all counts.

Subsequently (July 30th) Kutuzov sent a detailed report on the results of his own investigation in regard to the activities of the sect mentioned in Avigdor's charges, insofar as his province was concerned. In it the Governor of Lithuania stated that the Shabbatian sect which originated in Smyrna, Turkey, had never found followers in his province. He surmised, therefore, that the sect accused by Avigdor was not to be identified with the Shabbatian movement, but with the so-called "Karlinists" mentioned in the official records of his predecessor, Count Lopukhin, who in 1798 had received a denunciation relating to alleged inimical activities by that sect. The denunciation came from a certain Hirsh Davidovitsch of Vilna, where, however, no such person could be found. As a result of that denunciation, the report continued, the leader of the sect, Zalman Boruchovitch of Liozna, in White Russia, was arrested and sent to Petersburg, while twenty-two followers of the sect were also arrested in Vilna and its surrounding district. All the accused were eventually released and cleared. It is to be presumed that the "Solomon" identified in the complaint by the former rabbi of Pinsk was none other than this Zalman Boruchovitch.

Kutuzov's report goes on to refer to the late Elijah, who had been venerated by the Jews, and who was an enemy of the sect. Before dying in 1797, the said Elijah declared to the Jews present at his bedside that he was leaving them with one regret only, namely, his failure to stamp out the sect completely while be lived. Accordingly, the Jews swore at his grave that they would carry out their rabbi's request, and new persecutions against the sect began under the leadership of a committee of five members in Vilna, headed by a certain Moshe Osherowitz, one of the most zealous disciples of Elijah. This committee was subsequently dissolved in the same year, when the heads of the Vilna *Kahal* were ousted.[20] Referring to the incident of the burning of the book called *Tzavaat HaRiBaSh*, Kutuzov describes it as "the last will and testament of the founder of the sect, Rabbi Israel Baal Shem Tov, meaning 'Kabbalist,' a book containing a new code for his sect." This is followed by a brief account of the history of the movement. Kutuzov concludes his report by reiterating his opinion that the accusation of Avigdor was unfounded, and that his claim for damages had no merit whatever.[21]

It is not difficult to gather from the report, summarized above, how Avigdor had at first succeeded in confusing the authorities in regard to the identity of the "sect" and its contemporary leader, as otherwise his charges would have received no hearing at all in view of the failure of the first accusation only two years previously. Secondly, the report indicates that Kutuzov's information, in many respects detailed and intimate, could have come only from Chasidic sources close to him. His views, as well as those of the Governor of Minsk, point to the fact that the Chasidim were quite firmly entrenched in those provinces, and were looked upon with favor by the local authorities.

Notwithstanding the unfavorable—for Avigdor—reports by the local authorities, his suit was not dismissed. Whether Avigdor had succeeded in ingratiating himself in the eyes of the Czar, or whether the Czar suspected that the Chasidim exerted undue influence on the local authorities, or perhaps yet for some other reason, the Czar decided to keep the case open. He ordered the Attorney General to instruct the local authorities to look into Avigdor's claim for the return of a loan and payment which he alleged to have made. Instructions to this effect went out on October 7th (1800). However, Avigdor's demand to have Rabbi Schneur Zalman brought to Petersburg to confront him and answer his charges, elicited no action until October 30th (1800), when Attorney General Obolyaninov sent an urgent order to Governor Severin of White Russia to apprehend "the head of the Karlinists, or Chasidim, the Jew Boruchovitch," and to send him to Petersburg.

This order followed closely upon the heels of Derzhavin's report, which was submitted to Obolyaninov on October 26th, containing, among other things, the unfriendly reference to Rabbi Schneur Zalman, which we quoted earlier. From this sequence of events, some historians conclude that Derzhavin's report had a decisive effect upon the arrest of Rabbi Schneur Zalman for the second time.[22] Perhaps the most damaging reference to Rabbi Schneur Zalman in Derzhavin's report was the allegation that the leader of the sect was sending huge sums of money to Jews in Palestine, which, quite understandably, was all the more serious since only the year before, Napoleon had been in Palestine, and called upon the Jews to rally to his support, promising them to rebuild their Temple. At a time when Russia and France were at war, such an allegation had extremely serious implications. On the other hand, it is doubtful, in my opinion, whether Rabbi Schneur Zalman's second arrest was a direct result of Derzhavin's report, which, on the latter's own testimony in his diary, had not been received with enthusiasm, as we had occasion to mention. Moreover, the same accusation and insinuation had already been made by Avigdor. There is room here to surmise that the investigation into Avigdor's allegations was carried on independently of Derzhavin's report, and that the decision to bring Rabbi Schneur Zalman to Petersburg for the second time, had actually been taken earlier, through the Czar's personal interest in the case. This conclusion seems to be borne out by the account of Rabbi Schneur Zalman's second arrest preserved in the family tradition,[23] which relates that his committee in Petersburg had learned of the imperial order to bring Rabbi Schneur Zalman to the capital, and used their influence to alleviate the manner of his arrest. According to this account Rabbi Schneur Zalman was "requested" to come to Petersburg to appear before the Senate. He could travel on the post-chaise at the expense of the Government, instead of being taken in the black, grilled carriage reserved for the worst criminals and traitors, under heavily armed guards, as on his first arrest. Rabbi Schneur Zalman was in no hurry to go. He wanted to find out the full details of the new accusation against him, in order to prepare his defense in the best possible way. The delay irked the authorities in the capital, and the stricter order followed.

On November 9th, Rabbi Schneur Zalman left for the capital, accompanied by two special couriers, as Severin duly informed Obolyaninov by dispatch of that date.

Four days later Governor Severin of White Russia sent a dispatch to the authorities in the capital, reporting on "a careful and secret investigation" into the activities of the Chasidim which he had undertaken on his own initiative. He states emphatically that there was no basis for suspecting the members of the sect of any activity inimical to the government; that their leader Boruchovitch had never engaged in anything but the study of the holy books and in prayer, and is a successful arbitrator between disputing parties to their mutual satisfaction, never giving any cause for complaint.

It may be safely assumed that the Governor sent this dispatch at the behest of leading Chasidim in the area. However, in order not to appear too partial, the dispatch refers favorably also to the sect of the "dissident Russians" in that area, which had been the cause of some anxiety in the higher spheres.[24] This dispatch was eventually of considerable help to Rabbi Schneur Zalman in clearing himself from all the charges of a political nature, which Avigdor had brought against him.

On arrival in the capital, Rabbi Schneur Zalman was placed under a milder form of arrest than on the first occasion, being this time confined in the Secret Department of the Senate. Here he was confronted with Avigdor in order to answer his charges.

In the presence of the Senate committee which was designated to act as judges in the case, Avigdor began to outline his charges, to which Rabbi Schneur Zalman replied point by point. The debate that ensued between the two contestants was carried on in Yiddish and left the panel of judges completely in the dark, since they did not understand that language. The judges then ordered Avigdor to present his charges in writing in Russian, to which Rabbi Schneur Zalman replied in the same manner. These documents covered the first two of Avigdor's nineteen charges. These documents have not been discovered to this day, and their contents are thus not known.[25]

The document containing Avigdor's other seventeen charges has been preserved in its original Hebrew text. It contained the following brief preface and charges:

Concerning points one and two, they have already been presented by me in writing, in Russian, and Rabbi Schneur Zalman replied to them also in Russian. Here follow, in the Hebrew language, the other points which I charged against him and all the Karlinists:

3. In that same book[26] of the Karlinists it is written that man should fear no creature. Although it may happen that a man or beast cause certain harm to a person, it is all caused by G-d, Who is present in that creature and metes out the punishment for the person's actions. This is contradictory to the Jewish faith, for it would absolve any wrongdoer, inasmuch as the Creator was present in him and caused the particular harm.[27]

4. The same book contains an admonishment to fear no man or other creature, nor to praise or flatter any man, save G-d alone. This, too, is at variance with our faith and our Torah, for in our holy Torah we find that our Patriarchs Abraham, Isaac and Jacob, our teacher Moses, and King David, all feared men.

5. In the same book it is stated that if a person craves a certain thing, it means that that thing is necessary to him for the edification of his soul, inasmuch as in all things there is vitality. This is contradictory to our religion, for sometimes a person may crave a sinful thing.[28]

6. In some passages of the book of the Karlinists the terms "thought," "speech," and "vitality" are used to personify the Creator. This is contrary to the Jewish faith. Moreover, they write that a person may sometimes be in unity with the Creator, hence they call their rabbis "G-d."[29]

7. Although the rabbi of the Karlinists, Zalman Boruchovitch, justifies himself saying that from bygone

years it has been customary to donate money for the support of Jews dwelling in Jerusalem and praying there, it will
become obvious from an examination of the financial
records that the amount collected in olden days was only
about one hundredth of the amount collected nowadays.
They thus disregard the obligation according to Jewish law
to retain nine-tenths for the local poor, leaving only one
tenth to be sent for the poor of Jerusalem.

8. With regard to other matters in which the
Karalinists[30] deviate from the Jewish religion, and the evil
acts of the said sect, I do not wish to, nor can I alone, bring
the proofs concerning them. Therefore, I request that all
the rabbis of that sect be summoned here to face an equal
number of rabbis of the orthodox Jewish faith.

9. Rabbi Chaimovitch,[31] and others, call Boruchovitch
and his cohorts by the name of "Karlinists" because upon
the death of the two leaders, namely, the Baal Shem Tov
and Rabbi Ber of Miezricz, their leading followers were
Aaron and Solomon,[32] who lived in the community of
Karlin, in the district of Minsk. The appellation
"Chasidim" is one that they themselves apply to themselves. The reason they are called Kat ("Sect") is because
they have changed the customary Jewish ritual in their
prayers, and even in their dress, for they do not wear
woolen clothes.[33]

10. They sent three of their rabbis to the Land of Israel:
The rabbi of Shorpotovka,[34] Rabbi Abraham of Kalisk, and
Rabbi Aharon of Vitebsk,[35] to whom they send large sums
of money. Their rabbis and dignitaries spend large sums in
the communities where they settled; they arrange large
feasts and gather around them the local Karlinists. The said
emissaries, together with the prominent Karlinists, visit
every Jewish household, inducing them to contribute. Out
of embarrassment the Jews make written pledges in their
books for weekly contributions towards the Land of Israel
fund. In this way all the various communities are compelled to give them money for their trouble. As a result,

they encroach upon the per capita taxes collected by the communities, and the latter incur debts, while many indigents starve to death.[36]

The Karlinists also endeavor to become leaders in the community councils who manage all the needs, incomes and expenditures of the community, so that they could take from the communal taxes to send gifts to their rabbis for each festival and other occasions.

11. Oaths have no value with them. This can be ascertained from what happened in Vilna, provided the invited leaders of the community should not include members of the Karlinist sect, so that the latter should not intimidate the witnesses.

12. They do not recognize respect for parents, declaring that no respect is due to the father since he begat his son merely in the satisfaction of his sexual desire. The same in regard to the mother, though she deserves more credit for having suckled the baby.

13. They all steal money from their parents and wives, with the knowledge of their rabbis to whom they give the money. According to our laws, one under twenty years of age[37] is not permitted to give anything away as a gift without the knowledge of one's parents.

14. From what I have written, and from the things which I intend to substantiate according to my intelligence, I call them *Shabbatai-Tzeviniks*,[38] who have given license to all to do anything they wish.

15. For a holiday, some 1000 to 1500 or more followers of the sect assemble in Liozna, to be with their rabbi, Zalman Boruchovitch, so that much overcrowding results there. It is surely reprehensible to assemble so many people together. And who knows what they plot during such an assemblage, for if it were for the purpose of hearing Torah, surely he could give it to them in writing. What then is the purpose of such a large assemblage of people in one place! Besides, there is considerable expense involved in traveling long distances.

16. Similarly, when their rabbis travel to different places, they incur substantial expenses, for much feasting is arranged for them, as well as gifts.

17. All that I have written is common talk among people who are not of the sect.

18. And all things I have written are known to the people of Vilna and Slutzk.

19. 1 have also heard that when anyone wished to join the sect of the Karlinists, he must first appear before their rabbi, and he is obliged to give him a list of all his sins, transgressions and wrongdoings which he committed during his lifetime up to that day, upon which he must affix his personal signature. Thereupon he is obliged to commit his soul to the rabbi, for the rabbi claims that his soul embraces all the souls attached to his. Then he must give the rabbi as much money as demanded by the rabbi, for he is afraid of him, having signed the said list. For the same reason the Karlinists comply with all that the rabbi commands them to do. And we see it clearly that the commandments of our teacher Moshe of blessed memory have not been so well fulfilled as those of their rabbis. Moreover, when one rabbi dies, they appoint another one to take his place. To make it brief, he is also a complete ignoramus.[39]

Avigdor the son of Chaim of blessed memory.

Clearly, the above charges were, for the most part, abusive fabrications and insinuations based on hearsay. Rabbi Schneur Zalman apparently refuted them without difficulty. While all but two of these charges of Avigdor were preserved in the official records of the Senate, only two of Rabbi Schneur Zalman's answers are known, the eighteenth and nineteenth.[40] These are as follows:

In respect of the 18th:
The people of the community of Slutzk are also our enemies, who perpetrated serious persecutions against the Chasidim of Lachowitz,[41] as the matter is well known, for in this connection the authorities of Minsk issued a decision, as it has been clearly reported.

In respect of the 19th:

I can bear no longer his (Avigdor's) abuses, insults and lies, whereby he invents serious slander against us, the like of which have never been seen or heard, except in the days of Polish rule, whose clergy libeled the Jews that they use human blood for Passover, and similar libels, as a result of which much innocent Jewish blood was shed. Surely he (Avigdor) had never seen or heard (them), but it is nothing to him to go about freely wagging his tongue at will. Has he not himself conceded that it was hearsay and that he has no personal and positive knowledge of this matter, yet he troubles our merciful lord, his Imperial Majesty, instead of first ascertaining the matter through the local authorities. A truly obedient servant of his Imperial Majesty, as a devoted son to his father, should not have troubled his Majesty unless the matter was clear.

And now I rely on no one but our Imperial Majesty. But I am confident in the abundant kindness and humility of his Imperial Majesty, that in his great kindness he will look from his lofty seat upon a sufferer and will discern the truth; and finding me innocent, will liberate me and save me from distress.

> Schneur Zalman,
> the son of Baruch of saintly memory.[42]

Rabbi Schneur Zalman's answers were evidently convincing. Governor Severin's recommendation, coupled with the official documents, relating to his previous arrest and discharge, had their effect in establishing Rabbi Schneur Zalman's innocence of any political activity, let alone of any activity inimical to the government. The Secret Council recognized that the case had no political implications and was purely an internal religious strife within the Jewish community. Accordingly, the case was referred back to the Senate to be investigated in conjunction with the general question of the *kahal*. This was done on November 27th (1800).[43] At the same time Rabbi Schneur Zalman was released, after being under arrest for two weeks. He was, however, ordered to remain in the capital, pending the final outcome of the Senate investigation.

The turn of events did not please Avigdor, and during the month of December he submitted another memorandum, with excerpts from the *Tanya* which, Avigdor claimed, showed the "treacherous" tendencies of the movement, not only in relation to the Jewish faith, but also in relation to the government. He did not refrain from taking liberties with the original text. Thus, in his translation of the cited passages,[44] the words "idolators," or (more correctly) "peoples of the world," were substituted with the word "Christians," to make those passages more objectionable. By revealing such misrepresentations, Rabbi Schneur Zalman easily refuted Avigdor's accusations.

Avigdor had requested also that Rabbi Schneur Zalman's accounts be seized so as to reveal the considerable sums of money sent to Rabbi Schneur Zalman by his followers, and transferred by him to his followers in foreign countries. Avigdor also demanded that the leaders of the Chasidim in other Russian provinces be likewise brought to the capital, together with their accounts. Finally Avigdor repeated the allegation that these Chasidic leaders, "in their ignorance of Jewish law, were misleading their co-religionists and were especially harmful to Jewish youth, whom they incited to rebel against their parents and to take away their wealth."

The whole dossier was turned over by Obolyaninov to the so-called "Third Department" of the Senate for a final disposition of the case. Supplementing this material was a quantity of books, correspondence and records which had been seized from Rabbi Schneur Zalman's house by the local authorities on orders from the Attorney General, with a brief description of the contents of each item, translated by two official Jewish translators. Included was a declaration by the translators that they found nothing in the seized items which was contrary to the Jewish religion or the welfare of the country.[45]

About fifteen weeks passed without any final action in the case. Understandably, the delay caused Rabbi Schneur Zalman considerable distress, and it might have dragged on for an indefinite period had not Czar Paul been assassinated in the meantime (March 11, 1801) and succeeded by Alexander I. One of the first acts of grace of the new emperor was to order the release of Rabbi Schneur Zalman. On March 29th, 1801, an official document to that effect was sent from Petersburg to the governor of White Russia.[46]

Having been discharged and permitted to return home, Rabbi Schneur Zalman was not content with regaining his personal freedom. He was determined to obtain official recognition of his movement, so as to prevent, once and for all, the recurrence of such crises as had twice threatened his life and that of his movement. Moreover, the atmosphere now prevailing at the Court seemed more auspicious. Alexander wished to gain the popularity of all his subjects, including the Jews. Knowing that the Jews comprised three trends—the *Chasidim*, *Mitnagdim*, and *Maskilim* (the latter, "the enlightened ones," were advocating secular education for the Jews and were a small minority),[47] Alexander made gracious overtures towards all three sections. The release of Rabbi Schneur Zalman was an act of benevolence towards the Chasidim. A special financial grant for the Jewish community of Vilna was intended as a token of grace towards the Mitnagdim. Finally, permission was granted[48] for Jewish children to attend Russian schools, a concession to the Jewish secularists.

Being aware of the more favorable climate prevailing at the Court, Rabbi Schneur Zalman pressed his victory further. He stayed in the capital, now of his own volition, for another four months. During this time he filed two petitions with the Senate. In the first (May, 1801), he recounted the hardships which had been caused to him by the false accusations of Avigdor Chaimovitch. He recalled that two years earlier he had been similarly denounced by a prejudiced accuser, whereupon he was arrested, investigated and discharged. Yet the accuser suffered no consequences. This emboldened Chaimovitch to try the same thing again. The latter embarked upon the scheme, Rabbi Schneur Zalman said, in order to avenge his dismissal by his community, which had refused to renew his contract on the grounds that he was misusing his position, and also because of his frequent intoxication, as had been documented by the community register and by the Magistrate of Pinsk, and submitted in evidence. Hence—Rabbi Schneur Zalman went on—if the accuser would again get away with this evil attempt, he (Rabbi Schneur Zalman) would not know peace, and "there would be no fence against any evil schemer, while slander and hatred would proliferate abundantly." Accordingly, Rabbi Schneur Zalman appealed that the Senate should, by order of His Majesty the Emperor, call the said Chaimovitch to account, according to the law of the land, in order to "restrain him henceforth, from interfering with me and the rest of the Chasidim in the way of our Divine service according to our custom of old, and to indemnify me for the slander and damage he had caused me to suffer."

The full text of Rabbi Schneur Zalman's petition follows:

If it please the governing Senate to give attention to my petition, it will undoubtedly see my innocence in my trial which is before it, concerning the libelous accusation by Rabbi Avigdor, who calls himself "Chief-Rabbi," who slandered me and a great multitude of Jews whom he calls "Karlinists." For all the charges which he imputed to me were not only nullified by my refutations, but were not in themselves worthy of consideration, because they have no substance in them whatever.

The said Chaimovitch, through his false slander, is the cause of my travail. In my old age I was taken from my home under heavy guard, like a notorious criminal, and was sent to Petersburg. After painful suffering here for two weeks, held in secret imprisonment, I suffered further misery, to my great misfortune, for about fifteen weeks, being denied permission to leave the city, pending the outcome of my trial.

To the extent that I am entitled to lodge a complaint against the slanderer Chaimovitch for this, and demand compensation from him, I cannot equally pass in silence also over the following:

Two years ago, as a result of a false slander by one who sought to harm me, I was taken into secret detention for investigation. I was found innocent and released, and permission was given me to conduct Divine worship as before. However, justice was not fully served in the way of compensation. For this reason Chaimovitch came out with slander without fear, and he finds satisfaction in the fact that he can again subject me to investigation and new trouble without redress. The reason which induces him to do this is, as it was in the past, his hatred for the Chasidim—whom he calls Karlinists—because those of them who lived in the city of Pinsk, where Chaimovitch had leased the office of the rabbinate, declined, upon the termination of the period, to permit him to renew the lease. They did this because he used to extort money from them excessively, and also because they knew that he indulged in intoxicating drinks. All this was recorded in the community resolution at the time, and is mentioned also in the decision of the magistrate of the city of Pinsk (a copy of which was recently sent to the Chief of Civilian Affairs in Petersburg, to be shown to Chaimovitch).

Consequently, if the cause of strict justice will not compel Chaimovitch to repent of his hatred, my tranquility will surely begin to wander, and there will be no fence against any evil schemer, and slander and hatred will proliferate abundantly.

In light of the above I humbly petition:

That by order of his Imperial Majesty the governing Senate be instructed to accept my petition in the Third Department; and that taking into consideration all the matters explained therein, and considering also that the Chasidic sect—whose Divine worship and prayer conform to the order and custom of Israel as transmitted to them from antiquity—faithfully preserve their allegiance to the sole government; now therefore they should deal with Chaimovitch for his invented and completely baseless calumnies in accordance with his Majesty's laws, and restrain him henceforth from interfering with me and with all the Chasidim in the manner of our Divine worship according to our custom of old, and to indemnify me for the slander and damage which he has caused me to suffer.

Merciful Emperor! I appeal to our Imperial Majesty to issue an order concerning my petition.

On this . . . day of May, 1801

(The petition was officially inscribed:
Received on May 21st, 1801).

No action was taken on this petition, and before leaving the capital towards the end of July, 1801, Rabbi Schneur Zalman decided to lodge his second appeal with his Imperial Majesty. This new appeal, apparently submitted for him shortly after his departure from the capital, substantially reiterated the tenor of the first. It also expressed apprehension at the possibility of renewed attempts on the part of Chaimovitch to bring slanderous action against him. Rabbi Schneur Zalman appealed "that by order of his Imperial Majesty, the Third Department of the Senate be directed to act on my petition, reach a final verdict, and order that throughout the Jewish domicile none should dare molest me or the Chasidim, by any unfounded slander, so that I may live in peace and not be brought, together with my family and small children, to complete impoverishment in my old age; nor shall the Chasidim likewise be interfered with in their businesses and occupations, thereby leaving the government also in peace." The petition (as the previous one) concluded with a request that Chaimovitch be duly punished for his empty schemes and calumnies, and be adjudged to compensate for the damages he had inflicted.

For the sake of completeness, the text of the second petition is also given below:

The governing Senate is not unaware of the serious losses caused to me by Avigdor Chaimovitch, who calls himself the rabbi of Pinsk, through the baseless slander which was brought against me during the life of Emperor Paul, the son of Peter, of blessed memory, purporting that I and the Chasidim, whom he called Karlinists, are inimical to the government. As a result of this slander, I was taken into secret custody, where an investigation revealed that nothing inimical or harmful to the government or to society could be attributed to us. Consequently, the Emperor, of blessed memory, referred the matter to the governing Senate, while setting me free with the condition that I do not leave Petersburg. After the demise of Czar Paul, the son of Peter, I was freed completely, and the honorable Chief Prosecutor Alexander, the son of Andrei Baklishov, informed the Civilian Governor of White Russia that by order of the Emperor I was given complete freedom, and everything remained as it was. A certificate to this effect was furnished to me by His Excellency the Governor, a copy of which I append hereto.

Also several years ago slanderous charges were brought against the Chasidim, who were named "Karlinists" at that time, too. I was then also taken into secret custody. It turned out that there was no substance to the slander, whereupon I was permitted to return to my home. However, several citizens of Vilna did not rest. In their hatred they dared trouble the Emperor, of blessed memory, for a second time—at the time when the honorable Alexander, the son of Andrei Baklishov served as Chief Public Prosecutor—in an effort to destroy the Chasidim, called by them "Karlinists." On the basis of His Majesty's order, and in his directive sent to the Governor of Lithuania in order to inform the petitioners, it was said that the so-called Karlinists merit toleration, as is evidenced from the enclosed copy, the copy of Governor Frizel's order to the police of the city of Vilna.[49]

Inasmuch as my case, by reason of Chaimovitch's slander, is now in the hands of the Third Department of the governing Senate, where it was sent by order of the late Emperor for final disposition, together with other communal problems, and whereas I have reason to believe that the said Chaimovitch is again about to trouble the Emperor reigning over us, in order to harass me and the Chasidim, and to ruin us effectively, I make so bold as to petition:

That by order of his Imperial Majesty, the Third Department of the Senate be directed to act on my petition, reach a final verdict and order that throughout the Jewish domicile none should dare molest me and the Chasidim by any unfounded slander, so that I may live in peace and not be brought, together with my family and small children, to complete impoverishment in my old age; nor shall the Chasidim likewise be interfered with in their businesses and occupations; and the government be left in peace.

As for his empty schemes and calumnies, and for his troubling the late Emperor in vain, he should be dealt with according to the law, and be ordered to compensate me for the damages he had inflicted upon me, a thing which I can honestly attest to, and swear to it.

Merciful Emperor! I plead for a final judgment upon my petition.

Zalman the son of Baruch the Jew,
Rabbi of Liozna.
August . . . 1801.

The petition bore the post-scriptum: "The petitioner authorized the Jew Hertz the son of Israel of Polotzk, to submit the petition to its proper destination."[50]

The above petitions were apparently intended more for the record rather than for personal satisfaction in terms of damages. What Rabbi Schneur Zalman desired most was to secure the right of his movement's existence and freedom.

After spending altogether nine months and ten days in Petersburg, Rabbi Schneur Zalman left the capital. He did not, however, return to Liozna. At the invitation of Prince Lubomirsky, who had been greatly impressed with the venerable Jewish leader, and who perhaps was not unmindful of the benefits the latter might bring to his estates, Rabbi Schneur Zalman agreed to take up residence in the town of Liadi, one of Lubomirsky's possessions. The prince provided a fine carriage for the Rebbe with two mounted guards. Accompanied by an entourage of close Chasidim, in four additional carriages, augmented on the way by thousands of followers, (according to one report the number was about 5,000), Rabbi Schneur Zalman arrived in Liadi on the eve of *Shabbat-Nachamu* (14th of *Menachem Av*, 5561). Here Rabbi Schneur Zalman spent the remainder of his life—more than a decade—and became known as the "*Rav* of Liadi."

CHAPTER XII

THE FINAL YEARS

Rabbi Schneur Zalman's triumph over his adversaries was complete. He had not only succeeded in clearing himself and his movement in the eyes of the Czar and the Senate, but had also won considerable respect in those circles. Yet he was not content to let it rest at that; he wished to win over his opponents, being convinced that their opposition stemmed from a total misconception and ignorance of Chasidut. Soon after returning from Petersburg, the peace-loving leader undertook another round of visits to some of the leading rabbis of the opposition.[1] By this time, some of the opponents of Rabbi Schneur Zalman and of the Chasidim had become more moderate, others had terminated their opposition, and many had become admirers and followers.

Out of the new center of Chabad in Liadi, Rabbi Schneur Zalman embarked upon a new era of intensive activity divided between the interests of the Chasidic movement and those of the Jewish community at large. Many of his senior disciples were active in various parts of the Jewish pale in spreading the teachings of Chasidut. Some of his more erudite disciples were permitted to expound the discourses of the Rebbe according to their understanding, making the philosophy of Chabad even more accessible to the rank and file. The Rebbe's oldest son and successor was instructed to record the weekly discourse of the Rebbe which was given every Shabbat. Being an extraordinarily rapid writer, the task was usually completed by Sunday evening, and scores of copies were made and dispatched to Chasidic communities for study.

Rabbi Schneur Zalman, however, never considered himself as leader only of his Chasidic flock. He was just as vitally concerned with the well-being of the Jewish community at large. Now that he was liberated from the pressures and travails directed against him and the Chasidim by the Mitnagdim, he could devote more attention to the economic problems of Russian Jewry. He put his youngest son Rabbi Moshe in charge of these activities, and the latter was an able administrator. Rabbi Schneur Zalman sent special emissaries to stimulate migration from the overcrowded cities and towns to villages and rural areas, where many families found new opportunities for a livelihood in agriculture and trade. He also established a fund to offer financial assistance to the families who settled on land and engaged in agricultural pursuits. Hundreds of Jewish families thus became small farmers in White Russia, the Ukraine, and in the districts of Yekaterinoslav and Poltava. Through his influential representatives in the capital, Rabbi Schneur Zalman succeeded in calling the government's attention to this economic development and obtaining certain aid for the new settlers. In this connection Rabbi Moshe occasionally made trips to Petersburg to further this cause.

In 1811, Rabbi Schneur Zalman instructed his representative committee in Petersburg to undertake strong action to induce the government to grant free land and homesteads in the district of Cherson for Jewish settlers, and to provide them with agricultural implements and livestock on credit for a ten-year period, with the remission of taxes during the first five years. The necessary petitions were duly submitted and an active lobbying was instituted to see the matter through. However, in the tense atmosphere resulting from the imminent Franco-Russian war (which broke out the following year), the effort had to be interrupted.[2] Nevertheless, during the decade that had elapsed since his arrival in Liadi after his second arrest, additional thousands of Jews swelled the ranks of those who had established themselves in villages and rural areas; and though it was a meager livelihood that they were able to eke out, they were, at least, spared starvation.

Rabbi Schneur Zalman's hopes and strivings for peace and unity were not fully realized. Ironically, disunity reared its head within the Chasidic camp itself. Rabbi Schneur Zalman found himself in the position of having to ward off an attack against himself by other prominent Chasidic leaders, his own colleagues.

The first one to come out with open criticism against Rabbi Schneur Zalman and his Chabad system was Rabbi Abraham of Kalisk, who, like Rabbi Schneur Zalman, was one of the disciples of Rabbi Dov Ber of Miezricz. Rabbi Abraham did not share Rabbi Schneur Zalman's enthusiasm for intellectual inquiry in matters of faith. Rabbi Schneur Zalman's insistence on "wisdom, understanding, knowledge" (Chabad), asserting that one could not truly fear and love the Almighty without intellectual effort, met with Rabbi Abraham's distinct disapproval. The latter insisted that the virtue of simple faith should be stressed above that of intellectual inquiry. However, despite their differences, Rabbi Abraham and his younger colleague were ardent friends for more than a quarter of a century. In 1777 Rabbi Abraham settled in the Holy Land, and after the death of his senior colleague, Rabbi Menachem Mendel,[3] he became the acknowledged head of the Chasidic colony in Palestine. Their friendship was strengthened by the fact that Rabbi Schneur Zalman had organized, and was in charge of, a vast fund-raising system, whereby his many followers made regular annual contributions to a special fund in support of the Chasidic community in the Holy Land, as already noted. It was a well-organized philanthropic endeavor, whereby Rabbi Schneur Zalman's emissaries made their regular visits to the various Chasidic communities, collecting these funds and turning them in to their leader. He, in turn, remitted the funds, first to Rabbi Menachem Mendel, and later to his successor, Rabbi Abraham, for distribution. As has been noted, this philanthropic endeavor was one of the subjects of slander against Rabbi Schneur Zalman. Rabbi Schneur Zalman himself not infrequently took to the road, visiting the communities of his faithful in an effort to strengthen his fund-raising organization. Thus, the spiritual bonds between the two Chasidic leaders, separated geographically, were fortified by their mutual philanthropic activity in charge of their many dependents. They exchanged frequent correspondence and gave expression to their mutual affinity in the warmest terms. When Rabbi Schneur Zalman was reluctant to take over the leadership of the Chasidim of White Russia, Rabbi Abraham (in a letter of 1786) urged him to do so.

At that time, he wrote to his colleague, in most affectionate terms, of the great opportunity of spiritual leadership. The letter follows (in part):

> To G-d's beloved, may he dwell securely, The spirit of G-d hovers over him, this is Sinai, my beloved friend . . . great luminary . . . replete with the light of the Torah, the spirit of knowledge and fear of G-d . . . our teacher and rabbi, Schneur Zalman. . . .
>
> . . . In the abundance of mutual affection, your soul being bound up with mine, were I merely to inform you of the joy and delight with which I received the glad tidings of your well-being, through your rabbinical emissary . . . it would have sufficed. . . . He has shown me the letter written in your own hand, and I was gratified by it, but not by its contents. For it indicated your reluctance and intention to withdraw your hand from inspiring the hearts of our faithful brethren and teaching them the understanding and knowledge of G-d. But in my opinion, all the days of a man's lifetime, were he to live a thousand years filled with the service of G-d, would not compare to the merit of illuminating the eyes of the many, they and their children, generation after generation. And if this be too small in your eyes, put your trust in the Living G-d and taste of the very flavor of the World to Come, for the merit of the many is with you, so that there is no need of apprehension of the heaviness of the burden, etc. Indeed, it is quite beyond imagination and mental grasp how the light of the intellect gushes forth and the heart is like an everflowing spring in the dissemination of righteousness and the ways of G-d. Let your words shine forth, like an axe shattering rock, and the listeners will receive their sustenance, each according to his need.

The truth to tell you, my brother, had I weighed on the intellectual scale, before my journey to the Land of Life, the worth of this *mitzvah* and its flavor, perhaps it would have tipped the balance.

My beloved friend and the friend of G-d, I know full well the reasons why this matter weighs heavily upon you. . . . Go lead the people and sanctify them today and tomorrow, so to the living, to eternal redemption.

These are the words of your loving friend who seeks your peace with sincere heart and soul,

Abraham, the son of my master and father
Alexander Katz (Kohen-Tzedek)
of saintly memory.[4]

The great affection and intimate spiritual affinity which Rabbi Abraham of Kalisk felt for his colleague began to wane when Rabbi Schneur Zalman published his *Tanya* ten years later (in 1796). Despite the wide currency and reverence which the work gained among the Chasidim, or perhaps because of it, Rabbi Abraham felt impelled to criticize his colleague for encouraging the study of the esoteric among the Chasidim who, in his opinion, would be more secure in their simple faith. Rabbi Abraham was apprehensive lest the author had "poured too much oil into the lamp, which might extinguish the light altogether." Consequently he wrote to Rabbi Schneur Zalman in the following terms:

My beloved brother,

. . . I call the G-d of heaven and earth to testify for me that I have ever desired your righteousness, and my heart never ceased to cherish affection for you. . . .

However, as I live . . . were it not for the holiness of this land and my weakened strength, I would have willingly presented myself to you in person, to meet eye to eye to quench my thirst and fulfill my wish for a talk and discussion in accordance with the need. But now a mountain has risen, and a long distance separates us. So the words must be written, yet all the words are too tedious for the mouth to speak and for the scribe to write; and the words are too profound to be conveyed by messenger, for the words go after the intent of the heart. . . . For this reason I reconsidered my way, to put my hand to my mouth, for silence is good . . . but finally decided otherwise . . . since abundant waters cannot extinguish the love.

I shall speak only the most essential words, barely touching the edge, and privileged is he whose words fall upon attentive ears. . . .

As for me, I find no gratification in the effort by your Torah-excellency to push the sun into its sheath, namely, to clothe the words of our saintly and revered teacher of Miezricz—which are the very words of the saintly teacher, the Baal Shem Tov—within the words of the saintly Ari (Rabbi Yitzchok Luria) of blessed memory, although all diverge to the same place; the Torah speaking its own language, and the Sages speaking their own language. Particularly because of the danger that the rain drives deep, and the generation is not attuned. Hence a choice of careful language is necessary . . . in the ways of fear and love [of G-d], to purify the body and *midot* (attributes) that they be dedicated to G-d alone. I have much to recite upon the possible consequences of this, which cannot be put in writing, for I see what can come out of this, G-d forbid.

Now I see the *Sefer Shel Benonim*[5] which your Torah excellency has printed, and I find not very much use in it for the saving of souls, for they are trained with abundance of counsel . . . and the old is stronger [than the new]. By the level of the recipients, a single spark would suffice for them . . . and too much oil in the lamp may be the cause of extinguishing it, G-d forbid. . . . Such was also the custom of our teachers, who were most careful and wary in their words, not to let them be heard by the majority of the Chasidim, but only in the way of admonition, and to bring them into the covenant of faith in the leaders; for the word of Torah should be sparing and pure, little that contains much. . . .

I shall not conceal from my beloved brother what is in my heart. I fear that with the multitude of Chasidim perhaps it is, G-d forbid, the counsel of the *sitra achra* (the "other side") to lose the grain in the straw, the Merciful spare us. For men of excellence are few, one in a city and two in a family.[6] Especially in these times, when falsehood has grown exceedingly strong. Some wrap themselves in garments not theirs, speaking lofty words of wonder and hidden secrets, while mired in all sorts of low passions and evil traits, as I have seen at close range among newcomers to the Land from all the four corners. . .

Now, therefore, G-d be with you, man of valor, be strong and strengthen yourself for our people. Look into the individual, the one lowly of spirit and broken of heart, to vivify him with a spark of the Living Light, in sparing words that flourish within him—leaving the matter hidden to the eye. While, as for the community of the Chasidim, suffice for them faith in the leaders, and recognition of their own deficiency.[7]

The letter continues to take Rabbi Schneur Zalman to task for involving his young son Rabbi Dov Ber in the dissemination of the esoteric teachings of Chasidut. Rabbi Abraham particularly decries the fact that in every city the *Tanya* is being studied by Chasidic groups. "I fear for them that they will never see the bright light," he declares. He further claims that their saintly teacher Rabbi Menachem Mendel, before his demise, was much grieved to hear about the wide dissemination of the esoteric teachings of Chasidut carried on by Rabbi Schneur Zalman.

Rabbi Abraham sees dire consequences resulting from Rabbi Schneur Zalman's way, and suggests that his departure from the way of his forerunners was due to the fact that he had always been a person of extreme modesty and reserve, shunning leadership; hence he had not put his mind to learning the art of leadership from his superiors of blessed memory. Rabbi Abraham, therefore, strongly urges his colleague to change his method before the situation gets out of hand. He informs Rabbi Schneur Zalman that he intends to write a pastoral letter on the subject, for all the country, and suggests that Rabbi Schneur Zalman write a similar letter, so that both their views would harmonize.

The letter which Rabbi Abraham of Kalisk wrote to the Chasidim in the diaspora warns against the danger of intellectual pursuit, the delving in the Kabbala of the *Ari*, and the esoteric teachings of the Baal Shem Tov and the Maggid of Miezricz. The latter were meant, Rabbi Abraham claimed, for a few chosen and qualified individuals, and not for public dissemination to all and sundry. Here are some excerpts from this letter (written in the year 5557):

> . . . I am greatly concerned for you . . . lest your heart be deceived and you turn away from the essence of faith and truth. For all the words that touch the loftiness of the universe—all converge to one central point, the fear of G-d—the [true] wisdom. Whereas the reverse (i.e. when wisdom precedes fear) results in that "the wise have no bread," the latter ("bread") being the essence of fear and faith. . . . And in order to preserve this point, so as not to deviate from it, G-d has commanded us the practical *halachah* [to live] according to the Torah, through faith in the Sages . . . whereas the Torah and intelligences by themselves, without prior fear [of G-d], are abstracts, transient and destructive. . . .
>
> Therefore I do not approve of the publication of the heavenly secrets, the writings of the heavenly saints, whose every word is like fiery coal, reaching the loftiest aspects of the universe; for not every mind can absorb it. They are meant for those who possess a saintly soul, or whose Divine worship is out of pure love, having transcended the natural order . . . but he who is not worthy is endangered thereby; and who can say, "I am purified, my heart is cleansed; I will rely on my intelligence," G-d forbid. For the intelligence develops according to the purity of the body and spirit, and corresponds to the degree of their preparedness. On the other hand, faith and fear purify the body and cleanse the spirit to be irradiated with the light of Torah and Mitzvot. Were it up to my opinion, I would gather all the sacred books which are scattered among the beginners and I would put them in the custody of those who are pure of spirit, from whom the beginners would learn little by little, according to their intellect and after ample preparedness. . . .

The letter goes on to extoll at great length the superiority of simple faith in G-d and in the Sages, over intellectual pursuit, pointing out the pitfalls of the human intellect that could easily lead one astray into outright heresy.[8]

Thus the stage was set for a sharp division among the two Chasidic leaders in regard to method and approach towards the same goal—Divine service. The system of *Chabad* (*Chochmah, binah, daat*)—the *intellectual* approach, as propounded by Rabbi Schneur Zalman; and that of *Chagat* (*Chesed, gevurah, tiferet*)— the *emotional* approach by way of fear and love of G-d and simple faith which is "above the intellect." Not that one ruled out the other completely, for the distinction was more in the nature of emphasis, and the opinions differed merely as to which of the two systems was the most suitable one for the masses. Undoubtedly, the fact that Rabbi Schneur Zalman lived and worked in Lithuania and White Russia, where the intellectual level of his followers was higher than that of the Jewish masses in other parts of Eastern Europe, coupled with his own intellectual bent, had a great deal to do with his bolder approach to Chasidut and its dissemination among his followers.

Despite Rabbi Abraham's outspoken objections to Rabbi Schneur Zalman's publication of the *Tanya* and his method of spiritual leadership, these intellectual differences did not immediately result in a breach of their friendship. It was only when Rabbi Abraham decided to become independent of Rabbi Schneur Zalman's financial support, and create his own fundraising apparatus, that the rift widened, and their mutual friendship was disrupted.

As often happens in cases of a fall-out, a third party is involved. In the controversy that ensued between the two Chasidic leaders there were certain men who, for reasons of their own, wished to create discord between the two Chasidic leaders. One of the chief instigators in this case was a certain Elazar of Disna, a man of considerable learning in both Talmud and Chasidut, but of an impetuous and contentious nature. He came to settle in the Holy Land, claiming to be a devoted disciple and confidant of Rabbi Schneur Zalman. According to a lengthy letter of complaint which Rabbi Abraham sent to Rabbi Schneur

Zalman (in the year 5561),[9] this Elazar began a campaign of vil-
ification against Rabbi Abraham, not only among the Chasidim
in the Holy Land, but also among the Sephardic Jews. That
Elazar was a man of questionable character is evident also from a
letter[10] which Rabbi Dov Ber, the son and successor of Rabbi
Schneur Zalman, wrote to him, requesting him to desist from
slandering him (Rabbi Dov Ber), when Elazar turned against him
after the death of Rabbi Schneur Zalman.

In his campaign against Rabbi Abraham, Elazar of Disna
purported to speak in the name of Rabbi Schneur Zalman, creating in Rabbi Abraham the suspicion that his colleague bore a
secret enmity towards him, and intended to divert the financial
aid which he had been sending through him, and send it through
other channels.

In the year 5563 (1803), Rabbi Abraham sent two emissaries
to Rabbi Schneur Zalman, requesting him to abolish his fund-
raising system, so that these emissaries would themselves go
around collecting funds from non-Chabad Chasidim in
provinces beyond Rabbi Schneur Zalman's immediate sphere of
influence which centered in White Russia and Lithuania.

Rabbi Schneur Zalman saw in this attempt a serious threat
to the unity of the Chasidic community, dividing it up between
Chabad and non-Chabad adherents. He refused to accede to the
demand of Rabbi Abraham, and continued his work as before.
Rabbi Abraham, on his part, refused to accept these funds for
two years, and finally attempted to undermine the confidence of
many Chasidim in their leader in White Russia.

Rabbi Abraham also wrote a letter[11] to Rabbi Levi Yitzchak
of Berditchev, who had complained to him about the conduct of
his emissaries. In this letter Rabbi Abraham attempts to justify
his position by outlining what he considered were the basic
issues. According to Rabbi Abraham the underlying cause of
their strife was Rabbi Schneur Zalman's deviation from the way
of his teachers in matters of spiritual leadership and dissemination of Chasidut. Rabbi Abraham claimed that when he tried to
admonish his colleague in a friendly and confidential manner, to
make him change his ways, the latter turned his heart against
him, and confirmed his enmity towards him through the affair of

Elazar of Disna. This is why he, Rabbi Abraham, felt impelled to withdraw from the fund-raising arrangement which was previously in Rabbi Schneur Zalman's hands, much against his will and desire, and set up his own fund-raising.

In reply[12] Rabbi Levi Yitzchak totally rejects Rabbi Abraham's assertions that Rabbi Schneur Zalman has in any way deviated from the way of the Maggid of Miezricz. Thus he writes:

> In reference to the matter of the complaint by Your Eminence in regard to his (Rabbi Schneur Zalman's) ways [asserting] that they do not accord with the way of our master and teacher, the saintly Maggid of blessed and eternal memory, his soul rest in Eden—first of all, you have overlooked a clear and definite Talmudic principle appearing in many places, namely that after one has taken action in a situation, one's testimony is no longer acceptable.
>
> But apart from that, it is greatly surprising to me how it can occur to anyone to complain against the ways of our master and teacher (Rabbi Schneur Zalman), since such was the very essence of the ways of our saintly master and teacher the Maggid, whose main occupation was to teach the Torah and Mitzvot to his people, and this is the essence of (Divine) service, as we received it from our late teacher; and his (Rabbi Schneur Zalman's) ways are also on the same pattern. This is the holy way of our holy Torah, and in precisely this way the light of G-d dwells. Would that all the people be *tzaddikim* conducting themselves like him. On the contrary, whoever does not conduct himself in this way does not follow the way of our late teacher. And whoever complains against this way is as though he complains, G-d forbid, against our revered master and teacher of saintly memory, since essentially his whole service and saintly ways were precisely along this way. I am indeed very surprised at you, that you should not be aware of this way, since you were faithfully with us under our saintly master and teacher, his soul rest in Eden. . . . This I attest with absolute testimony that my *mechutan*,[13] the *Rav* and *gaon*, was held in extraordinarily high and boundless esteem by our late teacher, and he always praised him exceedingly. . .

But only wicked and unscrupulous men have carried evil slander to your ears for personal reasons, as the end attests to the beginning, for the men are empty-headed, devoid of Torah knowledge, as I have seen them. . . .

It is completely gratuitous on your part to praise them lavishly and to say that they are men of scholarship, piety and truth, for I have never seen among them men of scholarship, piety and truth. How can you write about them "men of truth," when Tzvi Hamar[14] has spoken many falsehoods in my presence; and if he is a scholar, I do not know who is an *am ha'aretz* (ignoramus).

As for the matter of money which you wrote, I am much amazed at your complaint, seeing that you yourself sent emissaries disrupting the system and increasing the discord, for they opened their mouths wide to discredit such a *tzaddik* as he, "the mouth of speakers of falsehood be stopped,"[15] saying in your name that you wished none of our money. How could he have acted otherwise? Surely he did the right thing.

In regard to your attendant Chaim, I do not know what judgment to make, for it is surely a lie, because Chaim said nothing to me. As for the wish which you expressed in your own words, namely "the mouth of speakers of falsehood be stopped," it is an imprecation which Your Eminence uttered against yourself. . . .

These are harsh words, coming from a man known for his extraordinary gentleness, affection, and saintliness. He was obviously greatly hurt by the unwarranted and unjust attack against his colleague, who had given so much of himself for the cause of Chasidut. The mutual affection and respect between Rabbi Levi Yitzchak of Berditchev and Rabbi Schneur Zalman was even further enhanced, since the two Chasidic leaders' families became united through the marriage of their grandchildren, Bela the daughter of Rabbi Dov Ber to Rabbi Yekutiel Zalman the son of Rabbi Levi Yitzchak's son-in-law Rabbi Yosef Bunim, which took place during the period between the years 5560-5563 (1800-1803), judging by the dates of their correspondence when they began to address each other as "my *mechutan.*" However, their mutual spiritual affinity and friendship dated back, of course, to the days when both of them were the disciples of the Maggid of Miezricz, and it remained consistent throughout. This is also evidenced from the fact that Rabbi Levi Yitzchak was the first person to whom Rabbi Schneur Zalman wrote of his miraculous acquittal in 1798, as we have already seen.[16]

Further light upon the controversy between Rabbi Abraham and Rabbi Schneur Zalman is thrown by the latter's lengthy epistle to Rabbi Abraham, written, apparently, in 5566 (1806), since it makes direct references to the latter's letter to him which was written in the previous year. Rabbi Schneur Zalman's letter is illuminating in many respects. It reads (in free translation) as follows, with but few abbreviations.

To begin with, there is the well-known dictum of our Sages, of blessed memory, that a covenant has been made with slander that it would be believed, if not fully, at least partly. For many years, during which those base individuals who descended from there (the Land of Israel) to here, and from here to there, have sharpened their tongue like a sword, year after year, [weaving strings] into heavy ropes, until the measure has been filled, and a mountain has risen between us, etc. Especially in the light of what I have heard in the name of the late Rabbi Menachem Mendel of saintly memory, that the place [the Holy Land] is susceptible to it, warning very earnestly to beware of groundless hatred, saying that the place does not tolerate it, since the Destruction took place because of groundless hatred, and a residue of it has been left, etc. Baseless hatred is due only to tale-bearing and slander, for it is not the nature of a person to hate another one, who has done him no harm, either by deed or word. Behold, need we cite anyone greater than Saul, the chosen one by G-d and His anointed. Yet, by accepting calumny, he destroyed Nov, the City of *Kohanim*.

As a result, you have changed your heart, as an error issuing from a ruler, and have raised your hand to write tedious and disparaging letters, seeking to entangle us in false accusations which are clearly transparent, in an effort to change what has been known, and well known, to all, in the area of spiritual matters, making a mockery of all the epistles sent to our Chasidic fellowship, and to me personally, over the course of twenty-two years[17] to strengthen and encourage me [such as]: "Open your mouth and let your words shine forth," and so on, and much more in a similar vein. These were recognizable words of truth, coming from the depth of the heart, and not just to gratify my wish. So you have also written to my *mechutan*, the saintly *gaon*, the Chief Rabbi of Berditchev. For I have never requested your approbation on my teachings of Chasidut, since they are the words of the saintly mouth of our great teacher of Miezricz and his son, of saintly memory. As a matter of fact, I tried to escape many years ago and to migrate to the Holy Land, whereupon I received the letters from the rabbis in the year 5546.[18] What fool can fail to understand this? For had you intended merely to gratify my wish, you could have confined your writing to our Chasidic fellowship, without writing to me in particular to strengthen and encourage me.

All the letters which you have written to me personally testify and declare that that they were truly genuine coming from the depth of the heart, especially the letter more recently transcribed, wherein you offer testimonial in my behalf in the name of "G-d Who searches the heart," and so forth. But many (letters) have been lost by me.

Now, how can one imagine that all your letters over the course of twenty-two years were only ostensible, for the purpose of strengthening the settlement in the Land of Israel, and not truly genuine? If this be so, how much more likely is it to assume that your present letters are designed merely for the strengthening of the settlement in the Holy Land, in compliance with the wishes of the men of Vilna, and Lachowitz, Lubavitch and Miedzibosz.[19] Indeed, this is what I think.

As for the letter which you sent to my *mechutan*, the *gaon* named above, and seeing that the letter failed, the messengers which you sent to him [to induce him] to take me to task in the matter of spiritual leadership, etc.—it is common knowledge that, much to the contrary, no sooner had they come to us in the winter of 5562, than they began to speak only well and to console me for your letters of the year 5558.[20] I did well to have consigned them to conceal-ment. They begged me to burn those letters in their pres-ence. I replied, "But the persons contradicting you declare that they are only ostensible!" Whereupon they bitterly lamented, saying, "How can anyone think such a thing of a great man like him, may they multiply in Israel, that for the sake of financial consideration he would cause thou-sands of Jewish souls to be abandoned, G-d forbid, were he not satisfied with [your] way, G-d forbid. Moreover, it would be rather wretched for the Holy Land were its foun-dation to rest on such a state, G-d forbid." They tried very hard to convince me of the truth of these words, and also obtained letters from me, requesting that they be written precisely in these terms. And when they made the rounds in many towns in our country, they loudly declared the same thing from the depth of their heart, as is known and well known to all.

Also in the winter of 5563, they challenged me only in the matter concerning the Holy Land, to abolish the emis-saries in our country, so that they themselves will make the rounds in our country; but they did not take me to account in spiritual matters, for they are not men of introspection, and are poor accountants.

The truth to tell, their words during the winter of 5562 did enter my heart, apart from the fact that "words of truth are recognizable." Besides, how can one even admit the thought that a G-d-fearing man could engage in such guile and deception, namely, to write letters of peace, affection and friendship every year for twenty-two years, in order to extract a gigantic sum year after year, reaching in the many thousands, while inwardly harboring evil, G-d forbid. Clearly, had most of our Chasidim known this, they would not have given so generously; perhaps a small amount as was customary in bygone days, but giving the rest to the renowned *tzaddikim* in the diaspora. Consequently, you do not degrade and vilify us, but yourself and your own honor.

It is a profanation of G-d's Name in the eyes of the masses; may G-d forgive it.

Furthermore, your writing to my said *mechutan* that you have repeatedly tried in various letters to correct me on one point, namely [the meaning of] "the *tzaddik* lives by his faith,"[21] is a matter that can easily be exposed. Your letters, year after year, show that you have written to me only once on this subject, in the year 5558,[22] after R.A.K.[23] journeyed thither (the Holy Land) and slandered our Chasidic fellowship in your presence. In the year 5559, because of the stringent times, I did not find time to answer you properly, until the year 5560. To this you replied nicely in the year 5561;[24] also in the year 5562 your letters to me were friendly. Likewise in 5563 came a friendly letter.[25] Only those critical of me did not reach me, as is known.

Now, the meaning of the verse, "the *tzaddik* lives by his faith" was well explained on *Shabbat-Nachamu* of this year, and it was in part alluded to in Chapter 33 of *Likutei Amarim*. However, according to your conception, the dictum of our Sages "Habakuk came and based [the 613 precepts] on one, as it is written, 'the *tzaddik* lives by his faith,'[26] is understood literally, that simple faith is all that is needed, as you wrote in your letters of 5558. But you have overlooked the dictum of our Sages of blessed memory, "The thief, upon breaking in, prays to G-d [for success]" (Ber. 63a). Thus one may believe in G-d, yet have no control over his passion to stop him from theft and murder; [murder, too] for the law is well known that killing a thief in the act of breaking in is not a capital offense, because the thief is himself prepared to murder the owner if discovered in the act. Thus, in order to attain fear of G-d, it is necessary to have deep contemplation, etc., as explained in *Likutei Amarim*. Anyone in the provinces of Wolhynia and the Ukraine who has the merest smattering of the teachings of the Baal Shem Tov, of blessed memory, and of his disciples, knows the meaning of the passage in the holy *Zohar* (Introduction to *Tikunei Zohar*) that "*Binah* (understanding) is the mother of the *banim* (children)," the "chil-

dren" being love [of G-d] and fear [of G-d] . . . and what
begets them is knowledgeable contemplation in depth on
the subject of G-d's greatness, each one according to one's
capacity. And just as no children can be born without a
mother, so it is impossible to be G-d-fearing without contemplation. You put your finger on it well in your letter of
5561[27] addressed to our Chasidic fellowship, especially in
the matter of contemplation. How, then, can one presume
to take issue with it?

According to your letter to my *mechutan* the *gaon*, you
sent [your emissaries] to investigate me in spiritual matters,
and to deal with me as they saw fit in the light of their findings, authorizing them to speak in your name whatever
they considered proper. If so, our pursuers were light
(unworthy),[28] these low-minded individuals of scanty
knowledge. You gave them authority because they consider themselves erudite in the Torah, but we recognize them
and know them from their youth and until now. They are
not versed in Torah learning, neither the revealed nor esoteric; suffice it to call them [merely] literate. I was tremen-
dously astonished—whoever saw such a thing: To place
such a great and tremendous matter, as that of taking issue
with thousands upon thousands of Jews, into the hands of
messengers, placing a sword in their hands to use according
to their mind and reckoning; messengers who are certainly
not qualified to determine and judge. . . . Even you yourself, with all due respect, cannot singly outweigh the many,
especially as you are partial in this matter, and after the
deed one's testimony is worthless, as my *mechutan* the *gaon*
has written.[29] Were you here, you would have to weigh
yourself on the scale of holiness whether to discourage
thousands of Jews and disturb them from the Divine service, G-d forbid, saying, "Accept my opinion."

Moreover, you are no longer trustworthy to recant your
letter of the year 5561 on the excuse expressed in your general letter, as has been ruled in the second *mishnah* of
Ketubot, that witnesses are not permitted to plead compul-
sion by reason of [threatened] monetary loss, because a per-

son is partial to himself, and no person incriminates himself to protect money in his possession, certainly not to enforce a monetary claim. Is complete license to be sanctioned for the sake of the love of the Holy Land, or, in the words of the Prophet Jeremiah (7:11), "Is this house become a den of robbers?"

I am further astonished how the living can deny the well-known occasion of my traveling together with you to Rovno to our great teacher, his soul rest in Eden, in the summer of 5532, and you feared because of our teacher[30] to enter the town, remaining in the outskirts. You asked me to see the late Rabbi Menachem Mendel, who had already been in that town for some time, to ask him to intervene in your behalf with our saintly teacher to permit you to come to him. The late Rabbi [M.M.] immediately went to our saintly teacher and obtained his consent. Thereupon I immediately went to the end of the town to call you. I went with you together to the room of our great teacher, and my eyes saw and my ears heard how he rebuked you sternly for your bad influence upon Chasidim in Russia, which led them to indulge in idle talk and frivolity, and to make fun of the scholars, degrading them with all sorts of insults; also turning somersaults head over heels in the market-places and streets, profaning the Name of Heaven in the presence of gentiles; and engaging in other kinds of foolish play in the streets of Kalisk. Consequently, during the dispute in Shklov in the winter of 5532, you found no defense for this and the like.[31] Then the rabbis of Shklov wrote to inform the late Gaon of Vilna, and persuaded him to condemn us in the category of those deserving to forfeit their lives, G-d forbid, and in the category of an *epikores*, humiliating Torah scholars; as for turning head over heels, he said it was of the idolatry of *Peor*, and so on. Whereupon they wrote from Vilna to Brody to that effect, and the pamphlet *Zemir Aritzim*[32] was published there that summer. It resulted in great distress for the *tzaddikim* of Wolhynia, and they could not stay at home, and flocked at that time in Rovno, to our great teacher, his soul rest in Eden, to deliberate and seek counsel. This is why you were so afraid to enter the town lest you incurred the wrath of our great teacher, G-d forbid. The Maggid of Zlotchev was also there at that time and he interceded in your behalf with our teacher the Maggid [of Miezricz], his soul rest in Eden. I know all this well, and it is common knowledge. Thus, all the troubles which were visited upon us in the year 5559 were by order of a *Beit-Din* who relied completely upon the personal signature of the Gaon of Vilna in 5532, as was made public there.

How could the *Rav* of Tiberias forget all this and remove the cover of shame from the face, and haughtily write against me to my *mechutan* that I do not walk in the path of our saintly teacher, but he does, etc? . . . As for mundane matters concerning the Holy Land, is this the way of a G-d-fearing man to let loose mouth and tongue with arrogance on the basis of mere hearsay, as you write in your letters,[33] "I have heard it," etc? What you have heard was only half of the matter, etc. And although according to scriptures and the teachings of our Sages in the early chapter of the tractate *Shabbat*,[34] it would be unworthy to answer you in any way, I am impelled to answer you at length and briefly, for the sake of remaining innocent before both G-d and Israel.

It was in the winter of 5563 that those lowly persons came to me and requested me to abolish in our country all the authorized collectors and regular contributions of old, so that they themselves would make the rounds and establish new regular sources among true friends not belonging to *Chabad*. I asked them, "How can you manage to cover all the provinces previously covered by my emissaries?" To this they replied that they would be content with the mission of R.Y.S. (Yaakov Smilianer),[35] approximating a third of the total collections, seeing that their numbers have decreased, for the majority have gone to their eternal rest and they did not need any more than that approximate amount. They told me explicitly that they were acting upon instructions of their rabbi, who ordered them not to accept [money] from those calling themselves as above [Chabad], since the latter give only because of my written appeal and not out of true love [to the recipients]. . . .

I refused to heed their request, so as not to increase dissension among the Jewish people and create separate groups in every town and congregation, as I had firmly announced in the winter of 5558.

To this they declared that if I would not let them make the rounds in our country, they would not accept a single copper coin from our country, of the money collected on my authority, for this is what you commanded them.

I asked them, "And if you say, what shall we eat?"[36] To which they replied that they have a firm assurance by the tzaddikim of Wolhynia and the Ukraine for the approximate amount that will take care of their needs, as mentioned above, and they would not depend on our country altogether, nor be subjected to Chabad. However, after a strenuous intervention by R.Y.S., he succeeded in inducing them to agree to receive [our help] at least this year, until the tzaddikim were able to fulfill their promise to deliver the money, and then they would receive no more from our country. With this they departed from me in peace.

However, after visiting Vitebsk, they changed their minds, and sent a stringent letter from that province, with a most stern warning that no emissary go around collecting for them in our country. Moreover, they spread the rumor in all the towns that the money given to our emissaries will undoubtedly not reach the Holy Land. All this they did in the name of their rabbi. They also hurled many insults at me and all our Chasidim and friends. . . . Upon hearing this, the contributors were very angry, and refused to give even a small coin for the Holy Land. But our emissaries implored and persuaded them to send the money direct to me to do with it as I personally will see fit. The gabbaim (local treasurers) sent letters to this effect for the emissaries to deliver to me. I still have all the letters from all the gabbaim, which can be produced. [One of my emissaries] Israel Chatzi-Rav[37] related to me that in some places he heard the following expression: "To give, we must, by order of the *Rav* of Liadi, but would that the money be stolen from you, so that none of it reaches the Holy Land because of the vilifications, may G-d spare us."

Nevertheless, my heart was filled with misgiving. Perhaps it was all done without your knowledge. And if they have sinned [why should others suffer]; perhaps the money should after all be sent to you. So I asked R.Y.S., and he replied that in his opinion it was quite impossible that they should have acted and spoken the way they did on their own accord, and undoubtedly they were commanded to do so by you. . . . I suggested that he should write to you to inform you that all the collected sum is in his, R.Y.S.'s, possession, but because your trusted emissaries declared in your name that you will certainly not accept it, he had not sent the money, lest it get lost, G-d forbid. But it is most astonishing that there should have been such an angry outburst to the extent of deeply offending all the donors by refusing to accept their contributions. However, if your Torah-eminence will wish to accept the money, then write to us a friendly letter to this effect, and all the money will be sent to you, both the principal and the profit, for it has been invested in most trusted hands. . . .

Rabbi Schneur Zalman goes on to reiterate his inevitable conclusion that Rabbi Abraham was intentionally seeking pretexts to create dissension in the Chasidic community. He concludes his long letter by warning the Chasidim, both near and far, to keep away from the mendacious and deceitful group, and speak to them neither good nor evil, and certainly provoke no strife or argument with them, but keep at a distance from them as "from a goring ox."

In the face of what clearly appeared as a calculated effort on the part of Rabbi Abraham of Kalisk to break away from the aegis of his colleague the Chabad leader, Rabbi Schneur Zalman was unable to heal the rift. Nor was he able to prevent a cooling off between the Chasidim of White Russia and those of the Ukraine and Wolhynia, who sided with Rabbi Abraham in this controversy.

The rift within the Chasidic community extended also in another direction, again as a result of jealousy. This time Rabbi Schneur Zalman's antagonist was Rabbi Baruch, a grandson of Rabbi Israel Baal Shem Tov. Rabbi Baruch objected to Rabbi Schneur Zalman's "trespassing" on his domain in Podolia, when the latter included it in his itinerary in his fund-raising campaign to help the numerous Jewish families who had been dislocated by new anti-Jewish measures on the part of the Russian government.

This new development in the economic position of Russian Jewry, which provides another instance of Rabbi Schneur Zalman's concern and work for the economic welfare of his co-religionists, Chasidim and non-Chasidim alike, calls for a brief review of the major events that affected the Jewish position in Russia at the beginning of the 19th century.

Ever since the Derzhavin report, the government was trying to find a way of "regulating" the position of Russian Jewry. By a *ukase* of Czar Alexander (November 9, 1802), a special "Commission on the Welfare of the Jews" was established, with Derzhavin as one of its members. Jewish communities were invited to send representatives to attend hearings by the Commission. A final recommendation by the Commission was made to the Emperor in October 1804, when the Commission recommended the expulsion of the Jews from the rural areas. The order to carry it out was duly given by the Czar, and caused great panic among the Jews. It meant the immediate expulsion of some 60,000 of the poorest Jewish families from the villages to the towns, without providing any measures to alleviate their plight, leaving this problem entirely to the Jews.[38] Owing to representations by local authorities concerning the hardships created for the Russian population, the cruel order was not fully implemented. In 1806 Alexander ordered the creation of a new committee to look into the matter. The following year this committee came up with a recommendation calling for the resettlement of the Jews from the rural areas to the towns of the Pale to be carried out in three stages, and completed in 1810. On October 19, 1807, an order was sent to the governor of Kamenetz-Podolsk to expel the Jews from the villages.[39] As a result, additional thousands of Jewish families found themselves suddenly uprooted, cut off from their means of livelihood, and crowded into the already overcrowded cities of the Pale of Settlement,[40] exposed to starvation and misery.

In the late winter of 1810, Rabbi Schneur Zalman set out to visit many towns of the Pale in an effort to raise financial support for the rehabilitation of the dislocated families. It was during his visit in Tultschin, in the district of Podolia, that Rabbi Schneur Zalman paid his respects to Rabbi Baruch, and the latter vehemently accused Rabbi Schneur Zalman of "trespassing on his territory," fearful that the latter's popularity might detract many of his personal followers.

Rabbi Schneur Zalman ignored the haughty attitude of the Baal Shem Tov's grandson, and went on with his mission of mercy. He was even prepared to ignore the malicious rumors spread by some jealous followers of Rabbi Baruch, designed to undermine Rabbi Schneur Zalman's influence. However, on the insistence of his children and disciples, Rabbi Schneur Zalman eventually decided to send an encyclical to his followers, pointing out the true facts about his controversy with Rabbi Baruch. In it, Rabbi Schneur Zalman stated, with characteristic candor, "I rebuked him [Rabbi Baruch] in his face for his ingratitude, for have I not been twice [summoned to appear] in Petersburg for the sake of his grandfather the Baal Shem Tov? I could have said, 'Is not his grandson among the living? Let him come and answer all the charges against him!'" Rabbi Schneur Zalman then went on to explain that he dismissed Rabbi Baruch's objection ("Why did you come to my province?") with a twofold answer: "First, it is written, 'The earth is the Lord's, and the fullness thereof.' Secondly, I could not bear the plight and suffering of the villagers who had been driven from their places to the towns, and are thrown into the streets in the throes of hunger, and are dying of starvation." Seeing that Rabbi Baruch remained unmoved and skeptical, Rabbi Schneur Zalman goes on to say, "I could only conclude that Rabbi Baruch had accepted the malicious slander originating from certain Chasidic quarters in Palestine."[41] Rabbi Schneur Zalman concludes:

At first I intended not to reveal the letter to our

Chasidim in order to avoid a *Chilul Hashem* in sight of the Mitnagdim, and others. Later, however, I changed my mind. Moreover, I gave instructions to have the said letter copied and sent to all our Chasidim, in order that all should know that the falsehood was with the other side. For in the said letter it was alleged that I requested of Rabbi Baruch his consent to my going to Petersburg, and he said that whoever goes to Petersburg must don German clothes and grow a hair lock,[42] whereupon I agreed to do this for the benefit of the Jewish people. But this is a well known lie, widely known in our province, for many [Jews] travel from our province to Petersburg and are not obliged to do all this. Besides, why should I need his consent, seeing that I have in my possession a document of freedom from his Imperial Majesty for all my practices?

With this I conclude and wish you *shalom* (peace) from the Master of Peace, for "their shadow (defense) is departed from them, and G-d is with us; fear them not,"[43] etc.

Thus, it would seem that jealousy, more than anything else, was at the bottom of the coolness that had set in among other trends of the Chasidic movement towards that of Chabad.

There were, however, also certain important doctrinal differences. Perhaps the most important of these was Chabad's tendency to play down the role of the *tzaddik* which was so basic among the Chasidic trends in Polish provinces, where various dynastic Chasidic groups had multiplied. Here, where the masses were on a much lower intellectual level than in Lithuania and White Russia, the Chasidic leaders placed more emphasis on the heart than on the mind, and on the simple faith in the Chasidic leader, or *tzaddik*, as the intermediary between the Chasid and his Heavenly Father. These Chasidic leaders believed that intellectual inquiry into matters of faith could be more harmful than beneficial to their followers, as we have already noted in the case of the opposition to the *Tanya* voiced by Rabbi Abraham of Kalisk.[44]

R abbi Schneur Zalman's life was a very busy one; his concerns and pursuits were many. He was, and always remained, an assiduous student; he was also a devoted teacher; a dedicated leader and a personal counsellor of a vast following, and a leader and defender of Russian Jewry as a whole; he was also a philanthropist and a benefactor on a vast scale. Yet, with all these claims on his time and attention, he was also a prolific author. His major contributions as already noted, were his *Shulchan Aruch* in the field of *halachah*, and his *Tanya*, or *Likutei Amarim* in the field of Kabbala, Jewish ethics, and philosophy. These were followed by the *Siddur* (Jewish prayer book), first published in Shklov, in 1803, in two volumes, arranged in accordance with Lurianic tradition *(Nusach Ari)*. Rabbi Schneur Zalman was particularly interested in ascertaining the correct recension of the text. He is said to have used and sifted as many as sixty different editions and versions of the Prayer Book for this purpose.[45]

Much of his literary work was edited by others and published posthumously. His published works[46] include *Biurei HaZohar* ("Commentaries on the *Zohar*"), edited by his son and successor, Rabbi Dov Ber (Kopust, 1816); *Torah Or* ("Torah-Light"), Chabad-Chasidic discourses on the first two books of the Pentateuch and on the Book of Esther, edited by his brother, Rabbi Yehuda Leib (Kopust, 1837); *Likutei Torah* ("Torah Gleanings"), in two volumes, on the remainder of the Pentateuch and on the Book of *Shir HaShirim* (Canticles), edited by his grandson Rabbi Menachem Mendel of Lubavitch (Zhitomir, 1888). The headquarters of the Chabad movement in Brooklyn, NY, is continually editing and publishing Rabbi Schneur Zalman's literary material which has not been published hitherto.[47]

One of the lasting contributions of the founder of Chabad was in the sphere of sacred music, or more precisely—Chasidic and liturgical music, known as *neginah*. Rabbi Schneur Zalman is the creator of a cadre of neginah with a distinctive character and temperament of its own, which has come to be known as Chabad-neginah. It stands in relation to general Chasidic neginah as the Chabad philosophical system stands in relation to general Chasidut. For, while Chasidic melodies in general are for the most part light and joyful, Chabad melodies are comparatively of slower movement, subtle and meditative, as well as richer in nuance and mood. If general Chasidic melody stems, so to speak, from the heart and appeals to the heart, Chabad melody has its source in meditation and the inner depths of the soul.

In the Chabad philosophical system of Rabbi Schneur Zalman, neginah receives considerable attention. He traces it to the Divine service in the *Beit HaMikdash* of old, where the Levites accompanied it by vocal and instrumental music. This, in turn, he explains as the counterpart of the Heavenly music with which the angels constantly serve and adulate their Creator. Indeed, the very existence of rhythm in nature is due to the fact that there is a Heavenly rhythm which serves as its supernal source, just as everything else in the material world has its counterpart and source in the spiritual world. Just as the human body responds to the rhythmic beat of the heart, so does the soul respond to the rhythm of sacred melody. The pulse of the heartbeat itself is but a reflection of the worshipful rhythmic movements of the angels in their constant swaying to and fro, in a manner of "advance and retreat," as described in the Heavenly vision of Ezekiel (1:14).[48]

Rabbi Schneur Zalman therefore made neginah part of his philosophical system, and here, too, we see how harmoniously he was able to blend the rational with the mystical.

To the soul, as the "lamp of G-d" (Prov. 20:27), neginah is a *natural* quality of communion with its Maker. Neginah is superior to the other forms of communion—thought and speech. Words are inevitably limited and limiting, and so are the "letters of thought," though to a much lesser degree. It is through neginah—pure melody, without words—that the soul can express its highest aspiration and come closest to communion with G-d, Rabbi Schneur Zalman explains. For this reason, most Chabad melodies are tunes without words. Sound and rhythm, beat and movement, meter and tempo—all have their place in the analytical exposition of neginah in the Chabad system of Rabbi Schneur Zalman.

Rabbi Schneur Zalman was a gifted composer of Chasidic neginah. He was also endowed with a fine melodious and awe-inspiring voice.[49] According to Chabad tradition, Rabbi Schneur

Zalman composed ten *nigunim*. They are greatly revered by Chabad followers. These are the "classics" of Chabad neginah.[50]

Most famous among them is the so-called "Nigun of Four Movements." It is also known as the "Nigun of the Alter Rebbe." This nigun is profoundly moving, rising in a crescendo of soulful outpouring. It is regarded by Chabad Chasidim as highly meaningful and expressive, full of mystic symbolism. This nigun is so hallowed by Chabad Chasidim that they only sing it on special occasions, and they are careful to sing it with meticulous faithfulness to detail and nuance. It is sung at the climax of only certain Chasidic celebrations ("*Farbrengen*"), such as those held on the final days of the Three Festivals (Pesach, Shavuot and Succot), as well as on Purim, on the principal Chasidic festivals of the 19th of *Kislev* and 12th of *Tammuz*,[51] at weddings and similar festive and solemn occasions.

The "Nigun of the Four Movements" is said to correspond to the "four worlds," known in Kabbala and Chasidut as *Atzilut* (Emanation), *Beriah* (Creation), *Yetzirah* (Formation) and *Asiyah* (Action), and to the four sacred letters of the Tetragrammaton, from which the "four worlds" emanate, and, finally, is related also to the four categories of the Divine soul, namely, *nefesh*, *ruach*, *neshamah* and *chayah*.[52]

The said nigun has been the subject of interpretation and exegesis by the successive heads of Chabad in the manner of a basic Chabad doctrine. It is said to reflect, generally speaking, four stages in Divine service according to Chabad teaching. The first movement inspires metastasis and introspection. In other words, a shift from the mundane atmosphere, clearing the way for intellectual inquiry into the real purpose and meaning of life. To put it more simply, disengaging the mind from the ordinary mundane affairs of the daily life, in order to engage it in clear and profound meditation on such questions as "Who am I?" and "Why am I here?"

The second movement of the nigun is an extension of the first, in that it inspires a sense of contrition, soon giving way to fervent hope and aspiration.

The third movement affects a sense of spiritual uplift and edification, or the outpouring of the soul.

The fourth and last movement expresses the ecstatic feeling of the soul's illumination as it comes closest to its Source.

Thus, the nigun is said to reflect the basic intellectual approach in Divine service, which is the corner-stone in Rabbi Schneur Zalman's Chabad system.[53]

It is assumed with certainty that this nigun was composed by Rabbi Schneur Zalman when he was under the tutelage and inspiration of his teacher the Maggid of Miezricz.[54]

In Chabad literature and lore, neginah in general, Chabad neginah in particular, and the compositions of the Alter Rebbe above all, receive a great deal of attention and are given an important place in the Chasid's quest for moral and spiritual perfection. It would take us too far afield to present here an exhaustive evaluation of the place of neginah in Chabad. Suffice it to quote some highlights of thoughts and *bons mots* on this subject.

Rabbi Schneur Zalman, while still a young man, is reported to have said on the occasion of a conclave of prominent Torah scholars: "Speech is the pen of the heart, while melody is the pen of the soul."[55]

This aphorism has been elaborated in Chasidic literature. The gist of it will give us an insight into the Chabad concept of a nigun:

Thought is the vehicle of the intellect, the latter being expressed in terms of thought; while speech is the vehicle of thought as well as of emotion, since words express both thought and feelings. But melody is the vehicle of the transcending powers of *desire* and *will*, which are more sublime than the powers of *reason* and *emotion*, as is fully explained in Chabad literature. For although the rational and emotive powers are the "inner" powers of the soul (in contrast to the powers of speech and action, which are termed the *"outer garments"* of the soul), the categories of desire and will touch upon the very essence of the soul.

A nigun, like speech, has "letters" too, though in a more subtle sense. But there is an essential difference between the "letters" of neginah and those of speech. The latter constitute a *descent*, while the former—an *ascent*. For the function of the letters of speech is to reveal and convey to others subtle thoughts and feelings in the process of which the abstract is materialized.

In the case of the "letters" of neginah the process is reversed: their function is to *elevate* the self. Under the influence of a nigun the person discards, as it were, his outer shell, at any rate temporarily, becomes absorbed in himself and reaches out to commune with his very soul in all its purity. Thus neginah has a cathartic effect, purifying the mind and heart, and elevating the Chasid to a higher level of Divine worship. Consequently Rabbi Schneur Zalman assigned to neginah not merely a secondary role, as an aid to spiritual elevation, but a primary role, as a mode in spiritual advancement, since neginah is capable of arousing and stimulating the most latent forces of the soul.

It is related that the Alter Rebbe made use of neginah to win "converts" to Chasidut. Thus, it is related, on one occasion, when Rabbi Schneur Zalman confronted a number of Talmudic scholars in Shklov, who challenged him with an avalanche of questions, the Alter Rebbe began to sing one of his inspirational melodies. The effect upon his audience was such that before he finished his *nigun* all their questions and doubts were dissipated.[56]

On another occasion, when some of his seminarians complained that they found the *Tanya* too subtle and profound, he is said to have advised them to try a Chasidic nigun . . . .[57]

Rabbi Dov Ber, the son and successor of Rabbi Schneur Zalman, is quoted as having said, "My saintly father could penetrate into the innermost recesses of a Chasid's soul by either a word of Chasidut or a nigun."[58]

Chabad tradition lists ten major contributions by Rabbi Schneur Zalman, among them the legacy of the ten nigunim which he composed. All of them are endowed with the quality of inspiring *teshuvah* and *devekut*.[59] When singing any of these nigunim, Chabad Chasidim identify themselves with the Alter Rebbe much in the way they experience spiritual attachment to him when they study the *Tanya* or any of his other literary works and teachings. The Chabad neginah is thus an integral part of the Chabad heritage.[60]

CHAPTER XIII

THE LAST JOURNEY

Rabbi Schneur Zalman was not destined to end his life in peace. In 1812 Napoleon invaded Russia, and the route of the invasion led through White Russia. The Jewish leader, who had twice been accused of high treason, turned out to be a most loyal patriot. Although the French conqueror was hailed in some religious Jewish quarters as the harbinger of a new era of political and economic freedom, Rabbi Schneur Zalman, to whom the ultimate criteria were spiritual rather than economic or political, saw in Napoleon a threat to basic religious principles and spiritual values.[1]

In a strictly confidential letter which Rabbi Schneur Zalman addressed to his devoted Chasid, Moshe Meisels[2] of Vilna, he writes:

> . . . It was revealed to me during the *musaf* prayer on the first day of Rosh Hashanah that if Bonaparte should be victorious, the Jews would prosper economically and politically, but their hearts would be separated and alienated from their Father in Heaven. But if our sovereign Alexander will be victorious, though the Jews would suffer economically and politically, their hearts will become more intimately and securely attached to their Father in Heaven.
>
> And this is your sign [confirming the prediction]: In the coming days your beloved will be taken from you, and they will begin to conscript some of our Jewish brethren for military service.
>
> Remember the subject on which we parted in

Petersburg, in connection with the explanation of [the verse] "Princes have persecuted me without cause, and [consequently] my heart feared Your word" (Ps. 119-161).[3]

While Napoleon's star had been rising with meteoric speed, and his armies swept through the continent of Europe, Chasidic leaders differed in their opinion of the "Little Conqueror." Most of the Chasidic leaders in Poland and Austria welcomed Napoleon's advance. The Jews of Poland in particular saw in him a ray of hope in their dismal situation, which had a long history of economic oppression and religious persecution. Indeed, after the Treaty of Tilsit (July, 1807), when new principalities were carved out at Napoleon's pleasure in Central and Eastern Europe, including the Duchy of Warsaw, the Jews were granted equal rights with all other citizens of these provinces, and they began to look forward to a new era of economic freedom and opportunity. It is not surprising, therefore, that the oppressed Jews were favorably inclined towards the victorious emperor of France. Those Chasidic leaders in Poland who were dubious about the new Napoleonic era were notably in the minority, and even they were prepared to accept the inevitable.[4]

Rabbi Schneur Zalman had nothing but contempt for the man whose arrogance and lust for power knew no bounds, and who represented to the Chabad leader the embodiment of the *kelipah* itself, the antithesis of humility and holiness.

Moreover, Czar Alexander, from the day of his coronation, had shown a new spirit of liberalism, as we had occasion to note, and in fact personally ordered the release of Rabbi Schneur Zalman from his second arrest. The Chabad leader undoubtedly felt a sense of personal gratitude and loyalty to Alexander. These feelings were widely shared also by the Jews of Russia, and resulted in important aid to the Russian war effort.

The moving spirit behind the genuine Jewish patriotism was Rabbi Schneur Zalman. He urged his numerous followers to help the Russian war effort against the invaders in every possible way. With the aid of his followers behind the enemy lines, some of whom were employed by the French Military Command,[5] Rabbi Schneur Zalman was also able to render valuable intelligence service to the Russian generals at the front.

Even as Napoleon's armies were poised for the invasion of Russia, Rabbi Schneur Zalman instructed one of his devoted Chasidim, the above mentioned Moshe Meisels, to be ready to render intelligence service to Russia's Military High Command. Being able to speak and write French, he was to offer his services to the French—in one capacity or another—gain their confidence, and pass on any information of military value through confidential Chasidic channels to the Russian High Command.

As the Rebbe had foreseen, the French, after their occupation of Kovno and Vilna, did in fact seek men with knowledge of Russian and French for various duties. Moshe Meisels then received a responsible position on the technical staff of the French High Command. Knowing the good feelings which the Jews of Poland harbored for the French, whom they welcomed as liberators, Napoleon had no reason to suspect the Jews of Kovno and Vilna, former Polish provinces, of disloyalty. Moshe Meisels won the confidence of his employers. He was given a job in the strategic department, where Russian maps were carefully studied and prepared for the commanders of the invading troops. He also assisted in the translation of various documents and proclamations into Lithuanian, Polish and Russian, and vice versa, since he was well versed in these languages. Thus Moshe Meisels had access to highly classified material in the French High Command at the front, which he passed on, at obvious peril, to the Russians, through trustworthy channels prepared by the Alter Rebbe.[6]

These patriotic and very valuable services earned him the grateful recognition of the Russian generals, and also reached the attention of Alexander. Eventually Moshe Meisels also became a "persona grata" at the court of Alexander, a position he used to good advantage whenever a personal intercession with the Czar in Jewish interests was required.[7]

Rabbi Schneur Zalman was convinced of the ultimate debacle of Napoleon's armies, and predicted that Napoleon's downfall would be brought about by his own compatriots.[8]

When the French armies approached Liadi, the Russian generals advised Rabbi Schneur Zalman to flee. In August (1812) Rabbi Schneur Zalman hastily left Liadi, leaving everything behind, and fled with his family towards Smolensk. No sooner did the refugees reach Smolensk than they had to continue their flight in the face of the advancing invader. For some five months Rabbi Schneur Zalman and his family suffered the hardships and perils of the road and of an unusually inclement winter, until they reached a village in the district of Kursk. Here the aged Rabbi succumbed to a severe illness which he contracted in the final stages of the harrowing journey, and passed away at the age of sixty-eight. Chasidic tradition has taken note of Rabbi Schneur Zalman's life-span, pointing out that sixty-eight is the numerical equivalent of the Hebrew word *chayyim* ("life").[9]

Traditions and records preserved in the family of Rabbi Schneur Zalman provide interesting details in connection with Rabbi Schneur Zalman's last and fateful journey.

From an account by Rabbi Nachum, the son of Rabbi Dov Ber, and grandson of Rabbi Schneur Zalman, relating his personal experiences, we learn the following details:

It was on Friday (the weekly *sidrah* being *Re'eh*), 29th of *Menachem Av*, the day before *Rosh Chodesh Elul* (5572/1812) that the Alter Rebbe fled from Liadi on the advice of the generals commanding the Russian armies in that area. Sixty wagons were put at his disposal, but they were not enough, and many had to walk on foot. A number of armed troops were assigned to accompany and protect the caravan. In view of the rapid advance of the French army, the generals suggested that the best route for the flight would be through the town of Bayev. But the Alter Rebbe decided to head for Krasna, urging the caravan to make the utmost haste, in order to cross the river Dnieper at the earliest possible time.

After covering a distance of about two miles, the Alter Rebbe suddenly requested the accompanying troops to let him have one light carriage with a team of good horses. He got into the carriage with two companions and, accompanied by two armed guards who acted as drivers, hastened back to Liozna. Arriving at his deserted house, he ordered his men to search the house carefully to make sure that nothing whatever, however trivial, had been overlooked. The only things found were a pair of worn out slippers, a rolling pin and a sieve, which had been left in the attic. He ordered these to be taken along, and to set the house on fire before the enemy arrived, first removing the sacred Torah scrolls from the adjacent synagogue. Then he blessed those of the townspeople that remained in the town, and speedily departed again.

No sooner had he left the town on the road leading to the Dnieper than the *avant-coureur* of Napoleon's army reached the town from the opposite end. Presently, Napoleon himself with his entourage entered the town on their galloping steeds. Napoleon inquired after the house of the Alter Rebbe, but when he reached it, he found it ablaze, the fire burning beyond control. Napoleon wished to have something which belonged to the Alter Rebbe and offered a rich reward to anyone who could bring him anything that belonged to the Alter Rebbe or his household. But nothing was there to be brought to him.

In the meantime, the Alter Rebbe reached and crossed the Dnieper and soon overtook his caravan. They continued the journey in all haste until about half an hour before sunset, when they reached a village. There they remained the entire Shabbat. At the termination of the Shabbat, they resumed their journey, travelling right through the night. The following day, the second of *Elul*, they reached Krasna and rested there.

The following Friday (*sidrah* of *Shoftim*), 6th of *Elul*, upon receipt of news of further French advancement, the flight was resumed. The wagon in which the Alter Rebbe traveled was the third in the caravan. At the head was the wagon in which Rabbi Nachum was traveling, together with two armed soldiers. Whenever the caravan reached a crossroads, Rabbi Nachum would halt and turn to his grandfather for directions. In most cases the Alter Rebbe would get out of his carriage and walk up to the crossroads. There he would lean on his walking staff, engrossed in contemplation, and coming out of the reverie, he would point to the way and give precise instructions as to the direction and road to follow.

On one occasion, after receiving such instructions, Rabbi Nachum, leading the caravan, took a wrong turn. Some ten miles later, the Alter Rebbe enquired if they had not passed a certain village on the way. Thereupon Rabbi Nachum realized his error and in great distress informed his grandfather of it. The Alter Rebbe sighed deeply, and remarked: "Good it is when the grandson follows the road chosen by his grandfather, and the reverse is the result when the grandfather is compelled to follow the road chosen by the grandson."

All the Chasidim accompanying the Alter Rebbe knew that he had expressed the fervent hope, "May the Almighty have mercy and enable us to reach the district of Poltava before Rosh Hashanah." Rabbi Nachum's error resulted in a great deal of added delays and troubles and perhaps was even the cause of the fatal illness which the Alter Rebbe contracted on the way. Rabbi Nachum never forgave himself for his error and suffered remorse all his life.[10]

According to a further account, Rabbi Schneur Zalman was very reluctant to leave Liadi for various reasons, not the least of them in order not to create any panic among the Jews of White Russia. That is why he waited until the very last moment, when he received word that Napoleon had crossed Borodino and advanced some thirty miles in one day. The Russian strategy was to harass the invaders rather than engage their huge forces in a decisive battle. So the main Russian armies fell back step by step, while they laid waste the country as they retreated. The rapid French advance compelled the Alter Rebbe to flee in great haste.

The Rebbe took with him all the members of his family who lived with him, numbering some thirty persons. Not included in the group were Rabbi Schneur Zalman's youngest son Rabbi Moshe, who was living with his father-in-law in the city of Ulla, and his brother Rabbi Yehuda Leib who was then in Yanowitz, in the district of Vitebsk. About ten of his closest Chasidim accompanied the Rebbe on his flight.

Rabbi Schneur Zalman had to abandon all his possessions, being able to take but a few light chattels with him. It has been related also that in the excitement of the hasty flight, one of Rabbi Schneur Zalman's grandchildren, a two-year old boy, was lost. Fortunately they had not gone very far. A search all the way back to the town discovered the missing boy by the wayside crying.[11] The flight was then resumed.

According to this tradition the French, upon entering Liadi, and finding his house in flames, were so disappointed and angered that they burnt down also the Rebbe's synagogue.

As already mentioned, Rabbi Schneur Zalman and his family and accompanying Chasidim, some of them with families of their own, spent nearly five months in their flight from the path of the invading French armies. On the 8th day of *Tevet*, in the midst of a severe winter, the caravan finally reached the village of Piena.

During all this long and arduous journey Rabbi Schneur Zalman kept in touch with the situation of Russian Jewry caught in the holocaust of the gigantic Franco-Russian war. He received detailed information on the terrible plight of his brethren in White Russia, the main invasion route of the enemy. The retreating Russian armies, using the scorched earth policy in order to deprive the enemy of vitally needed supplies, exacted a tremendous sacrifice from its own people. At the same time, the invading armies plundered everything they could lay their hands on. Starvation and ruination were the order of the day, and the Rebbe's heart went out to his suffering brethren, who were the most hard-hit victims of the invasion. Rabbi Schneur Zalman was also greatly distressed by the reports he received from the cities of Vitebsk, Kovno and Vilna, where there was a great deal of fraternization with the occupational troops, and the standards of morality and decency sank to a low ebb.

There was one bright note during this painful journey, as related by Rabbi Schneur Zalman's grandson, Rabbi Menachem Mendel, the famed "Tzemach Tzedek." On the termination of Shabbat (*Sidrah Vayyetze*), 10th of *Kislev*, when they were in the village of Zemievka, in the district of Tambov, the Rebbe predicted that during the following week Napoleon would suffer a debacle at Moscow, and his fate, which had been sealed on the previous Rosh Hashanah, would actually come to pass soon.

On the following day, 11th of *Kislev*, they left the village of Zemievka and, traveling from village to village, they came to the village of Yeseyevka on Wednesday. The following day, being the 15th of *Kislev*, the Rebbe observed the annual fast of the *Chevrah Kadisha*, being a lifelong member of that society. After the

222

evening service and breaking his fast, the Rebbe invited his followers to drink "L'Chayim" in celebration of Napoleon's miserable retreat from Moscow that same day. His joy at the defeat of the "Little Corporal," whom he considered the arch-enemy of the Jewish faith, was marred, however, by the painful thoughts of the renewed suffering of his brethren. For the Rebbe knew that the retreating, starved, freezing and bedraggled remnants of the once proud French army would plunder the vestiges of the Jewish settlements in their path. The thought of the untold new miseries awaiting his brethren sent tears streaming down his face.

Arriving in Piena on the 8th of *Tevet*, Rabbi Schneur Zalman decided to stay there for a rest. The village of Piena was a large one, with fairly large houses which were half empty, inasmuch as most of the male population had been mobilized into the Russian army. The villagers were friendly and offered the distinguished but destitute refugees relatively comfortable quarters and firewood without charge.

Without losing any time, the Alter Rebbe embarked upon a relief campaign for the Jewish victims of the war. He said that he would take up residence for the duration of this campaign in Little Russia. Faced with the problem of Jewish refugees from the stricken areas, and in order not to create a shortage in housing and food, the Rebbe planned to have them divided into three groups, to be settled in three places, namely the towns of Hadiacz, Krementchug and Romnia.

Rabbi Schneur Zalman appointed three delegations in order to implement his plan. One delegation, headed by his older son Rabbi Dov Ber, was sent to the said towns for the purpose of making the necessary arrangements to prepare housing for the refugees. A second delegation, headed by his son Rabbi Chaim Abraham, was dispatched to the districts of Poltava and Cherson to raise funds for the rehabilitation of the Jews of White Russia. A third delegation, headed by the prominent Chasid, Pinchas Schick of Shklov, was sent to Vitebsk to supervise the distribution of the relief and to arrange the most practical ways of rehabilitating the impoverished war victims, so that they could get onto their own feet.

For ten days following his arrival in Piena, Rabbi Schneur

Zalman worked feverishly on his plans and projects to alleviate the plight of his brethren. Then, on Monday, 18th of *Tevet*, he fell ill. His condition became steadily worse from day to day. At the termination of the following Shabbat (*Sidrah Shmot*), Rabbi Schneur Zalman recited the Evening Prayer and the *Havdalah* with complete lucidity of mind[12] then he requested pen and paper and composed the following cryptic letter:

The truly humble soul, at its root—its task is to practice Torah, for its [the soul's] own [benefit] and for [the benefit of] others, through material deeds of loving kindness, friendliness and good counsel from a distance, [and] in all family matters. Though the vast majority [of such acts] are [concerned with] false matters, it is impossible to practice true kindness otherwise, for the only Truth is the Torah, and Truth said "[man] should not be created" [for he is full of falsehoods], etc., while Kindness said, "Let him be created," for he is full of loving kindnesses. And Truth was thrown to the ground, and the world was created in loving kindness without the truth.[13]

In early generations, when the essence of Divine service was Torah, the quality of Kindness was mostly included in that of Truth, that is, in efforts to induce others [to do good deeds], in enforcing *Tzedakah* contributions,[14] etc., by authority of the Torah of Truth [taught] by the Sages. However in [these days of] the "footsteps" (imminent arrival) of Moshiach, when the Falling Tabernacle of David has fallen to the ground, in the realm of *Asiyah* and the essence of [Divine] service is in a category no higher than "footsteps," without the Torah of Truth, the *Mishnayot* and *Beraytot*, the "wings" and "thighs"—most of the kindness is not in accord with Torah of Truth in benevolent endeavor, but only through the favor and good will of the doer, which are far from genuine, and the end of the deed is rooted in the thought preceding it. But even if there be no other way and it is a lowly one, man's consolation is to accept it with love, or to search his deeds and return unto G-d in his distress, and then he shall have relief.

A few minutes after he penned this profoundly mystical message, the Alter Rebbe was finally granted relief from his weary sojourn on earth, and he returned his soul to his Maker.[15]

His body was taken to the town of Hadiacz, in the district of Poltava, where he was laid to rest. A tomb was erected over his grave, and it has ever since attracted numerous pilgrims who come to pray at his grave, especially on the anniversary of his demise (24th of *Tevet*).

The Hebrew inscription on his tombstone reads as follows:

Here is concealed the Holy Ark / The great and divine *Rav*, pious and humble / Holy and Pure, diadem of Ariel / Crown of the Truth, wellspring of wisdom / He practiced the righteousness of the Lord and His judgments with Israel / And many did he turn back from sin / Our master and teacher Schneur Zalman, the son of Baruch, his soul rest in Eden / Longing for holiness, his soul returned to the Lord / On the first day of the week, 24th of *Tevet* / In the year 5573 of Creation.[16]

Some details and insights relating to Rabbi Schneur Zalman's last days are provided in a long letter written by his son and successor, Rabbi Dov Ber Schneuri (known as the "Mitteler Rebbe") to Moshe Meisels. It reads, with a few abbreviations, as follows:

To my life-long beloved friend, whom I cherish like my own soul, a man of loyal spirit and great wisdom, etc.

I shall not conceal from my intimate friend all that has happened to us in the bygone year, in the time of the holocaust: the great miracles and wonders, and awesome Divine signs which, as we have witnessed, happened to the Light of Israel, our father of blessed memory, *may I be an atonement for his grave.*[17] Not a single word nor half a word that issued from his holy mouth failed; in the manner of true prophecy; as we now clearly see, for unto all Jews there is light, joy and gladness, etc. [at the defeat of Napoleon].

The beginning of the matter was as follows:

As soon as the enemy, the notorious oppressor and wholesale murderer, entered the borders of Poland, into

Kovno and Vilna, etc., [my father] began to deliberate with us about fleeing into the interior of Russia, and no other place. He said that if [Napoleon] will not wax too arrogant and act foolishly, it is possible that he will fortify himself and stay in Poland (but G-d frustrated his mind, and this was the root of his downfall . . .). At any rate, it is a great distress for the Jews, for not one will remain [steadfast] in his Judaism, nor retain his possessions. "I hate him with complete hatred" [my father said], "for he is Satan who opposes the good with every manner of evil; he is the force of the *kelipah* and stern judgment, the opposite of loving kindness and goodness, indeed death and evil. . . . But I am assured that he will not last, as it is written, 'Evil kills the wicked,' and 'the kindness of G-d [persists] all day,' and *chesed* (Kindness) prevails over *din* (Judgment). . . ." He said explicitly that . . . the war between *chesed* and *gevurah* is like that of water and fire, where water prevails. . . . The two essential aspects of the enemy are, first, his petulance and callousness, destroying countless lives without any feeling whatsoever, in his quest for victory at all costs, even to self-destruction; secondly, his arrogance and haughtiness, to claim all credit for his might and power and his unique military sagacity and prowess to conduct warfare . . . Concerning such it is said, The man who will not put his strength and trust in G-d, G-d will bring him down to the nadir of degradation, in order to show that G-d is He who gives strength and valor, etc. . . . Indeed it has been clearly shown that his [Napoleon's] downfall was due to his pride and arrogance. . . .

[Father] said *Tehillim* every day, praying with heart and soul that G-d may increase His kindness and expel the evil. When [the enemy] approached Borisov on the way to Minsk, [my father] said there seemed no way [to halt his advance], and he sent frequent messengers to consult with [General] Tolotchin, and so forth, as I will relate to you in detail personally. At the request of the latter's superior, he conveyed everything to Vitebsk; and all his efforts to arrange for the gathering of intelligence were done with all his heart and soul. But subsequently, be foresaw that the enemy will extend his invasion deep into Russia, and because of his hatred for the enemy he resolved to flee, saying he would rather choose death than life under him, so as not to see the evil that would befall his people.

It is impossible to describe in writing the great haste of the flight, though he was old and very weak, through the winter cold and prostration, much beyond his strength, with the infants of his four families. But he absolutely did not wish to remain even for one day under the reign and servitude of the enemy.

We [our family] fled in two wagons crowded with children and adults, twenty-eight souls, with only the small chattels we could take, while all the heavy household things and stores of grain and wood, and domestic animals, etc., in the value of some two thousand rubles had to be left behind. All this was with the knowledge of General Elianov stationed at Liadi—if he is in your proximity give him my regards, for he knows us, having stayed in our house for a whole week, and he saw how deeply my father of saintly memory was affected, which is impossible to describe in writing; also of his superior, General Nebrovsky, who was stationed in Krasna at the beginning of the war; as explained at length in our petition to his Imperial Majesty through Count Tolstoy, Governor of Mohilev.

And now, my beloved friend, who is like a brother to me, I will relate to you what we have seen of G-d's wonders on our way from Liadi to the time of his demise in the village of Piena, near Kursk.

When we learned full well of the conduct of the enemy Marshall Davnich (may his name be blotted out) in Shklov and Dubrovna, [Father] did not wish to tarry even for a moment, and we traveled to Krasna to be with Generals Elianov and Nebrovsky. They gave us good passports.

On Friday before *Rosh Chodesh Elul*, an entire army of the enemy, together with the army of Vitebsk, some 40,000 men in all, suddenly approached Krasna, while our forces numbered no more than eight thousand. At this time

General Nebrovsky, who was under the command of Marshall Count Burtinka, was stationed at Smolensk with seventy thousand men. The enemy avoided our larger force, proceeding via Liadi and Krasna. When the enemy reached Krasna about noontime on that Friday, a hue and cry broke out in our midst. We did not know what to do, whether to escape to the woods, etc. Our aged mother, and all the women and children, burst into wailing, something indescribable. Then Father, of saintly memory, sternly rebuked them and quieted them, saying we would not flee to the woods, but would continue our journey in horse-drawn wagons. Presently the General came personally and urged us to flee in all haste to Smolensk, since the enemy had overwhelming numbers and nearly three hundred cannon. We fled at once, passing through our eight-thousand troops stationed outside the city in the direction of Smolensk. They had no more than eighteen cannon.

No sooner had we passed, than the enemy engaged our force. For three hours, while we were making our escape, we heard the sound of heavy artillery. We came to within thirteen *versts* of Smolensk. The road led through woods, where we spent all that night. It is impossible to relate to you in detail the miracles we experienced. At dawn the following morning we entered Smolensk. Neither French nor our troops were to be seen in the city. No one seemed to know anything about the situation, and we were asked for information. We conveyed it to the Count. Quickly a large force was gathered by midday, about 30,000 men and 120 cannon. We were unable to leave the city, and we were terribly distressed at what seemed to be the end for us. Towards evening, however, we left by the street leading to the Moscow road. My father, of saintly memory, ordered us to continue our journey through the Shabbat, saying it was not only permissible but a *mitzvah* to do so to save ourselves from those who would hurt us.

On Sunday we escaped together with the Governor of the City, Tolstoy, to Vyazma. On Wednesday we fled to Mazaisk. From Mazaisk we traveled by a round-about way, for father was familiar with the topography and in his inspired discernment knew that the enemy would make a detour. . . .

Last Rosh Hashanah we spent in Tritza Zerka, and about that time the battle at Mazaisk took place. He called me in and said, "I am much grieved, my son, about the battle of Mazaisk raging these days. May G-d grant that it turn out well, for the enemy is getting the upper hand, and I think he will take Moscow." He wept bitterly, and I wept too, and left.

On the day of Rosh Hashanah he called us in and told us pleasantly and consolingly, "Today I saw in prayer that there has been a change for the better, and that ours have won the war. And although the enemy will take Moscow, he will have no respite. Relief and deliverance will arise for us . . . so it was inscribed Above. . . ."

Then we ate and drank in good spirits, and we rejoiced with gladness of heart.

We traveled on to the town of Yura, near Vladimir, some seventy *versts*.

On *Shabbat-Shuvah* before the *Musaf* prayer, he called me and my son-in-law Rabbi Mendel. He burst into tears which came streaming down his cheeks and he cried, "Woe and alas! The whole of White Russia will be devastated by the retreating enemy. It is the balance of the Chmielnicki calamity, for he had not been in Little Russia and Lithuania, but rather in Wolhynia and the Ukraine. There will be mortal terror and ravages…

I said to him, "But, father, the enemy has not taken Moscow as yet, and if he does, perhaps he will go back in another direction?" To this he replied, "He will certainly take Moscow, and soon, for although he is already exhausted, and is like a corpse, his hard-won victory will . . . lead him on to Moscow. But immediately thereafter he will suffer a fall of incomparable humiliation, for he will not last there, and will turn back precisely by way of White Russia and not by way of Little Russia. Mark my word." And so it was.

On the day before Yom Kippur we arrived in Vladimir. [We learned that] the enemy had taken Moscow on the Monday before Yom Kippur, and on the day before Yom Kippur the entire Senate, fleeing [from Moscow], passed through Vladimir.

When I saw their rushing carriages I ran to Father, heartbroken, and with tears in my eyes. I called him to the window, saying, "See, Father, the flight of the Senate. What about your promise that the enemy will suffer a debacle upon taking Moscow?"

He came up to me, embraced me, and said these words stemming from the depth of his heart: "You see that I am now wearing *tefillin*, and I will not deceive you. I assure you on my very life that the enemy will not go beyond Moscow, but will soon turn back. He will not turn to Petersburg, but his aim will be to return home, and to find provisions en route through White Russia. But they [the Russians] will not let him, and his debacle will come soon, believe me."

. . . We traveled to the town of Assi, where we rested securely on the banks of the river Oka. Thence we traversed the districts of Razan and Tambov and the Ural, until we reached Kursk, a distance of some 1200 *versts*. It was the middle of *Kislev*, at the height of the winter cold. [We were suffering] in great distress, pains of hunger and cold, living on but coarse bread and water, and sheltering in the smoke-filled huts of the peasants, and so forth. There is no worse exile than that. And in all the villages we were met with hostility, insults and curses. But by G-d's grace, we found favor in the eyes of the landlords, and they let no evil befall us, for we traveled in sixty wagons, etc.

At Kursk a runner came with a message from Tolstoy to the local Governor to the effect that the enemy was chased for four days, from Kaluga to Vyazma. We felt very happy and thanked G-d for the good and kindness, and our joy was boundless. My wife had given birth to a son at the gates of Kursk. I arranged the *Brit* (circumcision) with a feast of white millet and good radishes, and with plenty of good liquor.

Thence we traveled to the village of Piena. On the 19th of *Kislev* we received news that the enemy suffered a crushing defeat at Krasna, and he is being chased like a dog. Our joy was sustained, for everything came true; not a thing or half a thing failed.

Alas, our peace was shattered, for just as our spirits had recovered, the crown of our head was taken from us. For, because of his deep-felt and sustained bitterness, his gall became infected, etc. He also contracted a severe cold because of his old age and weakness. For five days he lay ill until he succumbed on the night of the termination of Shabbat, *Sidrah Shemot*, 24th of *Tevet* past. I was away, for he had sent me to Krementchug to find a dwelling.

Woe unto our loss! Israel's glory has departed. May his merits stand us in good stead always. . . .

After his demise, he was taken over eighty *versts* to the town of Hadiacz, in the district of Poltava, located some twenty *versts* from this city, at the river Psal. The cemetery is located there in a small wood, near the said river, some two *versts* from the town.

I told my friend Ziskind of Vidz, your brother-in-law, what was to be done in this matter with the aid of Count Lubanov, and others. . . . We built a nice wooden dome [over the grave], also a large house [nearby], and have prepared bricks for a permanent structure in his honor, as in the case of ancestral tzaddikim, where people came to pray in times of distress, for "*tzaddikim* are greater in their death [than in their lifetime]." Last *Erev* Rosh Hashanah sixty Jews from Romen and Krementchug, etc., prayed there and lit many lamps. A person (guard) is always there. . . .

The letter goes on to urge Moshe Meisels to follow in his Rebbe's footsteps, including devoted loyalty to the Russian Emperor. It expresses the fervent hope that he would use his good standing with the Emperor to intercede in behalf of Russian Jewry, especially as the Emperor would recognize the valuable patriotic services which they had rendered during the war.

Rabbi Dov Ber makes a point of emphasizing the coincidence of Napoleon's final retreat from Kovno to the border of

Prussia with his father's day of death on the 24th of *Tevet*, "for to his last breath, he never ceased praying to G-d [for Napoleon's complete defeat and expulsion]. But his [Napoleon's] final end will come when his own compatriots will rebel against him, as the Alter Rebbe stated frequently."

Rabbi Dov Ber further referred to many confidential and wondrous things which he had heard from his late father at the time of the battle at Mazaisk regarding the fate of Moscow, and the British. These he (Rabbi Dov Ber) conveyed to Meisels orally through his brother-in-law Ziskind of Vidz, "for such awesome and wonderful matters are not to be written down, and not to be revealed, except to individual men of trust and truth."[18]

Thus came to an end the eventful and productive life of Rabbi Schneur Zalman. It was a life sadly harassed to the end by events and circumstances beyond his control, but never lacking in inner peace and harmony.

Rabbi Schneur Zalman was a man of many colorful facets, all harmoniously complementing each other. The rationalist and mystic, the Kabbalist and Talmudist, the saint and the man of the world, the humble worshipper and the sagacious leader—all were harmoniously blended together into the unique personality of Rabbi Schneur Zalman, and each coming forcefully to the fore as the occasion demanded. He was known to attain the loftiest heights of mystical communion, so that in moments of ecstasy during prayer he could batter his knuckles against the wall to the point of bleeding (his disciples eventually affixed a soft pad on the wall), yet he would hear the cry of a child next door and interrupt his meditation or study to comfort it. Knowing as he did the consuming bliss of soulful devotion, he was heard to exclaim, "I do not want Your Paradise, I do not want Your World-to-Come; I want only You, You alone!"[19] Yet he could tear himself away from his supernal state in order to find time to receive and console a stricken widow, or help a poor innkeeper thrown out into the road for lack of rent. He was a humble and peace-loving man, humble enough to disclaim any originality for his philosophic system, and conciliatory towards his adversaries. Yet he was indomitable and ready to suffer martyrdom for his ideals and convictions.

These characteristics were in Rabbi Schneur Zalman more than natural traits of a noble character. They were the embodiment of his philosophic system, of which the "supremacy of spirit over matter" was a basic principle. He was not an abstract philosopher or moralist whose mind floated in a world of pure speculation; he truly practiced what he preached. He lived with his people and for his people, and this, perhaps more than anything else, accounts for the tremendous following which he had acquired in his lifetime.

The Chabad ideology and way of life which Rabbi Schneur Zalman introduced nearly two centuries ago, has well withstood the test of time. The Chabad system has not been shaken by all the transilience which characterizes the last two centuries of the history of mankind at large, and of the Jewish people in particular. Chabad today is as vigorous and dynamic a force in Jewish life as it ever was.

NOTES

Notes

Introduction

1. The term *Chasid* (literally "benevolent") is to be found in the Bible (Deut. 33:8; I Sam. 2:9; II Sam. 22:26; Jer. 3:12, et al.). In the Psalms, where the term is found frequently, it is generally used in the sense of saintliness and piety. In this sense it came down to rabbinic literature. (Rabbi Elijah of Vilna, the great opponent of the Chasidic movement, was given the title "*Chasid*.") In Talmudic literature the title is associated with one who goes beyond the call of duty in the performance of his religious and social obligations. According to Rabbi Schneur Zalman's interpretation, based on *Tosafot, Niddah* 17a, the term implied self-sacrifice. Cf. *Likutei Diburim* by Rabbi Yosef Y. Schneersohn, published by Kehot Publication Society (Brooklyn, NY, 1957), Vol. 1, p. 135.

As a characterization of a specific group of religious devotees, the term goes back to the so-called Second Commonwealth, when the name Chasidim, or Chasideans, was given to the pious Jews who resisted Hellenization, and suffered martyrdom (I Macc. 1:59-68; 7:12-14; II Macc. 6:9-11.). Cf. Victor Tcherikover, Hellenistic Civilization and the Jews, JPS (Philadelphia, 1959), pp. 196 ff; S. W. Baron, A Social and Religious History of the Jews, JPS (Philadelphia, 1952), Vol. I, p. 237.

In Chabad the term Chasid has an essentially mystical connotation, based on the *Zoharitic* definition, "Who is a Chasid? He who deals benevolently with his Maker" (*Zohar*, Vilna, 1937 ["Rom" ed.] II. 114b; III. 222b, 281a; *Tikunei Zohar*, Introduction) Cf. *Tanya*, end of chap. 10. It is primarily in the light of this definition that the followers of the Baal Shem Tov derived their name Chasidim. Cf. *Likutei Diburim*, op.cit., Vol. III, p. 1029.

2. *Chabad* is a term derived from the initial letters of the three Hebrew words, *chochmah* ("wisdom"), *binah* ("understanding") and *da'at* ("knowledge")-the first three of the Ten *Sefirot*. These terms will be defined later. Suffice it here to say that Chabad represents the "intellectual" school of Chasidut, founded by Rabbi Schneur Zalman.

3. We can pinpoint the exact year when it began to function as a movement. The Hebrew date of Rabbi Israel Baal Shem Tov's birthday was 18th of *Elul*, 5458 (known in Chasidic lore as the year of נח"ת-delight), corresponding to September, 1698. According to Chasidic tradition, the Baal Shem Tov "revealed" himself, i.e., emerged as leader of the new movement, on his 36th birthday, namely, in 1734.

4. *Evreyskaia enciklopedia*, ed. Dr. L. Katzenelson, Petersburg, Vol. XV, p. 561.

5. Cf S. A. Horodetzky, *Shelosh Meot Shanah shel Yahadut Polin* (Tel Aviv, 1946), pp. 97ff.

6. Aaron Marcus, *HaChasidut*. trans. M. Schonfeld (Tel Aviv, 1953), p. 36.

7. Cf. Solomon Zeitlin, *"The Am Haarez"* in JQR, New Series, Vol. 23, No. 1 (1932), pp. 45-61. S. W. Baron, *SRHJ*, Vol. I, pp. 278, 280; II pp. 242, 272, 282, 286.

8. S.W. Baron *SRHJ*, Vol. II, pp. 120 ff.

9. S.W. Baron *SRHJ*, Vol. 1. p. 278.

10. For a description of *yeshiva* education in Eastern Europe in the first half of the 17th century see *Yeven Metzulah* (Venice, 1653) by Rabbi Nathan Hannover, a contemporary.

11. The name "Adam," quite unusual among Jews, has raised doubts as to the historicity of Adam Baal Shem. The most prevalent opinion among scholars is that this is a purely legendary figure. The present writer, however, questions the validity of this conclusion on several grounds. Firstly, argumentum a silentio is generally considered a weak argument. Secondly, if it were fictitious, and invented for a particular motive, a more credible name would have been chosen. Thirdly, the tradition about Adam Baal Shem had an early acceptance, being current already among the Baal Shem Tov's disciples.

It has been suggested that "Adam" might be an abbreviation of Abraham David Moshe. This view, too, may be disputed on the ground that if "Adam" were an abbreviation. the full name would have been mentioned occasionally in the Chasidic literature.

At any rate, the authenticity of his existence and name cannot be disputed, since it has been conveyed by the heads of Chabad from generation to generation, without reservation.

12. About the activities of the *Ba'alei Shem* see Memoirs of Rabbi Yosef Y. Schneersohn, translated and edited by Nissan Mindel, published by Otzar HaChasidim (Brooklyn, NY., Vol. I [3rd ed.], 1956; Vol. II, 1960). Alphabetical Index at end of Vol. II. The Memoirs were originally edited in Yiddish by David L. Meckler and published in the Jewish daily *Der Morgen Journal*.

The title "Memoirs" is used in this case in a broad sense, as the material comprises oral and recorded traditions relating to the Chasidic and Chabad movements, mostly transmitted methodically from father to son (a practice instituted by Rabbi Schneur Zalman, the progenitor of the Chabad-Lubavitch dynasty), as well as material from other sources. Some of the material is not free from embellishment insofar as style and form are concerned, but basically it is an authentic historical source, which throws considerable light on the origins of the movement and contemporary life.

13. *Memoirs.* op. cit., Vol. II, p. xi.

14. *Likutei Diburim*, op. cit., Vol. I, p. 166.

15. Pantheistic though it sounds, it must not be understood in any sense of Spinozian pantheism, as will be explained in due course.

16. Beginning of *Sha'ar HaYichud VehaEmunah* (Part II of *Tanya*).

17. Exod. 3:2.

18. Cf. *The Commandments*, by Nissan Mindel, published by Kehot Publication Society (Brooklyn, NY, 1956 [3rd ed.]), p. 46. *Kuntres Chicago*, Otzar HaChasidim (Brooklyn, NY, 1944), pp. 22-24.

19. *Mal.* 3:12.

20. *Hayom Yom*, ed. Rabbi Menachem Schneerson, Kehot Publication Society (Brooklyn. NY, 1957 [3rd ed.]), p. 54.

21. A reference to Ps. 90:10.

22. *Likutei Diburim*, op. cit., Vol. III, p. 1126.

23. Deut. 28:47; Ps. 100:2.

24. Prof. B. Dinur in "Reshitah shel HaChasidut Visodoteha HaSozialiyim VehaMeshichiyim," *Zion*, Vol. VIII (Jerusalem, 1942-43), esp. chs. 12-15, and *Zion* Vol. XX (1945-55), p. 80, expressed the opinion that the Baal Shem did have Messianic aspirations. However, see G. Scholem's critique of Dinur's views in "Demuto HaHistorit shel HaBesht," *Molad*. Vol. XVIII (Jerusalem, August-September, 1960), pp. 335-356.

25. *Likutei Diburim*, op. cit., Vol. I, p. 164; Vol. II, pp. 572, 618.

26. For a partial list of source books containing the teachings of the Baal Shem see *Kuntres Torat HaChasidut*, by Rabbi Yosef Y. Schneersohn, Otzar HaChasidim Lubavitz (Brooklyn, NY, 1957), pp. 25.

27. *Likutei Diburim*, op. cit., Vol. IV. p. 1320.

28. Ibid., Vol. II, p. 522.

29. While the first Haskalah polemics against the Chasidic movement began much earlier (e.g., *Mirkevet HaMishneh*, by Solomon Helma, 1751; *Nezed HaDema*, by Israel of Zamosc, 1773; *Toldot Chayyai*, by Solomon Maimon, 1792), the real literary campaign was

launched by the Maskilim of Galicia during the years 1815-1840. Cf. Shmuel Verses' article, "HaChasidut be'sifrut Hahaskalah," *Molad*, op. cit., pp. 379-391. In Lithuania and Russia the first impact of the Haskalah came even somewhat later with the publication of Isaac Ber Lebensohn's *Te'udah b'Yisrael* (Vilna, 1828). The influence of the secularists on the Jewish community was hardly felt before 1840; cf. I. Levitas, *Jewish Community in Russia 1772-1844*, Columbia University Press (New York, 1943), p. 80. On the struggle between Chabad and Haskalah, see *Admur HaTzemach Tzedek u'Tenuas HaHaskalah*, KPS (Brooklyn, NY 1957 [2nd ed.]). At any rate, the limit of our present review is 1813, the year of Rabbi Schneur Zalman's demise. About Rabbi Schneur Zalman's encounter with the Haskalah see chap. VIII.

30. *Kuntres Torat HaChasidut*, op. cit., p. 25, n. 1.

Chapter One / Birth and Childhood

1. Boruchovitch ("son of Boruch") was Rabbi Schneur Zalman's surname in official Russian documents. His son and successor, Rabbi Dov Ber, adopted the family name Schneuri. Succeeding generations in line of succession adopted the name of Schneersohn, or Schneerson.

2. The 18th of *Elul* is also the birthday of the Baal Shem Tov.

3. Accordingly, the date of birth given by M. Teitelbaum and others should be amended.

4. Biographical data concerning Rabbi Schneur Zalman's parents and ancestral background will be found in the *Memoirs*. op. cit., vols. I and II. Cf. *Beit Rebbi*, Ch. M. Hilman (Berditchev, 1903), ch. 24, about the last years of RSZ. Also D. Z. Hilman, *Iggarot Baal HaTanya* (Jerusalem, 1953), footnote on p. 1. There is evidence to indicate that RSZ's father died ca. 1790.

5. Best known of RSZ's brothers was Rabbi Yehuda Leib of Yanowitz, author of a halachic work, *Sheirit Yehuda*, KPS (Brooklyn, NY, 1957 [2nd ed.]). He recorded many of RSZ's discourses and edited the latter's *Shulchan Aruch* as stated in the preface of that work.

6. On the significance of this and other communal institutions, cf. I. Levitas, *The Jewish Community in Russia*, op. cit., ch. IV.

7. *Memoirs*. vol. II, pp. 180 ff. The genealogy runs as follows: (1) Yehuda Lowe (Maharal); (2) his son Betzalel; (3) latter's son Shmuel; (4) latter's son Yehuda Leib: (5) his son Moshe: (6) his son Schneur Zalman: (7) his son Boruch, father of Rabbi Schneur Zalman, founder of Chabad.

8. Cf. Introduction, p. XV f.

9. *Likutei Diburim*, vol. IV, P. 956.

10. *Memoirs*, vol. 1, ch. 6.

11. The appellation *HaMalach* ("The Angel") was given to him because of his saintliness of character and aloofness from mundane affairs. Rabbi Abraham, the only son of the Maggid of Miezricz, (d. 1780, in Fastov, Russia) is the author of a Kabbalistic work *Chesed L'Abraham*, published by his grandson Rabbi Yisrael of Ruzhin (Czernowitz, 1851). Cf. Aaron Marcus, *HaChasidut*, pp. 282 f.

12. Cf. Lev. 19:27; *Makkot* 20b. According to this custom a Jewish boy receives his first haircut on, or soon after, his third birthday, when sidelocks *(peyot)* are left. The size and length of the peyot are the subject of halachic discussion. Polish, Galician, Hungarian and Yemenite Jews are noted for the length of their *peyot*. Chabad Chasidim, not given to conspicuousness in external appearance, use moderation also in this respect. To them the custom of the first haircut came to be regarded essentially as the day of the boy's initiation into elementary Jewish education and training. Until recent years many a Lubavitcher Chasid within reasonable distance, and sometimes even from abroad, used to bring his three-year-old to the Rebbe for the haircutting ceremony (in Yiddish: *Obsherenish*), so that the Rebbe would cut off the first tuft of hair. However, finding it increasingly difficult to take time out for this ceremony, the Rebbe later sent a letter to the parents in lieu of personal participation. The following is the text of an excerpt included in such a typical letter, which is quoted in the name of his father-in-law, the sixth Lubavitcher Rebbe:

... Regarding the matter of the haircutting-*Obsherenish*-it is a meaningful practice of Jewish custom. Essentially it is the ceremony of leaving peyot for the first time, and the occasion serves to inaugurate the boy, from that day on, into such religious practices as wearing a *Tallit-katan (Tzitzit)*, the recital of the Morning Benedictions, Grace after meals, and reading of the *Shema* before going to bed.

13. *HaYom Yom* (KPS 1998), p. 57.

14. Text of the entry is given in *Beit Rebbi*, ch. 1. According to the inscription, the pledge of the contribution was made by the boy's grandfather, without specification whether the paternal or maternal grandfather was the donor. Both were living at that time. Cf. *Iggarot Baal HaTanya*, p. 2, notes.

15. *Likutei Diburim*, vol. III, p. 964.

16. Lubavitch ("Town of Love") in the county of Mohilev, White Russia, has an early history of mystics, the forerunner of the Chasidim. (Cf. *Memoirs*, vol. I, chapts. I and II, and further.) It became the residence of the heads of the Chabad-Lubavitch movement in 1814, when Rabbi Dov Ber, son and successor of RSZ, settled there. For over a cen-

tury (until 1915) and four generations of Chabad leaders, it remained the center of the movement. Hence the leaders of Chabad became known as the "Lubavitcher Rebbes," and their Chasidim as "Lubavitcher Chasidim," *Likutei Diburim*, vol. 1, p. 230 f.

17. Also known as Rabbi Issachar Ber Kobilniker. He held the position of "Maggid" in Lubavitch. Subsequently he participated in Rabbi Schneur Zalman's communal activities. The latter loved and honored him as "the treasure of my heart and soul; a friend and brother he is to me." *Iggarot Baal HaTanya*, pp. 30-31, and footnote.

18. *Likutei Diburim*, vol. IV, p. 1204.

19. Cf. *Outlines of the Social and Communal Work of Chabad-Lubavitch*, KPS (Brooklyn. NY, 1953), p. 13. Henceforth abbreviated to *Chabad-Lubavitch*.

20. *Sefer HaMaamarim, 5709*, KPS (Brooklyn, NY), pp. 87-88.

21. *Memoirs* (unpublished), by Rabbi Yosef Y. Schneersohn. Only the first two volumes of Rabbi Schneersohn's Memoirs have appeared thus far (the Yiddish version was edited by D. L. Meckler), as already noted (Note 12, Introduction.) The remainder of the material is still in manuscript in the Schneersohn Library. It is not catalogued nor systematically paginated, but can be identified under the title "Memoirs (unpublished)." Future reference to this particular source will be made under this title.

22. *Memoirs* (unpublished), op. cit. The names of the two brothers are given as Yaakov Tzvi and Menachem Elia. At the age of ten, Schneur Zalman compiled a calendar for fifteen years (5515-5530, i.e., 1755-70), indicating the equinoxes, solstices, new moons, Jewish festival days, and other data for each year of this period. During the first few years, Schneur Zalman marked on it also the days of the annual fairs in Liozna. For many years this almanac was preserved in the family among other relics. It consisted of 30 pages of thick paper, written in green ink, and bound in brown leather. It was destroyed during a big fire on the fifth day of *Elul*, 5616 (1856), Ibid.

23. Text of this second entry in the *pinkas* will be found in *Beit Rebbi*. ch. 1. See also *Iggarot Baal HaTanya*, beginning. M. Teitelbaum, *HaRav Miliadi, uMifleget Chabad* (Warsaw, 1910), vol. 1, p. 3, note 1. The date given there is incorrect, however.

24. *Likutei Diburim*, vol. III. p. 967.

25. *Chabad-Lubavitch*, op. cit., pp. 13-14.

26. I. G. Orshansky, *Russkoye zakonodatelstvo o evreiakh* (Petersburg, 1877), pp. 167 f.

27. Memoirs (unpublished), where both episodes are related in detail.

28. Preface to his *Shulchan Aruch*. On the testimony of his sons, who heard it from their father, Rabbi Schneur Zalman went through the entire Talmud with all early and late codifiers sixteen times by the time he was thirty years old, "studying on his feet, night and day."

CHAPTER TWO / "CONVERSION" TO CHASIDUT

1. Rabbi Elijah (1720-1797) was recognized as the greatest authority on the Talmud and Jewish learning in his day. He held no official position, but his fame was widespread. He excelled also in Kabbala. When he was thirty-five years old, the famed Rabbi Jonathan Eybeschutz (then about sixty-five) appealed to him to mediate and render a decision in the dispute between him and the equally famous Rabbi Jacob Emden on the question of the former's amulets (*kameot*) for which he was accused of Shabattian leanings. See also Introduction, p. 11.

2. Rabbi Dov Ber was born in Lukatchi, Wolhynia (date unknown), and died in Anipoli, Ukraine, on the 19th of Kislev, 5532 (1772). As an itinerant preacher for many years he gained fame as The Great Maggid, and as an outstanding Talmudist. He never accepted a rabbinic post. When he was stricken with an ailment seriously affecting his legs, he was persuaded by friends to visit the Baal Shem Tov who had become famous as a miraculous healer. From then on he never left the Baal Shem Tov until the latter's death several years later. This period was sufficient for his brilliant mind to master the teachings of the Besht, which he eventually expanded into a mystico-rational philosophical system. He is credited with being the real organizer of the Chasidic movement during the twelve years of his leadership in succession to the Besht. His reputation as a Talmudic scholar attracted many other Talmudic scholars who became his disciples, giving the movement additional stature. Like his predecessor, he left no written works, but his disciples compiled his teachings in two books, *Maggid Devoro l'Yaakov* and Likutei Amarim.

3. *Likutei Diburim*, vol. III, p. 966.

4. *Beit Rebbi*, p. 3, n. 2.

5. Ibid., n. 3. *Sefer HaMaamarim 5708*, KPS (Brooklyn, NY), p. 176.

6. *Kuntres Torat HaChasidut* by Rabbi Yosef Y. Schneersohn, published by Otzar HaChasidim Lubavitz (Brooklyn, NY, 1951), p. 11.

7. Ibid.

8. See Chap. 1, note 11.

9. *Hatamim*, pub. by Tomchei Tmimim Lubavitz (Warsaw), vol. II, p. 46.

10. Ibid., p. 48.

11. *Sefer HaSichot 5700*, KPS (Brooklyn, NY), p. 171.

12. *Likutei Diburim*, vol. II, p. 492.

13. On the comparative positions and functions of a *Rav* (Rabbi) and *Maggid*, cf. *The Jewish Community in Russia*, op. cit., pp. 151 ff., 167 ff.

14. For a comprehensive list of the various publishings of the "Rav's" *Shulchan Aruch*, see Supplement at the end of this book.

It is significant that with the exception of the first section, published in 1794, the Rav's *Shulchan Aruch* was published posthumously. This would seem to refute the allegation current in opposition circles that the purpose of the *Shulchan Aruch* was schismatic, namely, "to provide the Chasidim with a *Shulchan Aruch* of their own."

15. *Kitzurim VeHaorot LeTanya*, KPS (Brooklyn, NY, 1948), p. 128. The first two parts of the *Likutei Amarim*, namely, *Sefer Shel Benonim* and Sha'ar haYichud vehaEmunah, were first published in Slavita, 1796. More about RSZ's literary activity later.

CHAPTER THREE / FIRST CRISIS

1. Rabbi Abraham ben Alexander Katz (Kohen Tzedek) was in his youth a student of the Gaon of Vilna. Subsequently he became a disciple of the Maggid of Miezricz. He held a rabbinic post in Kalisk, Prussia. In 1777 he emigrated to Palestine with Rabbi Menachem Mendel of Horodok and other Chasidic leaders. The Chasidic colony was at first established in Safed, but following some local opposition moved to Tiberias. Rabbi Abraham later became embroiled in a controversy with Rabbi Schneur Zalman (ch. IV).

2. *HaTamim*, vol. II, pp. 62 f.

3. *Likutei Diburim*, vol. II, pp. 471 ff.

4. *HaTamim*, vol. II, p. 58.

5. *Beit Rebbi*, ch. 4.

6. The pamphlet *Zemir Aritzim*, consisting of 32 pages, was printed in Alkesnik (near Brody) in 5532 (1772) by an anonymous author and publisher. The copies were soon sold out, but the buyers were Chasidim who destroyed them. Only two copies are known to have survived of the original publication, one in the British Museum and the other in the Library of the Hebrew University in Jerusalem. It was published again in the periodical *He'avar*, vol. II (Petrograd, 1918) from a manuscript copy of the first issue. The pamphlet contained: 1) A letter of condemnation from Vilna, dated Iyar 8, 5523, against the Chasidim and their customs, particularly against the local leaders of the *Kat*, the

Maggid Rabbi Chaim and Rabbi Isser, who had been "exposed" and publicly punished by order of the *Beit-Din*. 2) A manifesto in Yiddish issued in Brody on Sivan 20, 5532, including an awesome *cherem* (excommunication). 3) A scathing parody by the (anonymous) author. 4) A letter from Vilna to Brest over the signature of the Gaon and those of Rabbi Shmuel ben Avigdor, head of the *Beit-Din*, and other signatories. 5) A letter from the community leaders of Vilna to all communities, said to have been written with the approval of the Gaon. 6) An account of the "misdeeds" of the *Kat* in Vilna, of the public burning of Chasidic books, etc. 7) Enactments of the community of Leshnov against the Chasidim. *Iggarot Baal HaTanya*, p. 178, note 16.

7. Avigdor Chaimovitch ("son of Chaim") later was the main adversary of Rabbi Schneur Zalman during the latter's second imprisonment. (Ch. XI)

8. *Beit Rebbi*, ibid.

9. *Kuntres Chai Elul*, 5703. KPS (Brooklyn, NY).

10. *HaTamim*, vol. II, p. 41.

11. Rabbi Menachem Mendel was a native of Vitebsk, where his father Rabbi Moshe headed a *yeshiva*. A man of great learning and extraordinary humility, Rabbi Menachem Mendel was held in great esteem by his master and colleagues. After the death of the Maggid of Miezricz, he made his residence in Horodok (near Vitebsk), hence his name Horodoker. For the next few years until his emigration to Palestine, Rabbi Menachem Mendel was considered senior leader of the movement. He tried hard to bring about a reconciliation with the Mitnagdim, including an abortive attempt to confront the Gaon of Vilna in company with Rabbi Schneur Zalman. When all attempts for a rapprochement with the opposition failed, he left for Palestine together with a large group of Chasidim (in 1777), settling in Safed, and later in Tiberias, where he died in 1788. He is the author of a Chasidic work entitled *Peri HaAretz* ("Fruit of the Land"), compiled by his disciples, and published in Kopust, 1814.

12. See note 21, below.

13. Presumably the reference is to Avigdor (cf. note 7, above).

14. *Yebamot* 65b.

15. See beg. of ch. 10, and n. 1 there.

16. According to *Beit Rebbi* the reference is to *Tzavaat HaRibash*. This seems to be borne out by the words "it is not for you to fight for the cause of the Baal Shem Tov." See n. 19 below.

17. This doctrine, one of the basic doctrines in Lurianic Kabbala, and expounded at length in Chabad, will be discussed in the second volume.

18. In his Introduction to the Gaon's *Commentary* (first published in Vilna, 1821, and again in 1912) on the *Sifra diTzene'uta* (one of the earliest Kabbala works), Rabbi Chaim of Volozhin, leading disciple of the Gaon, indicates that the Gaon occasionally differed from the *Ari* (Rabbi Yitzchok Luria), or amended certain passages in the latter's writings as they come down through Rabbi Chaim Vital, believing that these writings included addenda by Vital's disciples who were not equal to their master in grasping the *Ari's* profound wisdom. Rabbi Chaim appears to defend the Gaon's independent interpretation of certain Lurianic concepts on the grounds that the Gaon's grasp of the profoundest Kabbalah doctrines was most wonderfully enhanced after he twice experienced *giluy Eliyahu* (revelation of the Prophet Elijah). Incidentally, it is interesting to note that Rabbi Chaim relates in the said Introduction various other marvelous supernatural experiences of the Gaon, on the order of those related of the Baal Shem Tov, the Maggid, Rabbi Schneur Zalman, and other saints and mystics in Chasidic, as well as Talmudic lore.

19. Presumably referring to Rabbi Pinchas HaLevi Hurwitz (1730-1805), author of *Haflaah*, Chief Rabbi of Frankfurt am Main. A renowned Talmudist, he became a disciple of the Maggid of Miezricz. In 1771 he was called to the rabbinate in Frankfurt, a position he held for the rest of his life. Equally renowned was his brother Rabbi Shmelka Hurwitz, Chief Rabbi of Nikolsburg in Moravia, who was also one of the Maggid's most distinguished disciples.

20. See n. 16 above.

21. The full text of the letter appears in *Iggarot Baal HaTanya*, p. 95, and *Beit Rebbi*, ch. 12, quoted from *Metzaref HaAvodah*, at end. The author of *Iggarot* dates the letter in the period between *Tevet*, 5557 (after the publication of the *Likutei Amarim [Tanya]* mentioned in the letter), and the death of the Gaon of Vilna, *Tishrei*, 5558 (1797), since RSZ refers to the Gaon with the customary "long may he live."

22. In 1786 Rabbi Menachem Mendel wrote to Rabbi Schneur Zalman (*Iggarot*, p. 26) urging his reluctant colleague to accept the leadership of the Chasidim in Lithuania and White Russia. In 1788, RMM wrote to the Chasidim calling upon them to recognize RSZ as their leader (ibid. p. 34). It was his last pastoral letter to the Chasidim before he died. In a letter which RSZ wrote to his senior colleague in the same year, RSZ humbly pleads incompetence to assume the leadership, but agrees to do so on condition that RMM remember him and the Chasidim in his daily prayers. (Cf. letter in *Mishnat Yoel*, by Yoel Diskin, ed. Isaac A. Orenstein, [Jerusalem, 1941, p. 82]).

23. A list of 52 of Rabbi Schneur Zalman's most prominent disciples,

with biographical data, appears in Ch. M. Hilman's *Beit Rebbi*, KPS (Brooklyn, NY 1953), ch. 56, pp. 111-120. Cf. also *Likutei Diburim*, vol. I, pp. 80 f., vol. II, pp. 413 f., 492 f.

24. Rabbi Israel of Polotzk (or Polotzker) was one of a number of notable Talmudic scholars who became disciples of the Maggid of Miezricz. Upon arrival in Safed, the new Chasidic colony, numbering over 300 souls (*Iggarot*, p. 7), found itself in dire need. Thereupon Rabbi Israel Polotzker was sent back to his native land as an emissary of the colony, for the purpose of organizing a permanent relief fund for the support of the Chasidim in the Holy Land. He was to carry out this task in cooperation with Rabbi Issachar Ber of Lubavitch (RSZ's former teacher) and Rabbi Schneur Zalman, (Cf. pastoral letters by Rabbi Menachem Mendel of 1778 and 1782, ibid., pp. 5 & 10 respectively). His task successfully accomplished, Rabbi Israel intended to return to the Holy Land, when death overcame him in the town of Fastov (some time between 1782 and 1784, ibid., p. 9). He was laid to rest next to the grave of Rabbi Abraham, "The Angel," son of the Maggid of Miezricz.

25. *Babba Metzia*, 62a.
26. *HaTamim*, vol. II, pp. 52 ff.

CHAPTER FOUR / CHASM WIDENS

1. Introduction, p. XX.
2. Rabbi Ezekiel Landau (1713-1793), famed author of the responsa *Noda biYehudah*, relentlessly opposed the Chasidic movement. He ordered the public burning of the *Toldot Yaakov Yosef*. He also challenged the authority of Rabbi Yitzchok Luria (responsum 34).
3. The *Nusach Ari* differed from the *Nusach Ashkenaz* in several ways: changes in text, in the order of certain prayers, and in the omission or substitution of certain prayers. In view of the Chasidic emphasis on prayer and *kavanah* (concentration, attunement of heart and mind), the Chasidim liked to take their time both in preparation before prayer and during the recital of prayer, which was frequently carried out with excessive emotion (cf. Rabbi Schneur Zalman's defense in his letter to Rabbi Alexander Sender of Shklov, *Iggarot Baal HaTanya*, p. 33). All this made it difficult for the Chasidim to join in the congregational services with the rest of the community, and impelled them to hold their own congregational services. Cf. also M. Teitelbaum, *HaRav miLiadi*, vol. II, pp. 208 ff.; Aaron Wertheim, *Halachot veHalichot beChasidut* (Jerusalem, 1960), pp. 83 ff., 110 ff.
4. Officially the Chasidim were permitted to have their own syna-

gogues by an edict of April 26, 1798. Actually they had their own synagogues already before 1770, during the time of the Maggid of Miezricz. *HaRav miLiadi*, p. 35.

5. Cf. Rabbi Schneur Zalman's defense in letters and responsa, *Iggarot*, pp. 204-211; cf. also *Halachot veHalichot*, pp. 200 ff.

6. Jewish Community in Russia, p. 170.

7. A list of sixteen innovations by RSZ in religious practices appears in *Beit Rebbi*, pp. 35 ff. None of them, however, constituted "heretical" reforms from the viewpoint of Halachah, and the early opposition to them was motivated mainly by objection to any innovation in accepted practices.

8. *Iggarot*, p. 204.

9. Ibid., p. 205 f.

10. *Babba Batra*, 8a.

11. Proverbs, 10:25.

12. *Berachot*, 64a.

13. An allegorical reference to Deut. 25:17-19.

14. *Kuntres Chicago*, pp. 21-24; *Likutei Diburim*, vol. 1, p. 262 f.

15. *Jewish Community in Russia*, p. 170.

CHAPTER FIVE / ENTRENCHMENT UNDER FIRE

1. *Iggarot Baal HaTanya*, p. 8. See also pp. 12, 13, 116.

2. Pinchas Reizes was the son of the celebrated *gaon* Rabbi Chanoch Henoch Schick of Shklov. The latter-once an antagonist of Chasidut-gave his approbation for the publication of RSZ's work *Hilchot Talmud Torah* (1794), the first part of RSZ's *Shulchan Aruch* to be published. (It was published anonymously.) The entire *Shulchan Aruch* was published posthumously with the aid of Pinchas Reizes. Pinchas Reizes was attracted to RSZ while a young man, when he came to Shklov together with a group of other young Talmudic scholars to witness the debate between RSZ and the scholars of Shklov. *Sefer HaToldot, Rabbi Schneur Zalman miLiadi*, ed. A. Ch. Glitzenstein, KPS (Brooklyn, NY 1967), p. 361. Eventually he became one of RSZ's outstanding disciples and Chasidim. He was a successful merchant and philanthropist, and left most of his substantial estate to charity. He died in Lubavitch about 1825. Ibid., p. 373. (cf. *Reb Pinchas Reizes*, S.B. Avtzon, Brooklyn, NY)

3. The two emissaries were Rabbi Shlomo of Karlin (see ch. 11, n. 30) and Rabbi Wolf of Zhitomir. See *Sefer HaToldot, RSZ*, p. 374

4. "Zalman the Lithuanian"—an affectionate appellation given him by the Maggid of Miezricz, by which he was generally known among his colleagues the disciples of the Maggid.

5. Shmuel Munkis was another one of RSZ's prominent Chasidim. He was celebrated for his wit and wisdom and Chasidic pranks. On one occasion, as he arrived at the house of RSZ in Liozna together with a large group of Chasidim, he jumped on the gate and, placing his feet in the rails, dangled in the air, to the amazement of his friends. Explained Shmuel Munkis: "When you see a sign with shears hanging in the street, you know where the tailor lives; and by the sign of boots you know where to find the bootmaker. A Rebbe should have a Chasid hanging from his gate. . . ." *Likutei Diburim*, vol. IV, p. 1521. Another characteristic episode is related in *Sefer HaSichot*, 5703, p. 175; *Sefer HaToldot*, RSZ, 390 f. See also ch. X, n. 15, below. (cf. *Reb Shmuel Munkes*, S.B. Avtzon, Brooklyn, NY)

6. Rabbi Aharon HaLevi of Strashelia was the most distinguished disciple of RSZ. He is the author of *Avodat HaLevi*, a brilliant and profound exposition of the teachings of his master's philosophical system, a work which "eclipses many a celebrated work in rabbinic literature" (A. Marcus, *HaChasidut*, p. 122). At the age of 17 he came, among others, to witness the debate in Minsk between RSZ and the Rabbinate, and ever since then became closely attached to RSZ. (*Sefer HaToldot*, RSZ, p. 88 f.) In his preface to his *Sha'arei haYichud vehaEmunah*, Rabbi Aharon speaks with boundless admiration of his master. He also states there that for nearly thirty years he sat at the feet of his saintly Rebbe "and only after strenuous concentration on every word issuing from his saintly mouth did I fathom his teachings.... I have had no other teacher but him." (Ibid, pp. 313 f., 371.) RSZ showed him particular attention and made him the constant companion of his oldest son Rabbi Dov Ber. When RSZ settled in Liadi, Rabbi Aharon moved there, too, and lived there for eight years. Subsequently he returned to his town Assaye, and later to Strashelia, where he taught and disseminated Chasidut. After the death of his master, many Chasidim of RSZ became attached to Rabbi Aharon, instead of to RSZ's son and successor, which created a rift between the two. In addition to the two mentioned works, he wrote other Chasidic treatises. He died in Strashelia in 1828 (Ibid., p. 371).

7. *Likutei Diburim*, vol. II, p. 511 ff.
8. *Chagigah* 3a.
9. *Likutei Diburim*, vol. II, p. 486 ff.
10. Ibid., p. 520 ff.

CHAPTER SIX / INTERNAL CRISIS

1. *Likutei Diburim*, vol. 1, p. 86, vol. IV, p. 1332 ff.

2. Moshe Wilenker was one of the leading Chasidim of Rabbi Schneur Zalman, who was highly respected for profound knowledge of Chasidut, general wisdom and eloquence. His brother Ze'ev Wilenker was also a prominent Chasid of RSZ and a man of substantial wealth, living in Vitebsk.

3. Rabbi Menachem Nachum of Czernobil (1730-1797) was a disciple of the Baal Shem Tov and later of his successor the Maggid of Miezricz. He is the author of homiletic works *Me'or Einayim* and *Yismach Lev*, both published posthumously in 1798. He was the father of the Czernobil dynasty, with numerous followers in Wolhynia and the Ukraine. His equally famed son Rabbi Mordechai (d. 1836) was said to have at least 100,000 Chasidim. (A. Marcus, *HaChasidut*, p. 213.)

4. *Sefer HaSichot*, 5700, p. 64.

5. Yiddish expressions of grief.

6. Rabbi Baruch Mordechai served as Rabbi of Bobroysk for decades. He was respected for his learning and piety even by the Mitnagdic Rabbis. His biography is related at some length in *Sefer HaToldot, RSZ*, pp. 378-384.

7. *Shulchan Aruch / Tur*, chapter 13

CHAPTER SEVEN / LIOZNA, CENTER OF CHABAD

1. *Russkaya enciklopedia*, op. cit.,

2. See *Iggarot Baal HaTanya*, pp. 7, 13-15, 30-32, 42-44, 47-48, 70, 117, 161, 191, 221-228 for various letters and encyclicals sent by Rabbi Schneur Zalman which have to do with matters of philanthropy.

3. See RSZ's letter in *Iggarot*, p. 61.

4. As already mentioned (Ch. 1, n.1), the surname Schneersohn, or Schneerson, was first adopted by Rabbi Menachem Mendel of Lubavitch, the grandson of RSZ. Consequently those authors who used the name 'Schneersohn" in relation to the first two generations are obviously in error.

5. See p. 7.

6. *Memoirs*, see Index, at end of vol. II.

7. Ibid.,

8. Ibid.,

9. See p. 36 f.

10. The Halachah provides a time limit within which the *Shema* should be read. Rabbi Schneur Zalman insisted upon the observance of the proper time, noting in his *Shulchan Aruch* (*Hil. Keriat Shema*) that in the Northern countries the time limit in the summer is about 7:45 a.m.

11. The reference is to Rabbi Aharon HaLevi of Strashelia, of the senior disciples of Rabbi Schneur Zalman. See ch. V, note 6.

12. RSZ's brother.

13. *Iggarot*, p. 58 f.

14. Ibid., p. 59.

15. The "four occasions" were *Simchat Torah*, *Shabbat Chanukah*, *Purim*, and *Shabbat Shuvah*.

16. A reference to I Sam. ch. 9.

17. The following section of this encyclical appears also in the *Tanya*, under *Iggeret HaKodesh*, ch. 22.

18. *Iggarot*, p. 60

19. The reference is to the oldest son Rabbi Dov Ber.

20. Rabbi Schneur Zalman had three sons-in-law: 1) Rabbi Eliyahu ben Mordechai, husband of his daughter Freida. 2) Rabbi Shalom Shachna ben Noach, husband of his daughter Dvorah Leah (see pp. 84 ff) who died in 1792, several years prior to these *Takanot*, and her husband no longer lived in Liozna. He financed the first printing of the *Tanya*. 3) Rabbi Abraham Sheines, husband of Rachel. His father, Rabbi Tzevi of Shklov was one of the most outspoken opponents of the Chasidim, yet his son became greatly attached to RSZ and married his daughter Rachel. (Beit Rebbi, p. 117 f.). Rachel died five years after marriage. Rabbi Abraham Sheines was a brilliant scholar in both Talmud and Chasidut. It is believed that the reference "my son-in-law" is to Rabbi Abraham Sheines. *Iggarot*, p. 65, n. 3. About RSZ's sons and daughters and sons-in-law, see *Beit Rebbi*, pp. 112-120. See also Rabbi Ch. M. Perlow, *Likutei Sippurim*, (Kfar Chabad, 1966), p. 46.

21. Some words are apparently missing from the MS.

22. Ibid., p. 66 f.

CHAPTER EIGHT / FIRST ENCOUNTER WITH HASKALAH

1. See Introduction, and note 3 there.

2. Introduction, n. 29.

3. Ibid.

4. A. Marcus, *HaChasidut*, p. 77.

5. Moses (Moshe) ben Menachem Mendel (hence Mendelssohn) was b. Dessau, Germany, 1729; d. Berlin, 1786. He is generally regarded as the "father of the Haskalah movement."

6. B. Dubno (Wolhynia), Poland, 1738; d. Amsterdam, 1813

7. *Sefer HaToldot*, RSZ, op. cit., p. 65.

8. Young child. See *Zohar, Parshat Balak* 186a.

9. The initial words of the *Kedushah, Shacharit* and *Musaf* in the

Nusach Ashkenaz and *Nusach Ari*, respectively.

10. A group of *Maskilim* who organized themselves into the Society for the Cultivation of Hebrew Literature and published the periodical *Hame'asef*, which first appeared in 1784.

11. See p. 6

12. A form of idol-worship. (Leviticus 18:21)

13. *Sefer HaToldot, RSZ*, p. 170 f.

14. Ibid., pp. 173-177.

15. Ibid., pp. 178-9.

16. Ibid., p. 180 f.

CHAPTER NINE / PUBLICATION OF TANYA

1. Written by Abraham Yagel ben Chananiah Gallico, who lived in Ferrara and Venice in Italy, 16th-17th cent. His best known work *Lekach Tov* (Venice, ca. 1595), a textbook on the Jewish religion, was written in the form of a dialogue between master and pupil. A popular work, it was translated into Latin, Yiddish, and German.

2. Rabbi Meshulam Zusia of Anipoli, better known as Rabbi Zusia of Anipoli, was the brother of the equally famed Rabbi Elimelech of Lizajsk. Spending many years wandering about in Poland, the two brothers were celebrated for their saintliness and humility, and were among the outstanding disciples of the Maggid. There was a particular attachment between Rabbi Zusia and Rabbi Schneur Zalman, and the latter considered him as one of the four "model" disciples of the Maggid, whom he characterized as follows: "Rabbi Aaron of Karlin-a model of love; Rabbi Zusia of Anipoli-a model of fear (reverence); Rabbi Menachem Mendel of Vitebsk-a model of Talmudic brilliance; and Rabbi Yaakov Shimshon of Shipotovka-a model of profound thinking." A. Marcus, *HaChasidut*, p. 92.

3. Author of *Or HaGanuz* ("Hidden Light"), Vol. I on Pentateuch, Vol. II on *Mishnayot* (Lemberg, 1866).

4. *Kitzurim veHa'arot l'Tanya*, pp. 137 ff.

5. Ibid.

6. His father Eliyahu Ze'ev was one of the young Chasidim in the town of Smargon who were actively engaged in spreading Chasidut in the community. Leading the opposition there was an old Talmudic sage, Elyakum Faivush. The sage once uttered an imprecation against Eliyahu Ze'ev, and ever since then a curse seemed to hang over the latter's children, who caught colds and died of pneumonia in infancy. When Tzvi was three months old, Rabbi Schneur Zalman was visiting Smargon. The infant was taken by his father to the Rebbe for a bless-

ing. The Rebbe stroked the child's head, saying *"a waremer yingele"* ("a warm boy"), and blessed him. The boy grew up with the appellation "Hirshel *der Waremer*." Indeed, his Divine worship was characterized by a profound warmth, though outwardly he showed no sign of it. Rabbi Hillel of Paritch (author of Pelach HaRimon), leading disciple of RSZ, used to refer to him as *"Hirshele Sneh"* (alluding to the Burning Bush), while some Chasidim called him *"Hirshele Bren."* (From a letter by the late Lubavitcher Rebbe, Rabbi J. I. Schneersohn, quoted in *Sefer HaToldot, RSZ*, p. 149.)

7. Ibid.

8. Ibid., p. 151.

9. The circumstances of RSZ's imprisonment are related in the following chapter.

10. *Sefer HaToldot, RSZ*, p. 151.

11. Ibid.

12. A selection of biblical verses which are recited on *Simchat Torah* before *hakafot*.

13. Ibid.

14. *Kitzurim veHa'arot l'Tanya*, pp. 118-126.

15. For a list of translations of the Tanya, see list at end of this book.

CHAPTER TEN / IMPRISONMENT AND VINDICATION

1. The two emissaries were Rabbi Chaim of Cherhay, a member of the Rabbinical Court of Vilna, and Saadiah ben Nathan Nota, one of the Gaon's prominent disciples. The latter (a brother-in-law of Rabbi Zelmele of Volozhin) recorded the Gaon's commentaries on the "Minor Tractates" of the Talmud, and also the Gaon's Customs in a tract called *Ma'aseh Rav*.

They visited many communities to publicize the Gaon's letter. While in Mohilev the letter was lost, and thereafter they conveyed its contents orally. In Minsk their testimony was questioned, whereupon a special messenger was sent to Vilna to obtain the Gaon's reaffirmation. The latter sent a letter calling upon the Rabbis of the districts of Vilna, Vitebsk, Polotzk, Minsk, Mohilev, Zhitomir, Kamenetz-Podolsk, and upon all faithful Jews, to suppress the Chasidim for the sake of the Torah (*Beit Rebbi*, ch. 12).

In the years 1809-10 both of them emigrated to Palestine with the so-called *Aliyah* of the Gaon's disciples. (*Toldot Chachmei Yerushalayim*, part III).

2. *HaRav miLiadi*, vol. 1, ch. 7.

3. Rabbi Elijah particularly objected to Rabbi Schneur Zalman's

interpretation of the doctrine of *Tzimtzum* and his concept of Divine immanence. Apparently, the Gaon did not accept the Lurianic Kabbala in toto, and interpreted certain of its doctrines differently. (See ch. III, n. 17, above). Opposition to the ways and customs of the Chasidim was fostered also by other factors, as already indicated. See also S. A. Horodetzky, *Yahadut HaSechel veYahadut HaRegesh* (Tel Aviv, 1947), vol. II, pp. 362 ff.

4. See RSZ's letter, p. 31 ff.

5. It is believed that Rabbi Schneur Zalman had met Rabbi Elijah before the former became a Chasidic leader.

6. *Mishnah, Sukkah* 5: 1-4.

7. The allegation that the Chasidim rejoiced during "the very time" of the Gaon's funeral (cf. HaRav miLiadi, vol. I, p. 62) cannot, of course, be true, for the simple reason that the funeral must have taken place during the day. Cf. *Aliyot Eliyahu*, by Rabbi Nachman of Horodno (Stetin, 1856), p. 89, n. 119. The traditional *Simchat Beit HaShoevah* usually takes place in the evening. It should also be noted that under Jewish Law mourning rites during the festival are curtailed.

8. Dubnow, *"Istoria Chasidskavo raskola"* (Voskhod, 1891).

9. Rabbi Schneur Zalman issued this "awesome warning" to his Chasidim after the death of Rabbi Elijah, and again a year later. *Iggarot*, p. 116.

10. See p. 34.

11. These terms will be discussed in the second volume.

12. *HaRav miLiadi*, vol. 1, p. 73 ff.

13. Ibid., p. 69.

14. *Likutei Diburim*, vol. 1, p. 58.

15. Ibid., vol. IV, p. 1499. *Sefer HaToldot, RSZ*, p. 195.

16. Ibid., vol. IV, p. 1498.

17. Ibid., vol. 1, p. 75.

18. Ibid., p. 76.

19. Ibid., pp. 32 ff.

20. Ibid., vol. IV, p. 1499.

21. *Beit Rebbi*, p. 57.

22. Ibid., ibid.

23. *Sefer HaToldot, RSZ*, p. 201 f.

24. *Beit Rebbi*, p. 58.

25. Ibid., ibid.

26. Ibid., p. 60.

27. *Likutei Diburim*, vol. IV, p. 1504 f.

28. See p. 186 below.

29. This is said to explain why after RSZ's release, there was a

notable change in his method of Chasidic dissemination. He began to deliver Chasidic discourses more frequently, and the discourses (maamarim) were lengthier and more elaborately explained, so as to make them comprehensible even to the unscholarly.

30. *Beit Rebbi*, p. 60, n. 2.

31. Ibid., p. 61.

32. *HaTamim*, vol. II, p. 56.

33. *Sefer HaSichot*, 5703, p. 62.

34. *Sefer HaToldot, RSZ*, p. 208.

35. See p. 72 ff. above.

36. See p. 2 above.

37. About Rivkah's father (RSZ's grandfather) see *Memoirs*, vol. 1, pp. 56 ff., 91 ff.

38. The youngest son of RSZ was born in 1780. From early youth he displayed extraordinary mental capacities, and his illustrious father personally instructed him in Talmud, Chasidut, and religious philosophy. At the age of sixteen he received instruction in Russian and French from Moshe Meisels of Vilna who came to visit RSZ in Liozna, and RSZ detained him for several months for this purpose. A brilliant student and avid reader, young Moshe not only mastered these languages, but also used them to broaden his general education. *Sefer HaToldot, RSZ*, p. 209.

39. *Beit Rebbi*, ch. 17, p. 63 ff.

40. Rabbi Schneur Zalman considered the day auspicious, since it is the anniversary of the demise of his master Rabbi Dov Ber the Maggid of Miezric twenty six years previously. (A *Yahrzeit*-anniversary of death-is considered auspicious by Chasidim because it is believed that on that day the soul of the departed ascends to a higher level in the heavenly spheres.)

41. Chabad Chasidim consider this number significant, as it corresponds to the number of chapters in the *Tanya*. *Likutei Diburim*, vol. III, p. 818.

42. *HaRav miLiadi*, I, p. 77.

43. *Beit Rebbi*, p. 65 f.

44. On each of the Six Days of Creation (Gen. ch. 1) the words "And G-d saw that it was good" are mentioned, with the exception of the second day-when they are omitted, and the third day-when they are repeated twice. For this reason the third day of the week (Tuesday) is generally regarded by Jews as particularly auspicious.

45. The Maggid of Miezric.

46. It was RSZ's custom, followed also by his successors, to recite after the Morning Prayer the daily "quota" of Psalms according to their

division into 29/30 sections, corresponding to the number of days in the Hebrew month. The Book of Psalms is also divided into seven major sections, corresponding to the seven days of the week. While in prison, RSZ evidently recited additional Psalms corresponding to the latter division, since Psalm 55 (to which the verse referred to in his letter belongs) falls into the section of the "third day." (The recital of the daily quota of Psalms after the Morning Prayer has become the universal custom of Chabad Chasidim, as well as of many non-Chasidim). *Sefer HaToldot, RSZ*, p. 218, n. 14.

47. *Iggarot Baal HaTanya*, p. 114 f., where another version is also quoted. See also notes to the above on p. 115.

48. Ibid., p. 115.

49. The encyclical, known by its initial word *Kotonti* ("I am unworthy") is included in the *Tanya, Iggeret HaKodesh*, ch. 2.

50. *Tikunei Zohar*, Introduction.

51. Song 2:3; 8:6.

52. Jer. 31:2.

53. *Zohar I*, 11b.

54. Micah 7:20.

55. Gen. 18:28.

56. Gen. 28:15.

57. *Sitra achra*, the "other side," i.e., the realm of evil.

58. Jer. 46:3, etc.

59. Micah 7:20.

60. Prov. 15: 1.

61. Prov. 27:19.

62. *Likutei Diburim*, vol. I, p. 38.

63. Ibid., p. 41.

CHAPTER ELEVEN / SECOND CRISIS

1. *HaRav miLiadi I*, p. 70 f.

2. Ibid., p. 86.

3. Ibid.

4. Ibid., p. 88.

5. Ibid., p. 89.

6. Ibid., ibid.

7. *Memoirs* (unpublished), op. cit.

8. G. R. Derzhavin, *Polnye sotschinenia* (Petersburg, 1876-78), vol. VI, p. 401.

9. Ibid., vol. VII, p. 284.

10. Ibid., pp. 696 ff.

11. A case in point is the complaint lodged against him by a Jewess from Liozna to the effect that during Derzhavin's raid on the distillery in that town, he beat her mercilessly with a cane, disregarding her state of pregnancy, and causing her to lose her child. The Emperor ordered that Derzhavin stand trial before the Senate. The complaint was quashed with the help of Attorney General Obolianinov. Derzhavin, op. cit., Vol. VII, p. 715. Although RSZ's direct connection with this case cannot be established, it is hardly likely that the case could have been instigated without his consent, if not initiative, in an effort to discredit Derzhavin by establishing his vicious anti-Semitism.

12. *Memoirs* (unpublished), op. cit.

13. Believed to be the *Toldot Yaakov Yosef* by Rabbi Jacob Joseph of Polonnoye. *HaRav miLiadi*, vol. I, p. 36, n. 2.

14. Ibid., p. 72.

15. Named after Rabbi Aaron of Karlin, one of the outstanding disciples of Rabbi Dov Ber of Miezricz.

16. The book ("*Testament of Rabbi Israel Baal Shem*") is a collection of sayings and customs of the Baal Shem and his successor Rabbi Dov Ber, recorded by their disciple Rabbi Isaiah of Yanov. It was published in Zolkiev (date unknown) and again in 1793. The title is a misnomer, for "it is not his testament, nor did he leave a testament, but a collection of his sublime sayings, variously collected. The language is not completely accurate, but in substance it is absolutely authentic." Rabbi Schneur Zalman in his *Iggeret HaKodesh*, beg. of ch. 25.

17. *HaRav miLiadi*, pp. 93 ff. *Iggarot Baal HaTanya*, pp. 125-153.

18. *HaRav miLiadi*, p. 96f.

19. Ibid., p. 98.

20. For the complete text of Kutuzov's report, see *HaRav miLiadi, I*, pp. 189 ff.

21. Cf. Dubnow's article, "The intervention of the Russian government in the anti-Chasidic struggle," *Evreyskaya Starina* (1st quarter, 1910). Also *HaRav miLiadi*, part I, p. 166. The documents relating to the official investigation, and the correspondence cited in these pages, were first published in the original (Russian) by Dubnow in *Evreyskaya Starina*, op. cit., from original documents kept in the archives of the Senate in Petersburg. They were subsequently published in Hebrew translation in *HaRav miLiadi*, and republished with additional original sources, in *Iggarot Baal HaTanya*. Because of the availability of the latter two sources, the references in these pages are generally made to these last two sources.

22. U. I. Hessen, "On the history of the religious struggle," *Voskhod*, 1902. S. Dubnow, in his article in *Evreyskaya Starina*, op. cit. Cf. also

HaRav miLiadi, part I, p. 101.

23. *Memoirs* (unpublished).

24. *Iggarot*, p. 142, letter of Governor Severin of November 13, 1800.

25. These documents have since been discovered.

26. *Tzavaat HaRibash*.

27. An obvious misrepresentation, since the doctrine of human freedom of action is strongly upheld in Chasidut. But as already noted, the book *Tzavaat HaRivash* lends itself to misunderstanding, since it often contains loosely translated sayings and teachings of the Baal Shem (Note 16, above.) Rabbi Schneur Zalman deals with the problem of Divine Providence and freedom in his *Likutei Amarim [Tanya], Iggeret HaKodesh*, ch. 25, while the problem of Divine Immanence is dealt with at length, ibid., *Sha'ar haYichud vehaEmunah*.

28. An unwarranted inference, since it is amply emphasized in the teachings of the Baal Shem Tov that no sinful thing can ever be sublimated. Cf. *Tanya*, ch. 37.

29. A refutation of the assertions charged in pars. 5 and 6 will be found in the above mentioned *Iggeret HaKodesh*, ch. 25, and elsewhere in Chabad literature.

30. Both spellings-"Karlinists" and "Karalinists'-appear in the official documents.

31. Referring to himself.

32. The reference is to Rabbi Aaron HaGadol (The Great Aaron) of Karlin, and Rabbi Shlomo of Karlin, both of them being among the most outstanding disciples of the Maggid of Miezricz. The former (1736-1772) was particularly admired by RSZ. Though he died at the age of 35, Rabbi Aharon HaGadol had attracted a considerable following, and he was the progenitor of the Karlin dynasty of *tzaddikim*. His colleague, Rabbi Shlomo of Karlin, was sometimes called "The Small Baal Shem Tov" because of the wonders he performed. He was fatally wounded by a Cossack bullet in the summer of 1812 during Morning Prayer, and he died three days later. A. Marcus, *Sefer HaChasidut*, pp. 98, 190. *Sefer HaToldot, RSZ*, p. 367 f.

33. It is not clear what the accusation is. Many Chasidim used to avoid wearing woolen clothes for fear of possible *shatnes* (mingled wool and linen fibers together. Deut. 22:11). Those who could afford it, preferred silk, but cotton garments have been used mostly. Since the Russian government wished to do away with the Jews' distinctiveness in dress (see n. 42, next ch.), one may presume that the purpose of criticizing the Chasidic dress was to arouse the government's displeasure against the Chasidim.

34. The father-in-law of Rabbi Yaakov, son of Rabbi Aharon the

Great of Karlin.

35. Perhaps erroneously mentioned instead of Rabbi Menachem Mendel of Vitebsk. *HaChasidut*, p. 14.

36. A particularly scathing accusation in view of the famine prevailing at that time. See p. 194 above, also *Iggarot*, p. 141.

37. There is no such law. The Talmud (B.B. 155b) discusses the age limit at which an heir may dispose of property left him by his deceased father. Ibid.

38. Cf. Introduction where it was noted that the early opponents of the Chasidim accused them of being followers of Shabbatai Tzvi. But, of course, by the end of the 18th cent. when this denunciation was made, hardly anyone could seriously entertain such a suspicion.

39. There is, of course, no substance whatever to these accusations, which were pure fabrications.

40. In 1991, all nineteen answers were discovered.

41. Rabbi Mordechai of Lachowitz, a disciple of Rabbi Shlomo of Karlin (n. 31, above) was among the 22 prominent Chasidim arrested in 1798 in connection with RSZ's arrest. He was released soon after RSZ was vindicated. In the controversy initiated by Rabbi Abraham of Kalisk against RSZ, he sided with Rabbi Abraham, and was appointed by him as head of the Chasidim of Lithuania in charge of collections for the relief fund which Rabbi Abraham endeavored to set up independently of RSZ. He also sided with Rabbi Abraham and Rabbi Baruch of Medzibosz in their criticism of RSZ's school of thought in Chasidut. *Iggarot*, p. 182.

42. Ibid., p. 145.

43. The Senate in turn decided to turn over the investigation to the Third Department, to be dealt with in conjunction with other matters pertaining to the Jews which were then under consideration. Ibid., 146.

44. Ibid., p. 147. Cf. also *HaRav miLiadi*, p. 107, n. 1.

45. *Iggarot*, p. 147.

46. This document was preserved in the government archives in Vitebsk. It appears in Hebrew translation in *Iggarot*, pp. 150-151.

47. On the subject of Jewish secular education during that period, see Jewish Community in Russia, op. cit., pp. 70 ff.

48. By edict of December 9, 1804.

49. See beginning of this chapter.

50. It would appear that RSZ had submitted this petition after he had left Petersburg on 11th of Menachem Av, 5561 (*Hayom Yom*, p. 4). This Hebrew date corresponds to July 21, 1801. However, since Russia did not adopt the Gregorian calendar until 1918, the Hebrew date would correspond to August 1st according to the Old Style, or Julian,

calendar then in use in Russia. Altogether RSZ spent 9 months and 10 days in Petersburg, of which two months were spent in the custody of the Secret Council of the Senate, and the rest in a private home.

CHAPTER TWELVE / FINAL YEARS

1. This he undertook in fulfillment of a promise to a prominent member of the *Mitnagdim*, Nathan Notkin, in return for the latter's cooperation to secure his release. Rabbi Schneur Zalman was to visit Rabbi Moshe Cheifetz of Tzaves, Rabbi Joshua Zeitlin of Shklov, and Rabbi Yoel of Amtzeslav. *Beit Rebbi*, pp. 22 f. *Likutei Diburim*, vol. I, p. 292. Nathan Notkin of Shklov was a prominent merchant and financier, who acted as purveyor for the government and had personal connections in the high spheres. He was also a confidant of Derzhavin, and the latter accused him of offering him a huge bribe to sway him in favor of the Jews when the Jewish question was under consideration by the Senate. Derzhavin, op. cit., vol. VII, p. 763.

2. *Sefer HaToldot*, RSZ, p. 249 f.

3. See p. 26 above.

4. *Iggarot Baal HaTanya*, p. 27.

5. Another title of the book *Tanya*, or *Likutei Amarim*.

6. *Yoma* 38b

7. *Iggarot*, p. 105 f.

8. Ibid., p. 108 ff.

9. Ibid., p. 155 ff.

10. Ibid., p. 159 f.

11. Ibid., p. 169 ff.

12. Ibid., p. 171 f.

13. Rabbi Levi Yitzchak and Rabbi Schneur Zalman became related through the marriage of their grandchildren. (See p. 216)

14. The "Bitter One," after the town Gorki (or Horki), meaning "bitter" in Russian. *Iggarot*, p. 172, n. 3.

15. Ps. 63:12.

16. Page 153 above.

17. This would indicate that RSZ began his leadership in the year 5544 (1784).

18. See page 34 above.

19. In Lachowitz there was Rabbi Mordechai (ch. XI, n. 39), and in Miedzibosz there was Rabbi Baruch, grandson of the Baal Shem Tov; it is not known, however, to whom RSZ refers in Vilna and Lubavitch.

20. Only one letter is extant of the year 5558 (1798) which Rabbi

Abraham addressed to the Chasidim, urging them to refrain from controversy and strife. It can be found in *Iggarot*, p. 112.

21. Hab. 2:4. The letters referred to here have not been traced.

22. See n. 20 above.

23. According to *Iggarot* (p. 178, n. 9) the reference is to Rabbi Aaron Katan (the "Small One") of Smalein, a close aide to Rabbi Abraham of Kalisk, who was sent as the latter's emissary in 5548 (1788), and on his return "slandered our Chasidic fellowship."

24. The lengthy epistle appears in *Iggarot*, p. 155.

25. The letters of 5562 and 5563 mentioned here are not available.

26. *Makkot* 24a.

27. Not the letter of 5561 referred to above. The letter mentioned here is not available.

28. A play on Lam. 4:19, where the word *kalim* means "swift." In Talmud and Rabbinic usage, the adjective connotes levity in a religious or moral sense.

29. See p. 193 above.

30. The episode referred to here is briefly mentioned in the beg. of ch. III above.

31. See p. 24 above.

32. See ch. III, n. 6.

33. See Rabbi Abraham's letter of (5565), *Iggarot*, p. 164.

34. *Shabbat* 32b. See *Iggarot*, p. 178, n. 18.

35. Yaakov Smilianer (RYS) was one of the devoted followers of Rabbi Menachem Mendel Horodoker. After the latter's emigration to the Holy Land, RYS was appointed by him as his personal representative in charge of fund-raising for the Chasidic colony in the Holy Land.

36. Lev. 25:20.

37. An unusual name; identity unknown.

38. I. G. Orshansky, *Russkoye zakonodatelstvo o evreiakh*, op. cit., pp. 274 ff.

39. Ibid., p. 277.

40. The official Jewish population in Russia in 1803 was 350,000 (25,016 in White Russia in 1772). In 1847 the official Jewish population in Russia numbered 1,441,363. As the statistics were unreliable, and the Jews usually refused to supply correct figures, the actual Jewish population is believed to have been much greater. While the majority of the Jewish communities were small (100 to 1,000 souls), about half of the Jewish population in the Pale was crowded in the larger cities. Cf. *Jewish Community in Russia*, op. cit., pp. 18, 19.

41. *Iggarot*, p. 192.

42. Apparently in reference to a decree (1804) permitting Jews to

visit cities outside the Pale on special permits from the local governors, provided the Jews were dressed according to the prevailing style of the Russians. *HaRav miLiadi*, p.

43. Num. 14:9, applying it here to his adversaries.

44. See p. 190 ff. above.

45. *Beit Rebbi*, p. 167, n. 1.

46. A partial list of his published works (including various editions) appears in *Sefer HaToldot, RSZ*, pp. 299-352. A comprehensive list appears at the end of this book.

47. Some twenty-three major compilations of maamarim by RSZ, published for the first time, are listed at the end of this book.

48. *Likutei Torah*, KPS (Brooklyn, NY 1965);*Pekudei*, 10a, *Tzav*, 18a; *Pinchas*, 154a; *Shir HaShirim*, 2a f. *Torah Or*, KPS (Brooklyn, NY, 1954), 14a, 124a, 225a.

49. *Likutei Diburim*, vol. II, p. 530.

50. Three volumes of Chabad *Neginah*, entitled *Sefer HaNigunim*, have been published by "Nichoach," an affiliate of the Chabad-Lubavitch movement, vol. I (Brooklyn, NY, 1948), vol. II (1957), vol. III (1980) edited by Rabbi Shmuel Zalmanoff, with a comprehensive Introduction to vol. I. Also L.P. records and audio tapes have been published so far by the same organization.

51. The 12th of *Tammuz*, birthday of the sixth Lubavitcher Rabbi, Rabbi Yosef Y. Schneersohn (1880-1950), is also the anniversary of his liberation from imprisonment in Soviet Russia (in 1927), when he faced charges of counter-revolutionary activity for his defiance of the anti-religious policy of the regime. The day is one of the notable Chabad anniversary celebrations.

52. These terms will be explained in vol. II.

53. See *Sefer HaNigunim*, op. cit. vol. I, Introduction, p. 43 f.

54. Ibid., p. 44

55. Ibid., p. 21.

56. Ibid., ibid.

57. Ibid., p. 22.

58. Ibid., p. 23.

59. *Likutei Diburim*, vol. IV, p. 1436.

60. See also *Sefer HaToldot, RSZ*, pp. 281-297.

CHAPTER THIRTEEN / LAST JOURNEY

1. Rabbi Schneur Zalman was not the only Chasidic leader who considered Napoleon a menace to the Jewish people. This view was shared

also by Rabbi Israel of Kozienice. A. Marcus, *HaChasidut* p. 114.

2. About Moshe Meisels' last years and emigration to Palestine see *Beit Rebbi*, p. 94 f. See also Finn, *Kiryah Ne'emanah* (Vilna, 1860), p. 247.

3. *Iggarot Baal HaTanya*, p. 238.

4. *HaRav miLiadi*, vol. 1, pp. 153-158.

5. *Beit Rebbi*, p. 94 f.; *Sefer HaToldot, RSZ*, p. 262.

6. Also Rabbi Moshe, youngest son of RSZ, participated in the intelligence service rendered to the Russian military. *Beit Rebbi*, ibid.

7. That Moshe Meisels had personal access to the Czar is evidenced from a letter written by Rabbi Dov Ber, son and successor of RSZ, to Moshe Meisels in connection with a problem that had arisen regarding the new cemetery at Hadiacz. In it the new head of Chabad specifically requests Moshe Meisels to intercede with the Czar personally. *Beit Rebbi*, p. 102 f.

8. *Beit Rebbi*, p. 101.

9. *Likutei Diburim*, vol. 1, p. 165. This tradition is significant in lending further support to the date of Rabbi Schneur Zalman's birth in 1745; not 1747 as stated in *Beit Rebbi* and other sources that followed it.

10. *Likutei Diburim*, vol. I, p. 28ft.

11. *HaRav miLiadi*, vol. I, p. 159.

12. Introduction to the *Shulchan Aruch*, by RSZ's sons.

13. *Ber. Rabba*, 8:5.

14. B.B. 8b, 9a.

15. See *HaRav miLiadi I*, p. 163, where author erroneously assumes that RSZ's sons were at his bedside. Actually, none of RSZ's sons was at his demise, for they had all been away, as mentioned earlier.

16. *HaRav miLiadi*, p. 165.

17. Customary expression of respect and sorrow for the demise of a parent during the first year of mourning.

18. The original letter appears in *Beit Rebbi*, p. 95 ff., *Sefer HaToldot, RSZ*, p. 264 ff.

19. RSZ is reported to have exclaimed these words in a state of rapturous ecstasy, lying prostrated on the floor. *Likutei Diburim*, vol. IV, p. 1556.

INDEX

INDEX

Dessau, 90, 206, 251
Devekut, X, XVI, 77, 215
Dikduk, 113
Dikduk Eliyahu, 100
Dinur, B., 239
Diskin, Yoel, 246
Disna, 165, 195-197
Dnieper, 219, 220
Dniester, 36
Dobromysl, 120
Dov Ber, Maggid of Miezricz—
see Maggid of Miezricz
Dov Ber (Schneuri), 52-55, 74,
83, 84, 109, 126, 127, 137,
152, 153, 193, 196, 198, 211,
219, 223, 225, 231, 232, 240,
241, 249, 251, 263, 293, 294,
296-299
Dov Ber Moshe, 165, 166
Dov Ze'ev of Yekaterinoslav,
148
Dubno, Solomon, 96, 98, 99
Dubno (Wolhynia), 43, 98,
251
Dubnow, S., 254, 257
Dubrovna, 61, 62, 64, 67, 120,
136, 227
Dvina, 10
Dvorah Leah, 6, 74-77, 152,
251

E

Eichel, Isaac, 106
Eizik "Mechadesh," 58-63, 68
Eizik of Homel, Rabbi, 127
Elazar of Disna, 195-197
Elia Avraham's, 67
Eliyahu Ze'ev of Smargon, 252
Eliyahu ben Mordechai, 251
Elianov, General, 227
Eliashowitz, Councillor, 163,

164
Eliezer, father of Besht, 17
Elijah (Gaon)—see Gaon of
Vilna
Elijah (the Prophet), 29, 31,
32, 58, 246
Elimelech of Lizajsk, 252
Elimelech Shaul of Polotzk,
128
Elimelech of Yanov, 124
Elyakum Faivush, 252
Emanation, Divine, 15, 16,
213
Emden, Rabbi Jacob, 243
En Sof, 12, 15, 46, 136
Ephraim Michel of Shklov, 61,
67
Epikores, 204
Esau, 113, 114, 158
Evreiskaia Enciklopedia, 238
Evreiskaia Starina, 257
Eybeschutz, Jonathan, XIII,
243

F

Falkin, Commandant, 163
Farbrengen, 112, 213
Fastov, 241, 247
Ferrara, 252
Finn, 263
Frank, Jacob; Frankists, XIII,
XVIII, XIX, 33, 115, 168
Frankel, David, 96
Frankfurt am Main, 98, 246
French, 96, 133, 153, 154,
216-223, 228, 255
Friedlander Brothers, 106
Frizel, Gov., 185
Frumeles, Aizik'l, 105, 106
Franco-Russian War, 188, 222
Freida, 251

INDEX

G

Gabbaim, 83, 87, 88, 92, 206
Galicia, XI, 30, 43, 95, 101, 102, 117, 120, 121, 240, 241
Gan Eden HaElyon, 75, 112, 114
Gan Eden HaTachton, 52, 64, 79, 112, 114
Gaon of Vilna, XX, 13, 24, 27-31, 33, 34, 43, 78-81, 95-100, 115-118, 120, 121, 204, 205, 244-246, 253, 254
Gedaliah, Fast of, 77, 107
Gedalia of Kalisk, 67
Gehinnom, 113, 114
German(y), 30, 32, 95-97, 100, 101, 117, 131, 165, 210, 251, 252
Gevurah—see *Chagat*, 195, 226
Glitzenstein (A. Ch.), 248
Golden Calf, 3
Gorki, 260
Greater Poland, 30
Guide, 110

H

HaChasidut (Sefer), 238, 241, 249-252, 258, 259, 263
Hadiacz, 223, 225, 231, 263
Haditch, 120
Haflaah, 98, 246
Hakafah, Hakafot, 57, 58, 62-66, 68, 129, 136, 253
Halachah, Halachic, 7, 14, 19, 20, 43, 44, 55, 194, 211, 240, 241, 248, 250
Halachot veHalichot beChasidut, 247, 248
Hamburg, 106
HaMe'Asef, 252
Hannover, Nathan, 238

Haskalah, XXI, 24, 95, 99, 100, 102, 103, 106, 114, 239, 240, 251
HaRav Miliadi uMifleget Chabad, 242, 247, 248, 253-259, 262, 263
Haskamah, XX, 122
Hatamim, 243-245, 247, 255
Havdalah, 77, 224
Hayom Yom, 239, 241, 259
He'Avar, 244
Hechalot, 2
Hellenistic Civilization and the Jews, 237
Helma, Solomon, 95, 239
Hena, Shlomo Zalman, 99, 100
Henoch Shklover—see Schick
Hessen, U.I., 257
Hertz (son of Israel), 186
Hilchot Talmud Torah, 248, 284, 290
Hillel of Paritch, 127, 253
Hilman, Ch. M., 240, 247
Hilman, D. Z., 240
Hirshele "Sneh" (Hirshele "Bren")—see Tzvi of Smilian, 123, 253
Holy Society, 15-17, 54
Hurwitz, Rabbi Pinchas, 98, 246
Hurwitz, Aharon HaLevi (of Strashelia), 52, 83, 85, 249, 251

I

Isaac, 175
Isaiah of Yanov, 257
Ishmael, 158
Islam, XII
Israel Chatzi Rav—see Chatzi Rav
Israel of Kozienice, 263

271

SUPPLEMENT

SUPPLEMENT

הלכות תלמוד תורה

חיבר קטון הכמות ורב האיכות
הלכות תלמוד תורה מחונך
ומלוקט מגמרא מן הירושלמי ומכל גדולי
הפוסקים ראשונים ואחרונים ומנופה בנ"ב
עשרה נפה באר היטיב דבר דבר על אופניו
בכדי שכל אחד ירווה למחונני וידע כל הדיני'
על בורי ועל מכונו ומסודר בלשון קל ונקל
לכל מעיין ובכדי לזכות הרבים הובא לבית
הדפוס :

נדפס פה קק

שקלאוו

תחת ממשלת האדון הגדול יעניראל...
מהייאר קאוואליער סעמען
גאוור יעלאוויץ זאריץ יר"ה :

בדפוס של ה"ה הרבני הקצין
מוהרר אריה ליב בהמנוח
מוהרר שניאור פייבוש
זלה"ה :

בשנת התקנ"ד לפ"ק

Facsimile of title page of Hilchot Talmud Torah, *by Rabbi Schneur Zalman, published in 5554 (1794)—first of his works printed in his lifetime.*

284

Facsimile of title page of the first edition of Likutei Amarim
(Tanya) by Rabbi Schneur Zalman, printed in 5557 (1796).

Facsimile of manuscript of first version of the Likutei Amarim (Tanya) (Agudas Chassidei Chabad Library).

Facsimile of a letter in Rabbi Schneur Zalman's Handwriting

287

THE HISTORY OF THE LETTER REPRODUCED ON PRECEDING PAGE

During the height of the persecution of the Chasidic community by the opponents of the movement, the followers of Rabbi Schneur Zalman in Vilna held a conference at which many of the younger Chasidim urged the adoption of strong counter-measures. This was contrary to the policy of the moderate Chasidim of Vilna, led by Meir ben Rafael, who had for five or six years (5551-56 / 1791-6) unsuccessfully endeavored to bring about peace. Moshe Meisels, a leading Chasid, supported the demands of the younger Chasidim, and under stress of a suffering and bitterly disappointed heart, voiced strong disapproval of the policy of Meir ben Rafael.

A special delegate of Rabbi Schneur Zalman attended the conference and brought a message from the Rav, to the effect that while their mood was quite justified, Chasidism taught that the mind should govern the heart. To have control over one's heart and feelings, and to reserve them for true love and fear of G-d, leading to practical deeds of kindness and charity to fellow man—this is the primary objective of every Chasid, the Rav said, promising the ultimate triumph of the cause.

In the month of *Elul* of that year, the Rav sent the letter to Moshe Meisels, in which be urges him to make a public apology to Meir ben Rafael.

IMPORTANT DATES
IN THE LIFE OF
RABBI SCHNEUR ZALMAN

5505 / 1745
18th of *Elul*, birth of Rabbi Schneur Zalman. Born in Liozna, Russia. His father was Rabbi Baruch, son of Rabbi Schneur Zalman; his mother was Rivkah, daughter of Rabbi Abraham.

5518 / 1758
At the age of thirteen awarded the title of *Tanna U'Pallig*.

5520 / 1760
Married Sterna, the daughter of Rabbi Yehuda Leib Segal, a wealthy and pious man from Vitebsk.

5524 / 1764
First journey to study under Rabbi Dov Ber, the famous Maggid of Miezricz.

5527 / 1767
Appointed *Maggid* (Preacher) of his hometown Liozna.

5530 / 1770
Starts working on his *Shulchan Aruch*.

5532 / 1772
Works out his system of *Chabad* philosophy.

5533-5538 / 1773-1778
Establishes (in Liozna) an academy of select disciples known as the First, the Second, and Third *Cheder*.

5543 / 1783
Successful public debate with leaders of the *Mitnagdim* in Minsk.

5554 / 1794
Published his first Halachic work, *Hilchot Talmud Torah*.

5557 / 1797
Publishes his main Chasidic work, the *Tanya*.

5559 / 1798
The day after Simchat Torah arrested and brought to Petersburg.

19th of *Kislev*, released from prison. Day celebrated, since then, as *Chag Hageuloh*.

5561 / 1800
Again brought to Petersburg and imprisoned. Subsequently released, but ordered to remain in Petersburg.

On the 11th of Av, set free and cleared of all accusations. From Petersburg he leaves immediately for Liadi.

5572 / 1812
End of Av leaves Liadi, on his flight from the French armies, accompanied by family and group of close disciples.

5573 / 1813
On the 12th of *Tevet*, he reaches the village Piena; in the District of Kursk.

Passes away on the night of the 24th of *Tevet*. He was laid to rest in the cemetery of the town of Hadiacz in the District of Poltava.

PUBLISHED WORKS OF RABBI SCHNEUR ZALMAN[1]

TALMUD TORAH

Laws concerning the study of the Torah, in four chapters. First published in *Shklov*, 5554. Subsequently published both separately and as part of the *Rav's Shulchan Aruch*. New revised edition with commentaries, published by Kehot in 5725, and subsequently with each print of the *Shulchan Aruch*.

LIKUTEI AMARIM

Famous as *Tanya*, after the initial word of the text.

PART 1: SEFER SHEL BENONIM (Book of the Middle Group of the Pious), deals with the service of G-d, love and fear of G-d, etc. 53 chapters.

PART II: SHA'AR HAYICHUD VEHA'EMUNAH (The Gate to G-d's Unity and Faith), deals with the doctrines of the Divine Unity, Providence, and faith. 12 chapters.

PART III: IGGERET HATESHUVAH (Encyclical of Penitence), dealing with the ways of true penitence. 12 chapters.

PART IV: IGGERET HAKODESH (Holy Encyclical), a selection of the *Rav's* letters dealing with such topics as charity, prayer, etc. 32 chapters.

KUNTROS ACHRON (Supplement), containing notes and com-

---

1. Excerpts from a Bibliography of Chabad-Chasidic Literature, compiled by Rabbi Menachem Mendel Schneerson. The works are listed here in chronological order of their first editions.

ments on passages of Part 1, and four additional letters.

Parts I and II were first published in Slavita, in 5557.

Parts I and 11 with the addition of Part III were first published in Zolkiev in 5559.

Parts I and II with Part III, the latter a revised edition, were published in Shklov, in 5566.

Parts I to IV, with the addition of *Kuntros Achron*, were published in Shklov, in 5574.

A revised edition of all the four parts was published in Vilna, in 5660, which edition was reprinted many times since.

A revised edition of the Vilna edition was published by Kehot Publication Society in Brooklyn in 5714 with supplements.

A pocket-size edition of same published by Kehot in Brooklyn in 5715 with additional supplements.

For a complete list of the close to five thousand editions of the *Tanya*, see *Tanya* published by Kehot.

LUACH BIRCHOT HANEHENIN

Later called *Seder Birchot Hanehenin* (Table of—later, Order of—Blessings). One chapter deals with the laws concerning the washing of the hands before meals; thirteen chapters deal with the laws concerning the blessings said on various occasions.
First published in Shklov, in 5560.[2] Later reprinted separately or together with the *Rav's* "*Siddur*."

SIDDUR (Prayer Book)

Arranged by Rabbi Schneur Zalman on the basis of *Nusach Ari*, after careful "study, comparison and selection of the versions of sixty different prayer books" (quoted from a Talk by Rabbi Menachem Mendel of Lubavitch, the *Tzemach Tzedek*).

First published in *Shklov*, in 5563.[3]

---

2. According to "*Bet Eked Seforim*" by Friedberg, it was first published in 5556(?). However, since Friedberg does not state the number of pages, as he usually does, it is evident that he never saw the book himself.
   In a letter (*Adar* 13, 5709, published in *Igrot Kodesh* vol. 10 p. 117) from Rabbi Yosef Y. Schneersohn of sainted memory, it is stated that it was first published in 5555.
3. According to the "*Shaar Hakolel*" by Rabbi Lavut, and "*Beit Rebbi*," Part I, p. 168. But see footnote 9 on p. 26 of *Torat HaChasidus*.

SHULCHAN ARUCH

Recodification of the *Shulchan Aruch* of Rabbi Yosef Caro, with revisions, additions and comments. It covers most[4] of the laws of the *Orach Chayim*, part of the laws of the *Yoreh Deah*, and selected laws from the *Choshen Mishpat*, and 43 responsa *(Shaalot Uteshuvot)*.

The part dealing with the Laws of Passover was first published in Shklov, in 5574.

The part dealing with the laws of *Yoreh Deah* and some of the *Shaalot Uteshuvot* was published in Kopust, in 5574.

The entire *Shulchan Aruch* was first published in Kopust, in 5576.[5]

Since then it was reprinted many times with various additions. A finally revised edition was published in Vilna, in 5665, which served as a standard edition for numerous reprintings without changes.

A new corrected edition with supplements has been published as follows—

Volume I published by Kehot in 5720.

Volume II published by Kehot in 5722.

Volume III-IV published by Kehot in 5725.

Volume V-VI published by Kehot in 5728.

A new revised edition with supplements was published by Kehot in 5745. A revised, newly typeset edition is currently being prepared.

SIDDUR

Same as above, with added commentaries and explanations in the Chasidic tradition as recorded by Rabbi Dov Ber, son of the Rav.

First published in Kopust, in 5576.

New revised edition with supplements, published by Kehot in 5725.

A new revised edition was published by Kehot in 5741, and subsequently in 5746.

---

4. The chapters 1-131, 155-6, 158-215, 242-408, 429-529, 582-651.

5. *"Ozar Haseforim"* by Ben Jacob gives the year as 5574. This is an error, as can be seen from the Introduction by Rabbi Dov Ber to the 5576 edition of the *Shulchan Aruch* (Part *"Orach Chayim"*) indicating that this is the first edition besides the Laws of Passover.

BIUREI HAZOHAR
(Commentaries on the *Zohar*)

Recorded by Rabbi Dov Ber.
First published in Kopust, in 5576.
Supplement to the above first published in Lwow, in 5621.
A revised edition with supplements was published by Kehot in Brooklyn, in 5717.

TORAH OR
(Torah-Light)

Chasidic discourses on portions of the Torah (on the Books of *Bereshit*, *Shemot*, and *Esther*), recorded by the *Rav*'s brother, Rabbi Yehuda Leib of Yanowitz. First published in Kopust, in 5597.
Supplement to the above, as recorded by Rabbi Dov Ber, first published in Zhitomir, in 5622.
A revised edition with supplements was published by Kehot in Brooklyn, in 5715.

A revised, newly typeset edition was published by Kehot in 5751.

TORAH OR

Chasidic discourses. Some of the discourses are the same as above, but with variations.
Published in Lwow, in 5611. (As far as is known, it is the only edition.)

LIKUTEI TORAH
(Gleanings of Torah)

Chasidic discourses on topics from the portions of *Beshallach* and *Pekudei*; from the books of *Vayikro*, *Bamidbar* and *Devarim*, and *Shir Hashirim*.
First published in Zhitomir, in 5608.
Revised edition published in Vilna, in 5664, serving as standard edition for further numerous reprints.
A newly revised edition with supplements, published by Kehot in 5725.

A revised, newly typeset edition was published by Kehot in 5759.

BONEI YERUSHOLAYIM
(Builder of Jerusalem)

Brief discourses and notes. Published in Jerusalem, in 5686. This is the only edition. See *Maamarei Admur Hazakein-Haktzorim*.

MAAMAR KETAPUACH BE'ATZEI HAYAAR
(As an Apple among Trees of the Forest)

Chasidic discourse on this passage of the *Tenach*. First published in Brooklyn, in 5714, by Kehot.

MAAMAR TZION BEMISHPAT TIPADEH
(Zion with Righteousness will be Redeemed)

Chasidic discourse on this passage of the *Tenach*. First published in Brooklyn, in 5715, by Kehot.

MAAMAREI ADMUR HAZAKEIN—HANACHOT HARAP ZAL
(Chasidic discourses by Rabbi Schneur Zalman. Notations from Rabbi Pinchus)

Chasidic discourses on various topics (portions of the Torah, *Tenach*, Sayings of our Sages, etc.). First publication from hitherto unpublished manuscripts, in Brooklyn, in 5718 by Kehot, with commentaries by Rabbi Menachem M. Schneerson

MAAMAREI ADMUR HAZAKEIN—ES'HALECH LIOZNA
(Chasidic discourses by Rabbi Schneur Zalman—delivered in the city of Liozna.)

Chasidic discourses on various topics.
First publication, from hitherto unpublished manuscripts, in Brooklyn, in 5718 by Kehot, with commentaries by Rabbi Menachem M. Schneerson.

MAAMAR YESOVEVENHU YEVONENEHU YITZRENHU
(He encircled them, He explained to them, He guarded them.)

Chasidic discourse on this passage of the Torah. First published in Brooklyn, in 5722, by Kehot.

MAAMAR BECHACHMAH YIVNE BAYIS
(With wisdom he will build a house).

Chasidic discourse on this passage of *Tenach*. First published in Brooklyn, in 5725, by Kehot.

MAAMAR PIKUDO LITEIN MACHATSIT HASHEKEL
(Commandment to give half of a *Shekel*).

Chasidic discourse on this passage in the *Zohar*. First published in Brooklyn, in 5723, by Kehot.

MAAMAREI ADMUR HAZAKEIN—5562
(Chasidic discourses by Rabbi Schneur Zalman—delivered during the year 5562).

First publication, from hitherto unpublished manuscript written by his son and successor Rabbi Dov Ber, with notations from his grandson, Rabbi Menachem Mendel, the *Tzemach Tzedek*. Brooklyn, 5725, by Kehot.

MAAMAR ANI YESHEINO
(I sleep)

Chasidic discourse on this passage in Tenach. First published in Bonei Yerushalayim (see above No. 10).
New revised edition published in Brooklyn, in 5724, by Kehot.

MEAH SHEARIM
(One Hundred Portals)

Collections of fifty letters and fifty short Chasidic discourses, selected from the writings of Rabbi Schneur Zalman, Rabbi Dov Ber and Rabbi Menachem Mendel (Tzemach Tzedek). First published in *Berditchev*, in 5673.
New edition with supplements published by Kehot, in 5727.

MAAMAREI ADMUR HAZAKEIN—HAKTZORIM.
(Short Chasidic Discourses by Rabbi Schneur Zalman.)

Delivered mostly prior to his arrest, on various topics. First publication from hitherto unpublished manuscripts, in addition to the short discourses previously published in *Bonei Yerusholaim* and *Meah Shearim*. Brooklyn, 5741, by Kehot.

MAAMAREI ADMUR HAZAKEIN—AL PARSHIOT HATORAH VEHAMOADIM
(Chasidic Discourses by Rabbi Schneur Zalman on the Torah Portions and Festivals.)

Unrelated to other categories above, namely, *Rabbi Pinchus, Liozna,* and unknown as to which year delivered.

First publication from hitherto unpublished manuscripts, written by his son and successor Rabbi Dov Ber, his grandson Rabbi Menachem Mendel, the "Tzemach Tzedek" and other transcribers.

Vol 1—Bereishit-Shemot, Vol 2—Vayikra, Bamidbar, Devarim. Brooklyn, 5743, by Kehot.

MAAMAREI ADMUR HAZAKEIN—NEVI'IM.
(Chasidic Discourses by Rabbi Schneur Zalman on verses of the Prophets.)

First publication from hitherto unpublished manuscripts, written partly by Rabbi Dov Ber, Rabbi Menachem Mendel, and mostly by transcribers. Brooklyn, 5744, by Kehot.

MAAMAREI ADMUR HAZAKEIN—K'TUVIM.
(Chasidic Discourses by Rabbi Schneur Zalman on verses of the Writings.)

First publication from hitherto unpublished manuscripts, written partly by Rabbi Dov Ber, Rabbi Menachem Mendel, and mostly by transcribers. Vol 1—5745, Vol 2—5746, Brooklyn, by Kehot.

MAAMAREI ADMUR HAZAKEIN—AL MAAMAREI RAZAL.
(Chasidic Discourses by Rabbi Schneur Zalman on the Talmud, Zohar and Prayers.)

First publication from hitherto unpublished manuscripts, written partly by Rabbi Dov Ber and his brother Rabbi Moshe, Rabbi Menachem Mendel. Brooklyn, 5744, by Kehot.

MAAMAREI ADMUR HAZAKEIN—INYONIM.
(Chasidic Discourses by Rabbi Schneur Zalman on topics unrelated to any of the above or any specific year.)

Topics arranged in order of the Alef Bet. First publication from hitherto unpublished manuscripts, written partly by Rabbi Dov Ber, Rabbi Menachem Mendel. Brooklyn, 5743, by Kehot.

MAAMAREI ADMUR HAZAKEIN—5562, VOL 2.
(Chasidic Discourses by Rabbi Schneur Zalman delivered

during the year 5562.)

First publication from hitherto unpublished manuscripts, written by Rabbi Dov Ber, with notations from Rabbi Menachem Mendel. Brooklyn, 5742, by Kehot.

MAAMAREI ADMUR HAZAKEIN—5563.
(Chasidic Discourses by Rabbi Schneur Zalman delivered during the year 5563.)

First publication from hitherto unpublished manuscripts, written by Rabbi Dov Ber and other transcribers with notations from Rabbi Menachem Mendel. Vol 1—5741, Vol 2—5742, Brooklyn, by Kehot.

MAAMAREI ADMUR HAZAKEIN—5564.
(Chasidic Discourses by Rabbi Schneur Zalman delivered during the year 5564.)

First publication from hitherto unpublished manuscripts, written by Rabbi Dov Ber and other transcribers with notations from Rabbi Menachem Mendel. Brooklyn, 5741, by Kehot.

MAAMAREI ADMUR HAZAKEIN—5565.
(Chasidic Discourses by Rabbi Schneur Zalman delivered during the year 5565.)

First publication from hitherto unpublished manuscripts, written by Rabbi Dov Ber, and other transcribers with notations from Rabbi Menachem Mendel. 2 Vol, Brooklyn, 5741, by Kehot.

MAAMAREI ADMUR HAZAKEIN—5566.
(Chasidic Discourses by Rabbi Schneur Zalman delivered during the year 5566.)

First publication from hitherto unpublished manuscripts, written by Rabbi Dov Ber with notations from Rabbi Menachem Mendel. Brooklyn, 5739, by Kehot.

MAAMAREI ADMUR HAZAKEIN—5567.
(Chasidic Discourses by Rabbi Schneur Zalman delivered during the year 5567.)

First publication from hitherto unpublished manuscripts, written by Rabbi Dov Ber with notations from Rabbi Menachem Mendel. Brooklyn, 5739, by Kehot.

MAAMAREI ADMUR HAZAKEIN—5568.
(Chasidic Discourses by Rabbi Schneur Zalman delivered during the year 5568.)

First publication from hitherto unpublished manuscripts, written by Rabbi Dov Ber with notations from Rabbi Menachem Mendel and Rabbi Yosef Yitzchak, the sixth Lubavitcher Rebbe.

Vol 1—5732, Vol 2—5742, Brooklyn, by Kehot.

MAAMAREI ADMUR HAZAKEIN—5569.
(Chasidic Discourses by Rabbi Schneur Zalman delivered during the year 5569.)

First publication from hitherto unpublished manuscripts, mostly written by transcribers with notations from Rabbi Menachem Mendel, apart from selected discourses by Rabbi Dov Ber. Brooklyn, 5741, by Kehot.

MAAMAREI ADMUR HAZAKEIN—5570.
(Chasidic Discourses by Rabbi Schneur Zalman delivered during the year 5570.)

First publication from hitherto unpublished manuscripts, written by transcribers; one discourse by Rabbi Dov Ber. Brooklyn, 5741, by Kehot.

MAAMAREI ADMUR HAZAKEIN—5571.
(Chasidic Discourses by Rabbi Schneur Zalman delivered during the year 5571.)

First publication from hitherto unpublished manuscripts, written by Rabbi Menachem Mendel and other transcribers. Brooklyn, 5755, by Kehot.

IGROT KODESH
A collection of letters by Rabbi Schneur Zalman.

Published together with letters by Rabbi Dov Ber and Rabbi Menachem Mendel.

Vol I-5741, Vol II-5753, Brooklyn, NY by Kehot.

LEKUTEI AMARIM (TANYA) IN TRANSLATION
Published by Kehot Publication Society

1. In Yiddish, translated by the late Uriel Zimmer. All parts of the *Tanya*, in two volumes. Kehot, 5716 (1956).

SHIURIM B'SEFER HATANYA. Containing lessons in Tanya studied on the New York Radio waves by Rabbi Yosef Wineberg. Reviewed by the Lubavitcher Rebbe before each broadcast.

Vol 1, Kehot, 5743, Vol 2, Kehot, 5745, Vol 3, Kehot, 5746

2. In English:

Part One, translated with introduction by Nissan Mindel. Kehot, 5723 (1962).
Reprinted, 1965. Third edition, new and revised, 1968.

Part Two, translated by Nissen Mangel, Kehot, 1965.

Part Three, translated by Zalman I. Posner, Kehot, 1965.

Part Four, translated by Jacob I. Shochet, with Introduction, Kehot, 1968.

Part Five, translated by Zalman I. Posner, Kehot, 1968.

Complete Tanya in one volume featuring page of translation facing page of hebrew text, Kehot, London, 5733

Revised edition, London, 5740

Revised edition, New York, 5743, Toronto, 5745, and numerous locations in Australia, 5744.

LESSONS IN TANYA. Translation of lessons in Tanya studied over the New York radio waves by Rabbi Yosef Wineberg. Translated by Rabbis Levi and Sholom Ber Wineberg.

Vol 1, Kehot, 5747, Vol 2, Kehot, 5748, Vol 3, Kehot, 5749, Vol 4, Kehot, 5752, Vol 5, Kehot, 5753

3. In French, Parts One and Two, Kehot, Paris, 1968. Part 3, Kehot, Paris, 5728, Part 4, Kehot, Paris, 5740

4. In Italian, Part One, Kehot, Milan, 1968.

Part 2, Kehot, Milan, 5729, Part 3, Kehot, Milan, 5730, Part 4, Kehot, Milan, 5734, Part 5, Kehot, Milan, 5739

5. In Spanish, Part 2, Kehot, Buenos Aires, 5744, Part 3, Kehot, Buenos Aires, 5730